LOSING IT

And Gaining My Life Back

One Pound at a Time

VALERIE BERTINELLI

FREE PRESS

NEW YORK LONDON TORONTO SYDNEY

FREE PRESS
A Division of Simon & Schuster, Inc.
1230 Avenue of the Americas
New York, NY 10020

First Free Press hardcover edition March 2008

First Free Press trade paperback edition November 2008

FREE PRESS and colophon are trademarks of Simon & Schuster, Inc.

For information about special discounts for bulk purchases,
please contact Simon & Schuster Special Sales at 1-800-456-6798
or business@simonandschuster.com

Designed by Ruth Lee-Mui

Manufactured in the United States of America

3   5   7   9   10   8   6   4   2

Library of Congress Cataloging-in-Publication Data

Bertinelli, Valerie
Losing it : and gaining my life back one pound at a time / Valerie Bertinelli.
      p.   cm.
   1. Bertinelli, Valerie.   2. Television actors and actresses—
         United States—Biography.   I. Title.
               PN2287.B4379A3   2008
   791.4502'8092—dc22   2007046179
   [B]

ISBN-13: 978-1-4165-6818-6
ISBN-10: 1-4165-6818-2
ISBN-13: 978-1-4165-6968-8 (pbk)
ISBN-10: 1-4165-6968-5 (pbk)

For Wolfie

CONTENTS

CONTENTS

Me

The Quickie Version

Name:	*Valerie Anne Bertinelli*
Age:	*Forty-seven*
Height:	*5'4½"*
Status:	*Formerly married, currently involved, always hungry*
Weight:	*Dropping*
Occupation:	*Mother, actress, Jenny Craig spokesperson*
Strengths:	*Honesty and integrity. I also see the good in other people and let most things roll off my back.*
Faults:	*Insecurity, tendency to procrastinate, overly judgmental, emotional eater*
If you were in my house, you'd hear Wolfie say:	*"Ma, don't go all Gandhi on me!"*
You will never see me:	*. . . without my clothes on*
Favorite meal:	*Anything Italian . . . or French . . . or Mexican . . . or . . .*
Happy or sad?	*Grateful*
Everything I know in ten words or less:	*Love, you always have a choice, exercise, portion control*

BRING HOME THE FUN

Some people measure depression by the medication they take or the number of times per week they see a therapist. For me, it was different. I measured my depression with baked jalapeño-and-cheddar-cheese poppers, the brand that advertises itself with the slogan "Bring home the fun."

I'd love to meet the person who came up with that line and ask him a question. Is it really *fun* to see yourself blow up three dress sizes?

I suppose they wouldn't sell as many if their slogan was "Pack on the pounds." On the other hand, they may do OK with a promotion that said "Forget your ex-husband" or "Eat these instead of having sex—since nobody wants to see your fat bare ass."

During the cold winter months of 2002–03, when I was making *Touched by an Angel* in Utah, those jalapeño-and-cheese poppers were my Prozac. I was on a significant dosage: at least nine a night and sometimes more. At the grocery store, I saw other women looking at me when I loaded the boxes into my cart from the frozen food case. I could almost hear them thinking *Oh my gosh, that's Valerie Bertinelli. And look: she's on those jalapeño poppers.*

It was true. There were nights when I OD'd on those poppers. My mouth burned because I couldn't wait for them to cool down after taking them out of the oven. Other times I savored the taste with tiny, almost sensual bites, drawing out the feeling of comfort and escape I got from eating. The bright smile that served me well for so many years went into storage. So did my size 8 jeans. And my 10s. And my 12s. And my—well, my weight soared past 170 pounds, the highest it had ever been outside of my pregnancy.

Those were some of the darkest days of my life, and I was eating my way through them. By 2001 my marriage to Eddie Van Halen was over after more than twenty years of competing with his rock-and-roll life-style for attention. Our fights about his drinking had taken a toll. Discussing and solving our problems used to bring us closer, but now it wore us out. Ultimately, when he failed to help himself by giving up cigarettes after mouth cancer had threatened his life, I knew, sadly, that one way or another I was going to end up on my own.

By then I was working and living in Utah eight months of the year. Full of anger and frustration, I spent at least three nights a week on a plane so I could see our ten-year-old son, Wolfie, who stayed home in Los Angeles to be in school with his friends. That wasn't the way I wanted to live or the type of person I wanted to be. But instead of helping myself, I did the opposite. I ate my misery and turned my misery into a reason for eating.

Overweight, alone, and horribly depressed, I kept eating poppers and everything else in my path. After *Touched* went off the air, I returned home and became a hermit. I hid from the world, hoping no one would see that I'd gotten fat. In reality, I was hiding from the one person who could help solve my problems: me.

That was hard to believe. Over the years, I'd tried every diet on the bookshelves—from the grapefruit diet, to Weight Watchers, to the lemon juice and cayenne pepper fast—and all of them had worked as long as I stayed on them. But once I stopped, the weight came right back, and, unfortunately with a little extra. While I hate to admit it, I was on the verge of giving up and accepting that I was never going to look the way I wanted to—or feel the way I wanted to either.

I used to say half-jokingly that I was going to give up, move to the mountains, and be the quirky old fat lady down the street with forty-some-odd cats.

I'm glad I didn't. Instead I ended up outing myself on the cover of the April 4, 2007, issue of *People* magazine by declaring, "I know what you're thinking—I'm fat." Publicly, it was the start of a diet where the stakes were total humiliation and embarrassment if I failed to reach my goal. Privately, it was, as my fellow Jenny Craiger Kirstie Alley promised, not just a diet but really the start of a journey. She was right.

By any standard, I've enjoyed a charmed life. Even though I gained notoriety by working on TV, I shunned the spotlight in favor of a normal life, driving carpools, volunteering in my son's classroom, making dinner, and trying never to miss my monthly book club get-togethers. Of all the roles I've undertaken, none has been more satisfying than motherhood. I'm as much of a regular gal as people seem to expect—and I like it that way.

If you walked into my house right now, you'd find my cat Dexter lounging on the sunny floor in the kitchen, a large bowl of fruit on the counter, delicious-smelling vegetable soup simmering in a tall pot on the stove, the recycling trash can ready to be emptied, and paperwork and schoolbooks spread across the dining room table. You'd also see my boyfriend Tom on the phone in the backroom, and me working the crossword puzzle, as is my daily routine.

Creating this happy picture was a puzzle that took my entire adult life till now to solve. By the time I went public as a size 14, I'd already done the hard work: confronting the fears, insecurities, disappointments, and frustrations that accounted for the three different sizes of dresses and pants I needed in my closet for my constantly changing weight. After that, it was just a matter of portion control, exercise, and self-discipline.

Since going on Jenny Craig in March 2007, I've surpassed my original goal of 30 pounds and set new targets for myself. But the weight I've lost doesn't compare to what I've gained—or regained—in my life. The weight loss and renewed zest for life go hand in hand. Kirstie had promised as much when she said, "Valerie, it's not about the weight. What's going to happen is you're going to quit hiding and discover the real you."

She was right. My relationships have never been healthier, including the one I have with myself, and I've finally found a joy that seemed beyond my grasp when I was reaching for those jalapeño-and-cheese poppers. Physically and emotionally, I'm a different person. It's like I'm hitting my stride. These days I really do bring home the fun.

In this book, you won't find me professing to have all the answers to life's problems. Hey, I'm still trying to figure out most of those. Instead this story is about the choices I've made, good and bad, and how I've grown and learned from them. There are also exciting times, emotional moments, and life as it happened. Through it all, you'll get me uncensored and unfiltered—the good, bad, stupid, stubborn, size

14 and size 4. It's nothing more complicated, though as you'll see, it was complicated enough for me. Isn't it always that way?

If you're starving right now because you're on a diet, ask yourself if your hunger has anything to do with food. I know the answer to that question. Look, we're all human. We go through the same things. If you're in a dark place over some problem in your life, I hope that reading my story will help you feel less alone when you see that someone else has made the same mistakes and gotten through them. I hope you'll relate to my story, learn from it, and, as I finally did, find the courage to change, shed any unwanted pounds, and gain all the good things you thought impossible.

Now where did I put that bag of chips?

Just kidding.

Valerie Bertinelli
November 2007
132 pounds

One

THE VISION

With only a few minutes before show time in Toronto, I felt the excitement pulse through me as I walked down a corridor in the bowels of the arena. I barely heard the sound of my heels clicking on the cement floor over the din of the crowd coming in through the doors. Out front, the Air Canada Centre arena was filled to the rafters with fans anticipating more than two hours of head-thumping, party-time rock from Van Halen. It was impossible not to feel the excitement.

Ed and the group's original lead singer, David Lee Roth, were almost three weeks into their first tour together since 1985, and, as in the several other cities I'd been to with them, it felt like a reunion—a gathering of old friends ready to whoop it up after having let too many years pass.

I smiled to myself, enjoying a flashback. The first time I wore an all-access pass to a Van Halen concert was in 1980. Now it was October 12, 2007, and the backstage atmosphere at this show was nothing like the hundreds of others I'd attended over the years. On previous tours, I'd hung out with Ed in his tuning room or by the bar in Sammy Hagar's room (lead singer after David left the band), or sat by myself at the hotel, wishing I had stayed at home. This time I opened the door to my sixteen-and-a-half-year-old son's dressing room.

It felt strange to be on tour as the mother of one of the musicians. Wolfie, who had taken over on bass for Michael Anthony, gave me a big hug when I walked in. The tour, postponed earlier in the year after Ed had entered rehab, had been in the works for months, and I had been a nervous wreck from worrying about sending my little boy (though he is bigger than I am) on the road with men who helped write rock's rule book on partying.

Before the tour, I'd tried to talk to him about drugs and groupies and hangers-on, but Wolfie would either cut me off by saying "Thanks, Ma, I love you too." Or he'd pick me up and carry me to another part of the house.

For months, I'd wondered how I'd deal with him at shows. Would our relationship change? Would he change? As it turned out, I dealt with him as I always have—like his mom. I was in his dressing room for less than two seconds before I asked if he'd eaten a good dinner and then brushed his teeth. In return I got a semi-annoyed *"Maaaaa!"*

Next to me was the bathroom door. I popped in to check my eye makeup after tearing up slightly just because I *am* his mom. I didn't notice that the adjoining dressing room shared the bathroom, but suddenly the door opened and in walked Ed, my husband for more than twenty years until we separated in 2001—and Wolfie's dad. Though no longer married, we tried hard to make our crazy version of a family work.

"Hey, we haven't shared a bathroom for a while," I joked.

He smiled. There'd been times when a lot of us thought Ed might not make it to this tour, so I was delighted to see that his eyes still twinkled.

"Look at my hair," he said. "Janie cut it." Janie was his girlfriend. "What do you think?"

"It looks good," I said.

A few minutes later, Ed, followed by Wolfie, walked onstage and rekindled the love affair between the band and twenty thousand fans with the opening chords of "You Really Got Me." That was followed by "Runnin' with the Devil," "Dance the Night Away," "Everybody Wants Some!!" and my personal favorite, "Romeo Delight."

The hard-rocking songs took me back to another time, but something was different. I noticed it while watching from the soundboard, and then again as I walked around, burning off nervous energy. Ed, though playing guitar spectacularly, was having equipment trouble. I saw him pushing buttons and talking to a tech off to the side of the stage. It was the kind of situation that used to set him off into an alcoholic-fueled rage, but he kept his cool while they tried to fix the problems.

As they hammered through a set list of hits, I ended up in front of the stage, right in front of Wolfie. He looked down at me and smiled. I mouthed, "I love you." He did the same to me. A few people came up to me and said, "You must be so proud." I was. I really was.

Unfortunately, there wasn't time to visit after the show. Hurrying onto their buses after a hug and a kiss, they made a quick getaway for the next city. My boyfriend Tom talked me through a few tears. There was no use hiding my feelings. My baby was on tour, and I needed consoling.

About a half hour later, after we'd gone back to our hotel room, the phone rang. It was Ed, who, despite the late hour, was wide awake as his bus sped along a highway. Years ago, I'd been on the bus with him, partying and talking as if we were in our own spaceship, separate and apart from the rest of the planet. Of course, those times were in the past, and our lives had changed. We'd gone in different directions and gotten involved with other people. Still, in some ways, we were becoming, dare I say it, friends.

"I just wanted to call you and say, What kind of son is that we have?"

"I noticed you had a difficult night but were able to work through it," I said. "I was impressed."

At that time, both of us were involved in our own efforts at self-improvement. I was seven months into my Jenny Craig diet, and Ed was working hard to stay sober after years of battling alcoholism. All the reviews of the tour had mentioned that he looked healthy. They also noted the grin that he wore through the entire show. He'd dreamed of playing with Wolfie from the moment he was born, and you could see his enjoyment—not an emotion normally associated with Ed, who can be the dark artistic type.

"When things were going wrong, I just looked across the stage at Wolfie and knew I didn't have any problems," he said.

"I'm proud of you," I said. "I'm glad it's going so well."

"What a kid."

"He is pretty terrific," I said.

"At least we got that one right."

"We did."

Our conversation was warm and supportive. It hadn't always been that way. Neither of us was a great communicator. Growing up as the only girl among three boys, I'd learned how to talk about football and cars, but my dad, Andy, an executive at General Motors, and my mom, Nancy, a full-time homemaker—though terrific parents who set a high bar for raising a family—didn't teach me how to deal with the personal stuff. When faced with a problem, I was expected to suck it up. Ed was no better. He expressed himself best through music.

So as we talked easily and honestly, I wanted to break into the conversation and point it out. "Hey, look, we're finally doing it—talking!" I didn't. Instead I thought fleetingly of difficult times we had put behind us and appreciated the harmonious moment we were in.

"Hey, Val, one more thing," said Ed.

"Yeah?"

"You looked great tonight."

"Thanks," I said. "Give Wolfie a hug, and I'll talk to you soon."

After hanging up, I walked into the dressing area outside the bathroom and allowed myself a moment of reflection before changing clothes. Tom was waiting for me to get into bed, and Wolfie and Ed were on the road. I felt fit, physically and emotionally. That day, I'd eaten three healthy meals and walked eighteen thousand steps. The jeans I stepped out of were a size 8. Slipping into a T-shirt, I allowed myself an approving look in the mirror. Things were good; I wasn't used to that.

And that's when I felt it: a moment of inner tranquility or, better yet, a moment of grace. It was the payoff of hard work and many prayers.

To be honest, I'd prayed a lot to feel that way. A year earlier, almost to the day, I had arrived at a crossroads where either I was going to get my shit together or spend the rest of my life disappointed with myself. The catalyst was *Claire,* a movie about a mother with psychic powers that I starred in for the Hallmark Channel. My longtime managers, Jack Grossbart and Marc Schwartz, sent a DVD of the director's cut to my house and told me to watch it and get back to them with comments. Within ten minutes of sitting down in front of the TV, I fought the urge to run into my room and cry.

Normally actors fall on one of two sides. Some don't mind watching themselves. Others hate it. That's me. But if need be, I can do it. I can detach myself from the idea that the person I'm watching is me. In fact, it's not me. I'm in character. Even when I played Barbara Cooper on *One Day at a Time* from 1975 through 1984, and it was clear that the two of us were nearly interchangeable, it still wasn't the real me. In my everyday life, I don't have my hair perfectly done, wear much makeup, or walk around in perfect lighting.

But not even professional coiffing, makeup, and lighting helped me in *Claire*. What I saw on the screen horrified me. Previously, my ability to go through life with blinders on had carried me through many situations that I should've walked out on. I have a high threshold for pain and punishment, or I'm way too forgiving, or I'm ungodly lazy, or all of the above. However, the sight of myself was too much even for me to tolerate.

"Who is that?" I blurted out. "Who is that fat, ugly, old woman?"

A few days later, without telling anyone, including Tom, I began to visualize a new me, the person I wished I could be *and* wanted to be both inside and out. I spent time every night after getting into bed picturing myself in this new guise. If it's true that your thoughts can affect your place in the universe, I was going to give the good ones a try. After a while, I found myself thinking about it at odd moments during the daytime, too. It's only with hindsight that I realize something else was going on in that vision beyond my desire to be much thinner.

See, there's the weight you see on the scale every morning, and then there's the weight you carry around inside that makes your feet drag, your shoulders hunch, and your eyes look down. As I know from experience, the two go hand in hand. One makes you look miserable, the other makes you feel miserable. Beyond the picture I envisioned in my head, I really prayed for a lightness of being.

I had no idea back then how I would get my fat ass to that place. But now, a year later, after talking to Ed from my Toronto hotel room, I finally felt it: that elusive, mysterious, and absolutely wonderful lightness I had conjured in my vision.

I got there through hard work, discipline, and faith. At that moment, I liked myself—which, more than the weight I'd lost, was what I'd really wanted the whole time.

Two

TINY DANCER

It was and remains the most awful thing that ever happened to my family, and I wasn't even born yet.

It was early fall 1959, and the trees in Claymont, Delaware, where my parents lived, were starting to turn. Brilliant orange, red, and yellow leaves gave the town a seasonal beauty before the gray days of winter arrived. There didn't appear to be any gray days for my parents, though. Married for four and a half years, following a chance meeting one rainy night outside a movie theater, they already had two boys, Drew, three, and Mark, seventeen months, and another one—me—on the way.

Having married at ages seventeen and twenty, they were still young and their life together full of promise. My dad was starting what would be a thirty-year career with General Motors. They had recently moved into a three-bedroom house in preparation for their latest arrival. They had a wide network of family and friends nearby.

One day they drove out to the country to visit their close friend Perina, a woman I'd later know as my Aunt Perina, even though we weren't blood relatives. She lived on a farm, a spread of land that was especially beautiful at that time of the year.

As far as I know, they were having a wonderful time until they noticed that baby Mark was missing. Panic set in.

Believe it or not, I was in my early teens before I was told that I'd had an older brother who'd died as a toddler. In Bertinelli fashion, my parents kept this tragedy locked inside them for years. Not a word was spoken about him. The subject was too painful for them to discuss. I don't remember the situation in which it came out, but I was stopped cold when I heard my mom reveal that piece of family history.

She didn't offer many details and seemed so fragile sharing the most basic pieces of information. I found out later from my older brother that Mark had wandered off from where they were visiting and, while unsupervised, had drunk poison that was stored in a Coke bottle. Rushed to the hospital, he died as my parents watched in helpless, guilt-ridden horror. Doctors were unable to save him.

I would have loved to ask my mom more about him. For instance, when I was growing up, there weren't any photos of Mark displayed next to all our other baby and childhood pictures. Why? My brother told me that it was too painful for my mom to have them out, so they were kept in a special album.

The next time Mark was mentioned, I was early in my pregnancy with Wolfie. When I said my due date was March 3, my mom said that had been Mark's birthday. At some point, she also hinted that she liked the name Mark for a boy. Looking back, I see those were subtle invitations to talk about the past, but for whatever reasons, I chose not to open that door.

More opportunities came and went. In late 1992 my paternal

grandmother died. We attended the funeral in Delaware, where she was buried next to my brother. I looked down at the grave, staring at the dates etched in stone that mark the beginning and the end of his life. I held Wolfie in my arms. At that time, he was seventeen months old, the same age Mark had been. I squeezed him tightly, as if by drawing him close I could protect him from anything bad forever.

I looked over at my mom and dad and wondered how the hell they'd survived losing their baby. That day I grew more in love with my parents, knowing what they must have gone through. I would have been a basket case if that, God forbid, had happened to me. But I would have talked about it—and that's something new to me.

For far too long, I kept my feelings bottled up. I was raised to be the strong-and-silent type. The drill was simple and straightforward: Don't complain. Deal.

That was my mother's philosophy as her early April due date for me came and went that spring of 1960. She was ready to pull me out of her if something didn't happen soon. Even before I was born, I was already a world-class procrastinator. Closing in on three weeks late, her doctor suggested drinking a cocktail of cod liver oil and root beer, an old-fashioned elixir that would either send her into labor or give her terrible diarrhea.

Let's just say that she ended up in the hospital, not on the toilet. Shortly thereafter, on April 23, I made my entrance. My parents, who had already been through two deliveries, heard something quite different this time when the doctor said, "It's a girl." As unique as that was for them, I was average height and weight at 20 inches long and 8 pounds, 14 ounces. I had such thick black hair that my mom used a barrette to keep it out of my eyes on the day they took me home.

That was perfect. Two days old, and I already had a new hairdo.

I love looking at old photos of my parents. Several sit in antique frames on the bookshelf in my living room. My mother was a red-haired beauty who, despite modest means, put herself together with a striking stylishness. That was in line with her natural artistic talent. She had dreamed of becoming a fashion designer or a painter. If she'd been born ten or fifteen years later, she probably would've ended up in New York or San Francisco, living a far different life.

I applaud my dad's excellent taste and keen eyesight for noticing her on that snowy night as she waited at a bus stop near the movie theater where she worked. He stopped his car and persuaded her to let him drive her home. She was, as he once told me, his Rita Hayworth. When they wed a short while later, she was already carrying their first child, my older brother Drew. Circumstances may have rushed them into marriage, but they lovingly grew into the arrangement and each other.

After a stint in Germany with the 11th Airborne, my dad got to work. He wasn't physically large, but as a former boxer, he jabbed his way up the ladder. A people person, he had an exceptional work ethic.

Together they made family a priority. Sixteen months after my arrival, my mom gave birth to my brother David. Two years later, in 1964, she had my brother Patrick. My early childhood memories are all pleasant and happy. I was fortunate. I liked school and made friends easily. My kindergarten report card noted that I arrived each day well groomed, something my mom took pride in, since she made the cute dresses I wore. (She also made matching outfits for my Barbies.)

There were lots of family gatherings and parties with friends. My recollection is that all of them, especially those with relatives, revolved around food. My dad is Italian, so naturally any family get-together started and ended with the women in their basement kitchen. My grandmother and aunts stood at the counter making gnocchi and other types of pasta by hand, as well as fried bread. I'm gaining weight just from thinking about the delicious aroma that rose from that stove. Meals were like some kind of Food Network fantasy. My nonni's everyday Italian would put Giada De Laurentiis to shame (and I love Giada). I joke that I was raised, like any good Italian, to believe in two things: God and garlic. And it's true.

I was also taught to celebrate good times with lots of food. During hard times, it also helped to eat. One way or another, I ended up in the kitchen.

The last memories I have of life in Claymont, Delaware, are from 1968 and show a growing awareness of the turbulent social and political climate at the time. First came the tragic news that April of Dr. Martin Luther King Jr.'s assassination. My parents sat in front of the TV listening to Robert Kennedy eulogize him with a reading of his favorite poem by Aeschylus, whose theme of wisdom through pain and grace continues to resonate with me as I go through my own journey.

> *Even in our sleep, pain which cannot forget*
> *falls drop by drop upon the heart,*
> *until, in our own despair,*
> *against our will,*
> *comes wisdom*
> *through the awful grace of God.*

Two months later Kennedy was slain at the Ambassador Hotel in Los Angeles while campaigning for the Democratic presidential nomination. I remember my mom crying quietly. A light had dimmed in the country and in our home. My parents hosted gatherings in support of

Hubert Humphrey's bid for the nation's top job. They infused me with a liberal bent, which eventually pitted me against my dad, who for some reason became a Republican. I assume that as a military vet, he was offended by the "hippie" war protesters.

Years later, we still argue about George McGovern versus Richard Nixon. I've forgiven him for Nixon, but not Cheney, Rove, Rumsfeld, or W.

That summer we moved to Detroit after my dad snapped up an opportunity to work in the heart of the auto industry. We lived in Pine Knob, a hilly area outside of Pontiac. We went skiing and sledding in the winter. Dad taught us to ice skate on a nearby lake. I can still picture him shoveling snow off it until there was enough room for us to skate. We also swam in the lake during the hot, sticky summer months. That lake was full of leeches, and I hated peeling them off my legs. Gross though they were, what better preparation for Hollywood?

The idea of a career wasn't even seeded in my brain when, in 1971, Dad was transferred to a new GM plant in Los Angeles. To me, the most exciting prospect of moving out west was the possibility that I might see one of my favorite teenage stars from one of my favorite TV series, *The Brady Bunch* or *The Partridge Family*. Otherwise I, like my brothers, was flabbergasted by our flight to L.A. on a 747. The plane was enormous, and we had first-class seats!

In my diary, I wrote that we were able to drink all the Coca-Cola we wanted—*for free!* I was blown away.

I didn't think life could get any more exciting. I was wrong.

Three

DAYDREAM BELIEVER

Acting is relatively easy. You have to show up for work.

The hard part is finding a way in.

For me, that "in" started on the school playground. Shortly after moving into our new home—a dream come true in a new development featuring fifteen-foot ceilings, a rock garden in the foyer, and a swimming pool—I made friends with a girl at school. When I found out that she worked in commercials, I asked her tons of questions. Where I came from, television was how we spent our leisure time at night; everyone gathered around the set to watch *All in the Family, The Carol Burnett Show, Laugh-In,* or *Sonny & Cher.* The people on those shows were all famous; they were stars, as were Marcia Brady and Keith Partridge. Oops, I mean Maureen McCormick and David Cassidy. The notion that ordinary people could be on TV—or, conversely, that those who starred on TV were in fact real people—had never crossed my mind. My new friend revealed a whole new world to me.

After that, I caught the acting bug, although, in truth, I don't know if I caught the bug as much as I thought it would be cool to be on TV.

To my mom's credit, she didn't laugh after I came home and told her. Initially, in fact, she thought it was a good idea and might help me overcome my painful shyness. Unfortunately, my dad had heard that some acting schools weren't legit, and he didn't want to hand his hard-earned money over to scam artists. He was just trying to be protective. But I refused to take no for an answer. Once I get an idea in my head, whether it's acting classes or, later on, making marriage work, I can be stubborn.

So I kept nagging my mom about it, until one day she was reading the paper, and noticed an ad for the Tami Lynn Academy of Artists. We showed it to my dad, who checked it out. After declaring the school on the up-and-up, my mom called and signed me up.

The school was in Sherman Oaks, a twenty-five-minute drive from our house, on the second floor of a small building located on a busy corner off Ventura Boulevard. I walked up the stairs with nervous anticipation. Once inside, I noticed the wall was full of framed headshots of her young students. Stacks of glossy teen magazines were spread on the tables. The atmosphere felt right.

Best of all—indeed, the thing that instantly sold me—was Tami herself, the founder. With her thick brown hair, porcelain skin, long eyelashes, and perfect features, she was one of the most beautiful woman I'd ever seen. Just looking at her, I was ready to follow and learn. I wanted to be her student as long as I could be around her.

There was one problem: I didn't like class. While I had no problem listening to or watching Tami, I struggled through the exercises and recitations, the tongue twisters and the routines we learned for auditioning properly. I balked anytime I did something that felt forced or unnatural. The same was true whenever it was my turn to step into the spotlight. None of this boded well for acting.

After the second class, I wanted to quit. My mom wouldn't let me, since she'd prepaid the entire month. It was fine if I wanted to quit after that, she said. At the end of the month, though, I signed up for more classes. I still didn't like being in class. Nothing had changed. But, being stubborn, quitting wasn't in my repertoire. I wanted to be on TV—or at least try to get on—and I hadn't yet given it a shot. One day I got a boost when Tami followed my mom and me out of class and said she thought I had some talent. She called it a spark, something that made me stand out.

No one else seemed to see it, though.

After six months of study, I was ready for auditions, and Tami sent me out on jobs. As it happened, I got one of the first jobs for which I tried out: an Easter-themed commercial for JC Penney. To my recollection, they chose me because I fit into the dress. It was as simple as that. I wish I could say I had the time of my young life shooting the spot, but I didn't. The director barked at me for not eating a chocolate bunny with enough enthusiasm, and, when I overheard one of the lighting guys say that I looked "flat," I assumed that he meant my face.

You'd think I would have thought he'd meant my lack of boobage. But, no, I thought he meant my face. I had a squatty, little, flat nose that my brothers made fun of. I think they called me "pig nose." And I thought my profile was flat.

The point is, not once did I think he might have been referring to the lights. How's that for a stop on the road map to my life's insecurities?

Following that first success, I went on nearly one hundred auditions without landing a single part again. That process of trying out and getting rejected, which went on for more than a year, brought out the worst in me, although I didn't think so at the time. I hated the process and resented my mom for taking me out of school in order to make the auditions, which were always scheduled in early afternoon when I was in art class with my favorite teacher, Mr. Hamill.

Understandably, I went through a rollercoaster of emotions. You take a normal kid and send her to offices where she smiles at adults, shakes hands and spends at most fifteen minutes trying to make people fall in love with her, only to be rejected, and it's going to have an effect. At the least, it will chip away at the kid's self-confidence. At worst, it will leave lasting, more serious psychological scars.

Without the grounding of a strong family, I probably would've ended up a pile of emotional sawdust, but my acting was just one activity among all the sports my brothers played, and so it wasn't given undo emphasis by my parents. If I was down, they buoyed my spirits at the dinner table with jokes and encouragement right off the football field: "Hang in there. You'll get 'em next time." That was all good.

The bad part was the way I perceived the constant rejection. Even though Tami and my mom emphasized that none of the rejections was personal, I saw it differently. I didn't just tell myself that the girls getting the parts over me were prettier; I decided that that was fact. To me, they all did appear to be cut from the same mold: lean, blonde surfer girls with perfect little bikini figures. In other words, they were everything I wasn't.

Obviously that wasn't true and couldn't have been true, but it made sense to me then. As a result, I went to war with myself. When I stood in front of the mirror, it was like the GOP going after Hillary Clinton. I didn't see anything I liked.

In truth, I'd begun worrying about my body years before I hit puberty. It started with one of my elementary school teachers. One day as I was talking to two of my girlfriends, he came by, asked how we girls were doing, and then patted my tummy—not theirs or all of our tummies, just mine—and said, "You'd better watch this."

Though he meant it innocently, that simple gesture was completely insensitive. If he was kidding around, he wasn't funny. He had no clue about the imprint he left. Was I fat? Did I have a big tummy? Why did he say that to me if it wasn't true? Those were my immediate thoughts. Long term, I never felt again like a perfectly normal, skinny little kid— which I was. The perception I had of myself was forever changed.

Self-esteem is a tricky thing, especially in young girls. We develop a sense of who we are from the way other people react to us. I think most women will agree, you can get a thousand compliments, but it's the one criticism that will stick with you. That's the way it was for me after my teacher's comment. From then on, I tended to see only the negative about myself. I focused on the worst.

As I went from thirteen to fourteen I focused on my hips—or my big Italian child-bearing hips, as I referred to them. In reality, they weren't big. They were perfect for a thirteen-year-old. I look back at pictures and wonder what the hell I was looking at. But back then all I saw were curves. It was as if I woke up one day with a new lower half of my body. They were like crop circles—mysteries. Where'd they come from? Their appearance was a cruel joke. I wanted to be straight. I wanted longer legs. Why couldn't I have grown more that way, up and down, rather than around?

What is it with the way girls are brought up that they look in the mirror and see only what they don't have and what they aren't?

It wasn't anything I talked about with my parents. We were Bertinellis after all. We didn't show or talk about our emotions, which made my desire to act—and get paid to show and talk about my emotions—deeply ironic. My parents were unaware of the hours I spent stewing about my body, wishing I looked different.

Even with the amount of time I spent with my mom going on auditions, my insecurities were still my secret. My preferred antidote to a bad day was a giant Hot Tin Roof sundae at Farrell's, an old-fashioned ice cream parlor. Two scoops of vanilla, thick hot fudge sauce, and a spoonful of salted peanuts. But sometimes I starved myself for a day or two. I wouldn't feel "worthy" of eating then.

But those extremes were few and far between. More often than not, when word came in that I didn't get a part or there was some other disappointment, I grabbed a bag of chips from the pantry. It was as if that bag of Ruffles called my name and knew what I was thinking. "Hey, kid, come here. Let me help you."

Like many girls, I had a few conversations with God about those sensitive issues. I was like the girl in Judy Blume's novel *Are You There God? It's Me, Margaret.* I can't remember how many times I asked, "Are you there, God?" The only response I got, though, came from my brothers, who, being normal boys, got pleasure from teasing me. They called my breasts little quarters, acorns, or pebbles. Even their gossip about the hot girls at school bothered me. All the so-called foxes they mentioned were blonde surfer girls, the same types that got all the parts.

When all you want is to be something you aren't, which in my case was "hot," the whole world can seem as if it's conspiring against you. Even my unwitting dad added to the problem.

One summer day, I was swimming with my friend Robin, the daughter of friends of my parents. A couple of years older than I was, she had the looks that I envied: blonde hair and a perfect body, which looked even better in a bikini. While I was envying her hot bod, my dad came into the backyard with his camera and said he wanted to take a picture of us.

Oh, great, I thought, as he posed the two of us next to each other on the diving board. The last thing I wanted was to sit next to Robin in a bikini. She had a figure like a pinup model, and mine was—well, mine was like the diving board on which we sat. As my dad focused his 35 mm camera, I glanced at Robin out of the corner of my eye. All I saw were boobs. Suddenly I heard my dad's perturbed voice.

"Valerie, sit up straight!"

"I am."

"No you aren't. You're hunched over."

He was right. I *was* hunched over—and if given the opportunity, I would have buried my head in the sand, except *that* would have put my butt straight in the air. That's the way I thought. But I recently looked at pictures of myself from that time and just about screamed, "What was wrong with me?" The truth was, I had an adorable figure for a fourteen-year-old girl. Neither fat nor curvy, I was perfectly fine. Why couldn't I see it?

Better question: Why didn't I like myself? Where did those seeds of dislike come from?

Even now there's no single answer I can point to. I think the normal self-doubts I had from puberty were exacerbated by the auditions I went on without any success. I was a glutton for punishment. And I kept too much inside. I would've done a whole lot better long-term if I'd opened up more and discovered that just about every other girl on the planet felt the same way.

Then came relief. In 1974 we moved to Oklahoma, where my dad was brought in as part of the team assigned to build a new GM plant. All of us went except for my brother Drew, who was in college in L.A. I was glad for the break from Hollywood. Even my mom recalls me being down on myself at the time, so I must've been seriously dispirited. I needed to step away from the constant negativity. Something clearly wasn't working. I had no intention of quitting my dream of acting, though.

My dad estimated that we'd be in Oklahoma for a few years, but plans changed suddenly and unexpectedly when OPEC—the Organization of Petroleum Exporting Countries—created a gas crisis by embargoing oil shipments to the U.S. and its Western European allies. As a result, GM pulled the plug on construction of the plant, and after just three months in Oklahoma, we moved back into our old neighborhood in L.A., but on a different street.

My new bedroom had ugly green jungle-themed wallpaper that I immediately covered floor to ceiling with posters of Elton John, my new obsession. During the three months we were gone, I'd gotten into rock (Elton, Linda Ronstadt, and the Eagles), developed an interest in fashion, and realized that I missed acting.

After a lot of soul-searching, I came to several important conclusions: I was more serious about acting than I'd previously thought. It wasn't just about wanting to be on TV, it was something I felt inside me. I also told myself that I couldn't take the rejections personally. All of a sudden I sounded like Tami, my mom, and the chorus of other people who told me that everyone went through the same thing.

For me, the net result was a change in attitude. Independent of anyone else, I decided that I could do it. I could succeed. It was as if, without knowing it, I'd visualized what I wanted to happen. I put it out in the universe with a new resolve—and a new self-assurance about the choice.

One of the things I know about performing is that you have to give yourself over to it completely. Whether it's acting, singing, or playing onstage, you must yield whatever reserve you have to the experience. If you're going to do it, you do it. You don't do it halfway. People can see through that. I think, in my own way, back then as a teenager, I realized that.

After those three months in Oklahoma, I returned with something new. Along with purpose, I added passion.

Mom took me back to meet with Tami, and something was different when I told her how much I wanted to be an actress. Now, in addition to meaning it, I felt it, too.

I sensed it was going to happen.

Four

YOU'VE GOT THE PART

I didn't get the first job I went out on after returning to L.A., but I got the next one, a commercial for corn chips, and somehow I stopped jumping and screaming long enough to snag commercials for StarKist tuna, Wyler's lemonade, and a public service announcement with Jack Lemmon.

Then, toward the end of 1974, I made the leap onto episodic TV by landing a guest spot on the series *Apple's Way,* a family-oriented show starring Ronnie Cox, Vince Van Patten, and Kristy McNichol. Getting that part was a monumental step forward. It also resulted in a colossal humiliation. But how else do you learn?

I was one of a handful of girls brought on for an episode titled "The Flag," and we were standing in our positions on the set. We waited while various people conferred with one another about the way the scene looked. Finally, after lighting and sound were given a last check, the director said, "Action!" Nothing happened. No one said a word. There was an awkward silence.

I looked around, wondering who'd screwed up. Thank God it wasn't me, I thought. I knew my lines perfectly. Even so, everyone was staring at me.

"Valerie," said the director, "I said action."

"Yes, I know," I replied.

"You have the first line."

I thought back to the script, wondering if I'd missed a line. No, I knew the part.

"No, I don't," I started to say. "I'm Sal"—

He interrupted.

"No, sweetheart, you're Peggy, not Sally."

Just then the girl playing Sally, Pamelyn Ferdin—a beautiful blonde girl who worked all the time—stepped forward.

"That's my part," she said.

And so it was. Though I'd read for that part when I auditioned, no one told me that they'd cast me in one of the other, smaller parts. I assumed wrongly that I'd gotten the larger one. Those were the lines I'd memorized.

If I could have dug a hole to the other side of the earth, I would have done it and jumped in. But I had to stay on my mark. That's what professionals did. Mortified, I turned every shade of red and tried not to cry. It must've been as uncomfortable for everyone else too. Earl Hamner, the show's executive producer and the man behind the hit *The Waltons,* walked onto the set and calmed me down. He was wonderful.

Later he wrote me a sweet letter, reminding me that everyone makes mistakes and wishing me luck in the future. It meant a lot to me.

In the meantime, I quickly learned the lines for *my* part, which weren't many or difficult, and finished the day. Looking back, I know that experience gave me some important seasoning: I got stronger from knowing I could survive such an embarrassing gaffe. But I could have done without it. I get queasy thinking about it even today.

I wish I could remember what I ate when I got home that night. I'm sure it wasn't pretty.

In June 1975, a few months after I'd turned fifteen, Tami sent me pages from a new sitcom auditioning girls my age. She was excited because Norman Lear was producing the series, and his casting director, Jane Murray, had seen my picture in an actors' directory. Noticing a resemblance I had to the youngest of Norman's two daughters, Maggie, Jane specifically asked to see me.

That request translated into excitement. Norman Lear had given TV *All in the Family, Maude, Sanford and Son, Good Times,* and *The Jeffersons*—all hits—and going up for one of his shows was a mega opportunity.

But Tami learned that Norman was having trouble with this one. Titled *All about Us,* it featured a divorced mother and her teenage daughter. He'd shot a pilot with Bonnie Franklin, a New York stage actress, playing the mother, Ann Romano, and Mackenzie Phillips, the daughter of John Phillips (of the sixties rock group the Mamas and the Papas), as her daughter, Julie Cooper.

Now he was reworking the show by giving Bonnie a boyfriend, a part that went to Richard Masur, and adding a second, younger daughter, Barbara Cooper—the part that Jane called me in to read for. Of course, I wasn't the only girl they wanted to see. The net was cast far and wide. On the day of my first audition at CBS, I was one of several hundred girls who showed up.

But I was one of only about twenty girls called back for the next round. I made that cut too. The next and final reading was for Norman. A half dozen of us were called back, and, like me, the other girls arrived with their families. Some brought their managers or agents too. The waiting room was crowded, and the atmosphere tense. One by one, we were called in to meet Norman.

My mood was positive. When my turn came, I walked into the room feeling nervous but good that I'd made it this far on such an important project. I also felt something at work that was beyond me, a coming together of pieces in a puzzle. Sometimes you hear people talk about a moment being right, everything falling into place; this was one of those times. I felt like the part was perfect for me and vice versa.

For those reasons, I was able to be myself when I met Norman. Not nervous, not insecure, not worried. Just myself.

And Norman was Norman. He wore his trademark white golf hat and had white hair, eyes that danced behind his glasses with brilliance, enthusiasm, and warmth. His manner was both firm and gentle. By this time, I had had enough experience to know that there was no use trying to win over a producer or director. They'd look at me—and in fact would start to assess me from the moment I walked into the room—and make a decision based on criteria that were beyond my control.

So there was nothing for me to do at this point other than to present myself as I was in real life. That also put me at ease.

Norman asked if I was ready and cued me to read my line. Then he gave me some notes and had me read again. After fifteen minutes of additional conversation, something about sports and music, he thanked me for coming in, and I joined my parents in the waiting area.

"How was it?" my mom asked quietly.

"I felt good," I said. "But I'm not sure."

To this day, I say the same thing after my managers ask me about an audition. I'm never sure what to think. The producers or casting people can tell you that you're brilliant. Then they'll call your agent and say you sucked.

In any event, after all the girls read for Norman, Jane opened the door and joined us in the waiting area. All of a sudden the tension in the room went way up. I sat by the door, with my parents farther down on my left. Jane casually touched my shoulder and while trying to look as if she were merely saying hi, she whispered, "Stay here after everyone leaves."

I realized that I'd been chosen. So did everyone else. I turned to my mom and cupped my hands over my mouth. My eyes were screaming what I wasn't able to: *oh my God!*

Jane thanked the other girls and told them that they could go home. My parents and I sat in our seats without moving. After the room emptied, we followed Jane into her office. There she said the words that changed my life: "Congratulations, Valerie. You've got the part." We jumped up and down and screamed. My mom hugged me. My dad swung me around.

"I can't believe it!" I screamed. "I got the part!"

Though I'm sure we had a nice dinner, I don't remember any other celebration. There was no time. A full script was sent to me the next day, and I immediately worked on it with Tami. Then work on the show began a few days later at CBS's Television City studio. My mom drove me to the set, as she would every day for the next three years. By law, I needed a legal guardian present until I turned eighteen.

As we waited for the elevator, Mackenzie arrived. The biggest name on the show, Mac was its only marquee-level star. She'd earned raves two years earlier in George Lucas's hit *American Graffiti,* and over the summer had starred with Sally Kellerman and Alan Arkin in the road trip movie *Rafferty and the Gold Dust Twins.* Off camera, she'd lived a life that made her seem a decade older than I was, even though her birthday was only six months before mine.

I'd worried about meeting her for the first time and what I should say. I wanted her to like me. But after stepping into the elevator, she gave me a serious once-over that, quite honestly, intimidated the hell out of me. That left me no choice other than to smile and say hi.

She nodded. I looked at Mac's face for a glimmer of potential friendship while I introduced my mom. As I said, "This is my mom, Nancy Bertinelli," all I could think was, Oh God, I am so not cool.

My first meeting with Bonnie was better. She gave me a warm hug and said, "I'm going to be your new mother." Then she introduced herself to my mom. "I'm her new mother." We loved her immediately.

But the only thing my mom and Bonnie had in common were red hair and freckles. Only thirty-one, Bonnie wasn't old enough to be my mother. Raised in Beverly Hills, she had started out doing episodic television and moved to New York, where, in 1970, she earned a Tony nomination for the musical *Applause.* Within a few days, I recognized Bonnie's immense talent and felt privileged to work with her. Off camera, too, she had a special way that drew me in and made us close. She was like a hip, younger complement to my real mom.

As for Pat Harrington, who played our apartment building's meddling handyman, Schneider, he was nonstop funny. As I got to know him, he got even funnier. He could do amazing impersonations—Ed Sullivan, Jack Benny—that always had me on the floor laughing. He also did a great drunk. I tried to recreate his jokes and invariably did them a little bit wrong; just wrong enough that I'd crack him up.

The show, renamed *One Day at a Time*, was created by the husband-and-wife writing team of Alan Manings and Whitney Blake. Whitney was also a busy actress (she played the mom on the 1960s hit sitcom *Hazel*) as well as the mother of actress Meredith Baxter Birney, who later starred on the hit *Family Ties*. As we rehearsed the new pilot, I remember some of the producers worrying that calling it *One Day at a Time* might cause people to think the show was about alcoholism. Clearly Norman didn't share that concern.

Thinking back on that first show, I marvel at Norman's smarts as a producer. He took a concept that didn't work in its initial draft and retooled the premise into something that tapped into the nervous system of mainstream America as it wrestled with issues such as rising divorce rates, single motherhood, women's liberation, and a reexamination of the family. His genius was finding the funny in it.

Our pilot episode, "Ann's Decision," introduced Ann Romano on her own, raising her two daughters, Julie and Barbara, and having to decide whether to let her eldest go on a coed sleepover. It was trademark Norman Lear television, with strong characters, conflict, humor, and social commentary.

"Here I am. Use me," Schneider (Pat) says to Ann Romano (Bonnie) in his first scene.

"I'd rather recycle you," she says, annoyed at being hit on by the handyman.

"Go ahead," he smiles. "I'm just as good the second time around."

I tried to absorb everything as I went through rehearsals with these pros and saw how scripts were rewritten daily, characters created and nurtured, and shows built from the ground up. Norman once said he saw in me "an original in a world of copies." I interpreted that to mean he could shape me. And I needed it. I worked hard on my technique, particularly projecting my voice, and I nearly danced a jig one day when Pat complimented my "instinct for comedy."

"You can't acquire it," he explained. "You've got to be born with it. And you're lucky because very few people *are* born with it."

Getting laughs in rehearsal—laughs from pros at the top of the business—was powerful stuff. It was more addictive in front of an audience. After the first time, I thought, Whoa, I'll take more of that! I was hooked.

On the night we taped the pilot in front of an audience, I experienced the same comfortable, slightly nervous feeling I had had auditioning for Norman. It was like stepping into a déjà vu moment. Everything felt as it was supposed to, and I was able to give myself freely and fully to the moment. As a result, I enjoyed one of the most powerful experiences of my life.

I can still picture myself standing behind the doorway where I would make my entrance, breathing slowly, feeling confident, and spotting my family in the audience. I held a basketball against my hip, a prop that showed I was still part tomboy. My first line was "Mom, I made the team!" No problem. I'd made the team in real life, too. The whole thing was too much, and yet somehow I kept it in perspective.

I don't know how that was possible, except that everything seemed to be falling into place as if it were meant to be. I keep saying that, but it's true. I knew the show would be a hit. People with more experience said the same thing. That feeling was in the air. There was a vibe on the stage that started the first day of rehearsals and continued into the pilot.

Right before stepping on stage, I took one last calming breath, as I'd been trained to do, and said to myself, "Get ready, this is going to change your life."

Five

TUMBLEWEED CONNECTIONS

My earliest memory of working on *One Day,* outside of the pilot, is not a pleasant one. It was during rehearsals for the second episode, and director Don Richardson yelled at me for not projecting. That's so ironic now, since I'm always being shushed and told to use my "inside voice," as if I'm a six year old in school. But back then I was shy and unsure of myself, working on my first real job, where there was pressure and responsibility, and I didn't always understand the mechanics of acting whether it was on a stage or a set. So I delivered my lines in the same voice that I used at home, and as a result Don's voice rang through the sound stage, cutting me off mid-sentence.

"Valerie, project! I can't hear you."

We tried it again. Again, he interrupted me.

"Valerie, *project!* We want to hear you on television."

On the third take, even though to me it sounded like I was screaming my lines, it still wasn't loud enough for Don. He lost his temper.

"Jesus Christ, raise your fucking voice so a human being can hear it!" he said.

I was upset enough at not being able to deliver what the director wanted, and his harsh words put me on the verge of tears. But I wouldn't allow myself to break down in front of everyone. That wasn't permitted at the network level, where standards were very high and everyone felt the pressure. No, as I learned, I had to take the direction and try to do better. There's no crying in television—at least not in front of anyone else.

Fortunately, as a Bertinelli, I knew how to suck it up. With supportive looks from Bonnie and Pat, I kept myself together and tried again. After several more takes, I gave the director a performance he liked. Then I hurried to my dressing room, shut the door, and cried my eyes out. Legendary Green Bay Packers football coach Vince Lombardi may as well have been talking about TV when he said that the dictionary was the only place where success came before work.

The producers and writers were trying to live up to the high standards Norman had set with *All in the Family,* and I think they turned out something special and groundbreaking merely by focusing *One Day* on a divorced woman successfully raising children on her own. They went further by exploring sex, politics, drugs, and all aspects of male-female relationships.

It was much more work than I anticipated. We rehearsed Monday through Thursday and taped on Friday, which was by far the longest and most strenuous workday. We performed two complete versions of the show in front of audiences, taping one at five-thirty and one at eight. After the audience left, we did reshoots and pickups until everyone was satisfied. Sometimes we didn't leave till midnight.

In addition, Mac and I received three hours of on-set tutoring a day. Our class, taught by Gladys Hirsch, started an hour before everyone else arrived. Then we squeezed in two hours in the afternoon. My toughest lesson was figuring out Mac. I wanted to be her friend, but I had an almost impossible time cracking the code.

Despite our closeness in age, we were extremely different. Her background gave her a guardedness that I hadn't encountered before. Then again, few teenagers had her history. Raised in a rock-and-roll milieu, she had learned to roll a joint when she was still in grade school and by twelve had used both pot and LSD. Her own stardom and success catapulted her from the fast lane to the faster lane.

Compared to my upbringing, she was from another planet. At sixteen she lived with her aunt Rose Throckmorton—her mother's sister—in a house atop Beachwood Canyon. Eager to make friends with Mac, I was excited when we finally arranged a sleepover at her house. We had a wonderful time. Once past her toughened exterior, I found a fun, sensitive teenage girl with many of the same interests I had, including food, boys, clothes, and music.

And of course I was impressed by Mac's adultlike setup. In her beautiful, hilltop home, she told exciting tales of late-night partying and celebrity-filled Hollywood escapades that made me envy her freedom. By contrast, my parents were on my back constantly. There were times when I came home five minutes after my eleven o'clock curfew, only to find my dad in the hallway saying, "You're late."

Naturally, at that young age, I resented my parents for hounding me that severely, but today I'm so happy they did. Their vigilance kept me out of too much trouble.

What's funny, though, is that when I went back home and called my friends Marci and Karen to tell them about Mac, I told them about her cable television, not her wild lifestyle. I remember saying, "She has HBO!" At that time, cable TV was still new and cool, HBO was more commonly known as Home Box Office, and nobody had it, nobody I knew—except for Mac. That made her even cooler.

It was strange when September rolled around and my friends returned to Granada Hills High for tenth grade without me. I saw my friends on weekends and assured them that my glamorous job wasn't changing me. That was true. As they knew, I still helped with the dishes, did chores around the house, and adhered to an eleven o'clock bedtime. My only indulgence was a white Chevy Chevette, with a burgundy tweed interior, when I got my learner's permit.

As a treat to myself, I had the back pinstriped "I love EJ." EJ was Elton John, and my obsession with the flamboyant genius was well-known on the set. One of the show's producers used his connections to take me to see Elton in a surprise VIP-only gig at the Troubadour, the small club in West Hollywood, where he'd blown people away five years earlier in his celebrated American debut. Now he was one of the biggest stars in the world, and I was among those lucky enough to see him. I had to pinch myself the whole night. I liked the perks of show business.

My real life provided *One Day*'s writers with the details that made Barbara such a relatable character, including my Elton obsession. Barbara's bedroom, like mine, was decorated with Elton posters. We also did a show where I dressed up like Elton, sang a song, and someone sent the tape of me to Elton. Much to my delight, I received an autographed photo in return.

"You look more like me than I do," it said. "Love, Elton."

A year or so later I was incensed when a teen magazine wrote that I'd given up on Elton because he'd recently confessed in a magazine interview to being gay. I didn't understand the press. Neither did my family. I'd given an interview, one of my first, in fact, but I'd never said that. I suppose I wasn't interesting enough. The writer should've seen me when I read her story.

"Bull crap!" I shouted, flinging the magazine against my bedroom wall. "I still love him! How dare you write those lies!"

Unfortunately, that first time wasn't the last time that lies would be printed about me. Excuse the rant, but it boggles my sense of right and wrong that publications get away with writing totally false stories. Every week you see magazines and tabloids lined up on newsstand trumpeting half-truths and total falsehoods about celebrities. It's worse online.

Why in the world is that permitted? It ingrains the practice of lying in our culture—as if it's not already a cancer.

On December 16, 1975, *One Day* finally aired for the first time. Family and friends gathered at our house to watch, and relatives called to congratulate me. I was a mixed bag of nerves and excitement. The show surpassed expectations, a winner in the ratings, shooting into the top ten. Overnight I became famous, though between the demands of work and my parents' effort to keep life as normal as possible, I was shielded from most of the attention.

I know that's hard to believe, but I had little awareness over the years that girls copied my hairstyles or that guys thought I was hot. I could have used a little more of the latter. Even today, guys tell me that they had a crush on me. I say, "That's great, but where were you when I needed to hear that?"

We shot fifteen episodes that first season, and I went out, as far as I was concerned, on a low note. Our last show was a two-parter. In the first, Ann learned her ex-husband (played by Joseph Campanella) was remarrying, and in the second, Julie and I tried to get them back together.

In part two, Julie and I had to face the fact that our effort at reuniting our family wasn't going to happen, ever. It was a touching, emotional scene. As written, it required me to cry. I tried umpteen ways to put myself in a sad mood and pop some tears, but nothing happened. My eyes were drier than the Mojave.

Ask any actress. They'll tell you that crying on cue is a skill. At the time, I wasn't remotely close to being a skilled actress—and I felt it. With everyone waiting for me, I hated myself for not being able to deliver. Sensing my frustration, Bonnie took me aside and cried for me, explaining her tricks for summoning tears. It was an instant acting lesson from a masterful teacher. Unfortunately, it sailed over my head, and we worked around it.

Afterward, Norman came to the set and took me aside and said that he wanted me to take acting lessons during the spring and summer break. Interpreting that as a warning, I thought my job was on the line. The opposite was true. Knowing that the network had picked us up for a full season of twenty-two episodes, Norman wanted me to get better for the next year. He saw my potential even if I didn't believe in myself enough to agree.

But it was little prods like that from Norman, Bonnie, and others that got me through that first season and helped me into a long career. However, outside of work, I was on my own; lots of difficult lessons lay ahead.

Six

BLUE-JEAN BABY

Perhaps one reason I was slow to come into my own as a woman has to do with the way I learned about being a woman. I know it's a different experience for each person, but mine was essentially a solo expedition. If I have one piece of advice, it's to implore mothers to talk to their daughters—about *everything*.

Mine didn't. I don't blame her, though. In a pre-*Oprah* world, she may not have known any better. Her mother died when she was eight years old, robbing her of a model for how to raise me. Frankly, by the time I was thirteen, I didn't want to talk to my mom about that stuff. So I got my period before anyone told me what was going on, and I learned about sex from kids at school.

I also learned about the facts of life through experience. In ninth grade, I had the hots for Doug. I don't remember anything about him except that he dumped me for the foxiest girl in school, yet he kept calling me, and for some stupid reason I agreed to go out with him

43

again. Big mistake. As soon as he got me alone in his car, he unzipped his pants and pushed my head into his crotch.

Hell-ohhh?

I don't know where that horny little dirtbag got the idea I was interested in going in that direction, but I quickly wriggled out of his grasp and leaned away, disgusted. At the same time, I tried not to show how completely grossed out I was by him. Wasn't I the polite, considerate girl? Wasn't I also the conflicted, confused girl? I told him to take me home; that much I knew.

I never could figure that one out. I wasn't good enough to date, but he wanted my face in his lap. What was up with that?

After Doug, I went more than a year before I was interested in another boy, or, rather, until a boy was interested in me. It was 1976, and I'd returned to Granada Hills High for the remainder of eleventh grade after *One Day* went on hiatus. Between my shyness and the notoriety I'd gained from the show, I had a tough time fitting back into school. Then my friend Karen's ex, a curly-haired boy named Ron, asked me out. We got along fine until Karen insisted he take her to the prom.

That was one of those situations where we could've used an intermediary, since it was too weird to deal with logically. Although Karen had dumped Ron—ostensibly, she said, out of boredom—she claimed he'd asked her to the prom earlier in the year, prior to their breakup, and she was holding him to it. Except that screwed me.

"Why can't I go?" I asked her.

"Because he didn't ask you," she said emphatically.

"But he's not dating you anymore," I replied.

"Yeah, but he still asked me," she said. "So I'm still going."

Believe it or not, I called Karen after she got home from the prom. I wanted to know how it went. They'd had fun. Then Ron came back

44

to me, and we dated through the summer. I didn't know other girls at school referred to him as "the cherry picker," but I definitely knew that he wanted to get more intimate with me and I felt my body urging me toward that special moment.

At the same time, I wasn't sure. I was scared. I can't remember if I'd even seen a guy naked before, so I wasn't clear about what *really* happened under the covers. I'm sure I would've performed well on a multiple-choice test, but I had doubts about being on my own in the field. It was the classic struggle between childhood and maturity, the insecurity of saying no and desires that made me want to say yes.

It was at that crucial time I could've used a good talk with my mom. But let's be real. What teenager talks to her mother—even when her mom wants to talk? Truth be told, Wolfie opens up more with the driver of his tour bus and my brother Patrick than he does with me. Teens just don't talk to their mothers the way they talk to other adults. Though I've needed to overcome some hurt feelings to get to this point, I know it's good he's talking to someone. And at least they're people I trust.

That's the situation I found myself in too. Early that summer, Bonnie had me spend a weekend with her in New York. I had the time of my life. She took me to the cool boutiques in SoHo and Greenwich Village, where I purchased a heavy red coat. I felt sophisticated carrying a shopping bag through New York City. After dinner, Bonnie and I sat outside on her fire escape, talking about everything under the sun.

We didn't move from that perch until five in the morning. I was surprised at how much I had to say, but Bonnie wanted to know me better and I was eager to win her approval, so I answered her questions more candidly than I would've had my own mother asked me.

At some point, I opened up about Ron and told Bonnie that I was debating about whether to go all the way with him. When she asked how experienced I was, I said that except for my ninth-grade boy-friend shoving my head in his crotch—"actually, he'd already dumped me by the time he tried that," I laughed—I was still a virgin.

After much talk and some graphic descriptions, Bonnie left the decision up to me and suggested that my heart would lead me to the best decision.

Back in L.A., feeling more mature and independent, I knew that I was going to do it with Ron. Those thoughts consumed me for days as I waited for our next date. I tried to imagine a romantic scenario, but the way it really happened still makes me cringe. Ron and I were in the back of his truck at the drive-in theater. Whatever movie was showing, I don't remember seeing a single frame of it. We started out fooling around under a blanket as usual. But this time, when he got to the point where I usually stopped him, he didn't encounter any resistance.

Like everyone, I wondered if I'd done it correctly. That curiosity prompted a few careful confessions to my closest girlfriends. After I admitted that the first time hurt, I found out everyone else pretty much felt the same way. None of us had a particularly enjoyable first—or second—time. Our stories were too much about the guy and not enough about us going slow and learning what felt good.

I don't think anyone has yet provided a good source of advice for girls on the topic of going all the way for the first time. Even after I'd done it twice, I still was pathetically ignorant. I'm embarrassed as I write this, but I actually told my girlfriends that I'd finally done it be-cause I was tired of wearing pads and wanted to switch to tampons, and I thought having sex would make it easier.

I know: too much information.

That summer, just before *One Day* went back into production on the second season, I decided to break up with Ron. Though I liked him, I didn't want to be tied to one guy at a time when my life was filling up with options. My girlfriends supported that decision. It felt right to all of us.

Then I switched into business mode. I had Ron come over to my house. I led him into my bedroom, put an Elton record on the stereo, and then matter-of-factly broke the bad news to him. It was like a scene from *The Godfather*—it's business, not personal.

"I'm starting work again, so I'm not going to be able to see you," I said.

"What?" asked Ron, surprised. "What are you saying?"

"We're going to have to break up," I said.

The split notwithstanding, we saw *Gone with the Wind* together the next night. I don't remember why. I was resolute about the split. But maybe once you made plans with Ron—à la Karen and the prom— you didn't break them. Or maybe I wanted to see the movie without the commitment of a boyfriend.

During the second season, I revealed my irrational concerns about my weight. "Let's face it," I told a newspaper reporter with utmost seriousness. "I have a very bad weight problem. When I stand next to Mackenzie, I look like a tub of lard."

Oh my God, when I read that today, I want to reach back in time, grab that ignorant, insecure teenager and shake some sense into her. I don't want to describe myself as out of control, because that gives the impression of someone with an eating disorder. My problem was different, though in its own way it was equally serious. I had no perspective in what was normal or healthy. Someone should have stepped in and contradicted me when I first said I was fat. I didn't have a weight problem. If I had any problem, it was in my head. I needed a stern talking to, someone to explain that the attention you got for who you were inside was more important than the attention you got for how you looked.

One might argue that it's different in Hollywood. But over the long term, I think substance always beats mere style.

At any rate, like most sixteen-year-olds, I was concerned with the superficial. I was stepping into the spotlight, getting my picture taken, showing up at events, and wanting to be thought of as desirable, if not sexy. I wanted to turn heads as the "blue-jean baby / L.A. lady" Elton John sang about. What did that fox look like? I don't know. All I knew was that she wasn't me.

I was reminded of that every day when I came to work and looked at Mac, who was built like a beanpole. Her Ditto jeans fit her perfectly with her 26-inch waist. My jeans were 30 inches. My waist was actually 23 inches, but I had to compensate for my hips. So even though I wasn't overweight, I felt obese next to her. If I saw her laughing with her cousin, I assumed they were making fun of me.

It makes me sad to remember how much irrational, needless pain I caused myself by thinking that I had a weight problem. I look back now and see that my focus on weight was just an ineffective way of trying to deal (or not deal) with the other issues going on inside me.

In reality, I was a svelte, shapely 110-pound girl. I looked the way I was supposed to. I was able to eat anything I wanted without gaining an ounce of weight. I enjoyed food. My mom, like all the women in my family, was an incredible cook whose repertoire included lasagna, Chinese food, caramel apples, and the best Christmas cookies ever! Instead of eating normally, though, I put myself on a diet.

Which diet? It changed from week to week. It didn't matter. It was more about restriction and punishment. I ate, or didn't eat, in response to emotions—not hunger. I starved myself in order to feel good, and I ate whenever I felt bad. Both had the opposite results. Eating made me miserable, and not eating put me in a bad mood. To my constant frustration, my body stayed the same regardless of my efforts and it led me to try a more drastic means of getting results.

It was still summer, and I turned to my older brother Drew for help. He was in college, and had his own apartment. The previous spring I sometimes went there after school with friends to smoke pot. Getting high didn't interest me as an everyday activity, but I had fun the few times I did it. Since I figured Drew had connections, I asked him if he could get me diet pills, and he came up with a bottle of black beauties.

Uncertain of how much to take and scared of OD'ing, I came up with my own regimen. Before I went to bed, I took half a pill. I know that sounds absurd, considering they're uppers and supposed to keep you buzzing for hours. But I went to sleep without any problem and woke up with enough energy to get me through the day without feeling like I wanted or needed to eat until I got home for dinner.

Very quickly I noticed the kind of results that I was unable to get on any diet. I lost weight. I looked thinner. There was a downside, though. I hated the way the pills made me feel. They also made my face break out in huge, honking zits. There were mornings when I walked into the makeup trailer and my makeup artist looked at me as if I'd turned into a leper. I can still hear him ask, "What's going on with you?"

I'm sure he knew. But neither he nor anyone else said anything. After losing 10 pounds, I had enough of feeling crappy and looking worse. Before anyone saw through the flimsy excuses I gave about being stressed or hormonal, I quit. I sensed the possibility that I might get hooked on either the pills or the feeling, which I liked, of my stomach being empty, and I knew that was dangerous, if not potentially deadly, territory.

In general, I liked my life. My body was the problem. You know what I think really saved me from getting into trouble? I simply loved to eat. At a certain point, I wanted my hot fudge sundae.

The show brought attention to my body whether I liked it or not. In the second season's fifth episode, a show titled "Barbara's Emergence," my character tried to attract boys by tarting up her appearance. Those scenes were difficult and uncomfortable for me.

There was also a kissing scene, my first one. The producers brought in Christopher Knight—Peter on *The Brady Bunch*—as the guy. Nothing against Chris, who seemed nice, but I hated kissing him. The moment the scene ended I hurried to my dressing room and brushed my teeth, as if erasing the experience from my memory bank. I know that making out with good-looking people is one of the perks of being an actor, but it creeped me out to be intimate with a stranger— and it still does.

In the next interview I did, I declared that I'd never do a nude scene. Not that the reporter even asked. I simply felt compelled to take a position in public. My dad clipped it, as he did every one of my articles and photos, and in the margin he wrote, "Yes! Yes! Hold fast to this statement." It hasn't been a problem. The only place I'm apt to be seen naked is in my bedroom—and then it's got to be with the lights out. The raciest photo I ever took was during an otherwise demure session with famed photographer Herb Ritts. I freaked out because one of my nipples kept poking through the loose weave of the sweater I was wearing.

The closest I ever came to baring it all was in the 1984 TV movie *Shattered Vows,* a true story about a nun who leaves the convent and falls in love with a man. I had a love scene with actor Tom Parsekian in which I had to take off my shirt. I did it from the back and wore ginormous pasties over my boobs. They covered everything, not just my nipples, and yet I still felt uncomfortably bare.

Then Ed walked onto the set in the middle of the scene. His timing was very strange, though Ed tried to put me and everyone else at ease by cracking, "Honey, every flick's got some tit in it."

True enough, I thought. But they didn't have mine—and they still don't.

Mac and I talked about boys all the time. We also chased them, especially those who guested on our show. On the first season, both of us went after Robby Benson. My more experienced costar won the friendly competition. Soon after, one of the teen magazines ran a story headlined "Valerie & Mackenzie: What to Do When You & Your Best Friend Like the Same Guy."

In the middle of season two, Mark Hamill came on the show as Schneider's criminal nephew, and Mac and I flirted with him like crazy as he told us about recently finishing a space-themed movie called *Star Wars* with director George Lucas. Mac, who'd worked with Lucas on *American Graffiti,* immediately lit up, and they compared notes on the director's brilliance, which made me, whether imagined or not, feel left out of the conversation.

Before leaving, Mark gave me a publicity still of himself as Luke Skywalker. I went, "Oh my God, that's so cool!" I had it blown up to poster size and drove to his beach house in Malibu, hoping to give it to him as a surprise. That was so pathetic in a sweet, naïve way. What would Mark have wanted with a poster of himself? In any case, I felt too weird about leaving it, even with a note, so I stuck it back in my trunk. Then I forgot to give it to him a few weeks later when we went out to lunch. I was probably too embarrassed.

When Mark came to the door to pick me up for lunch, I let him in and then immediately ran back to the kitchen, barely saying hello before leaving him to stand there on his own. I didn't want him to discover what was going on in the kitchen: that my dad was making me sign hundreds of fan club pictures. I felt like such an idiot. How uncool was I?

Mark and I had a fun time at the Farmer's Market. We went as friends, nothing more. Then *Star Wars* came out, and I never saw him again. The poster I had made got thrown out when I sold the car.

The point of revealing my young dorkiness is that, at that moment, I was ready to connect with someone special. That statement sounds like a plotline from a *One Day* episode. "Barbara feels ready to fall in love, but doesn't know how to go about finding the right guy." I can envision it, with a scene toward the end where my mom or Schneider provides the all-important life lesson by saying, "Barbara, as you get older, you'll learn the truth about love. You don't find it. It finds you."

My love life was a source of interest whenever I did press. I cringe when I picture myself sitting across from grown women, describing my Mr. Right as a man who "cares about my feelings, and is concerned about what I do. He must have an outstanding sense of humor. Someone who will always be there when I need him. And he must also need me a lot, because I need to be needed. Looks are what draw me at first—but if there's nothing in his head, that's that."

The teen press fueled many a naïve fantasy by linking me with Anson Williams (we hosted an American Heart Association event together), Parker Stevenson (we appeared together on a *Battle of the Network Stars*), and Shaun Cassidy (I played his girlfriend on one episode of *The Hardy Boys*). I didn't date any of them. But I did go out with singer Bo Donaldson after meeting him in December at the annual

Santa Claus Lane parade. A teen magazine ran a photo and asked if it was love.

No, it wasn't.

Before another photo op materialized, I began seeing another musician. I met Paul Shaffer—yes, the same Paul Shaffer who's now famous as David Letterman's bandleader—through actor Greg Evigan. They were costarring in the sitcom *Year at the Top,* the pilot of which was being shot in a studio next to the *One Day at a Time* set. We struck up a neighborly friendship.

Paul was a doll—nice, witty, and immensely talented. What really got me, though, was that to me he looked like Elton John. We went out twice, including New Year's Eve. Then his girlfriend called, and I never heard from him again. Thanks, Paul. In reality, there were no hard feelings, and we laughed about it years later.

Fortunately for me, the most intimate, personal, and sometimes painful material about my love life never became public.

Seven

LOVE WALKS IN

Our work schedule was the same each week. On Monday the entire cast and production crew, including the director, producers, and writers, gathered like a giant extended family around a long conference table and read through the latest script from start to finish. The idea was to find the jokes (that was always the most important part), feel the story arc, and discover the parts that worked and didn't work.

Through the weekly repetition of that process, I learned the technical part of my craft. The hard stuff about tapping into my emotions came later and over time. My mom was there every day taking notes for me. Bonnie was always interested in the story, trying to find the truths, while Pat looked for the jokes. I learned so much just from being around them.

I also liked the routine and the easy, familial manner in which all of us traded gossip about our weekends. In the predictability, I found myself surprised.

It was in mid-February 1977, and the script on the table was "Barbara Plus Two," an episode in which Barbara accepts her best friend's (John Putch) invitation to the school dance, but then says yes to another boy on whom she has a crush. She doesn't know what to do. Scott Colomby played that other boy, and from the moment I laid eyes on him at the table read I was a goner. Scott was handsome, with dark hair and a lean build. He was also twenty-four.

We sat next to each other at the table. By Wednesday's read-through, I flirted with him openly, drawing pictures of little hearts in the margin of the script for him to see. On Thursday, in case he hadn't gotten the message, I hauled out the big guns. I wrote the lyrics to "Lost Inside of You," a song Barbra Streisand sang to Kris Kristofferson in *A Star Is Born* ("I'm . . . lost in your eyes"). That worked.

After work we went for coffee and had one of those wonderful first date nights when everything clicked between us. We talked endlessly, as if the details of each other's life were as essential as air and water. Later that night, we ended up at Mac's house, where we continued talking until three, at which point he went home, and I fell asleep. My strict parents allowed me to sleep over at her house as long as I called and let them know where I was.

I had good dreams that night, and the next day started out even better. When I got to work, I found a single rose in my dressing room with a note that said, "Love, The Kid."

On the following Saturday, we went antique shopping and then to Scott's house. He shared a modest place in Hollywood with another struggling actor. I was impressed with his sophisticated taste in art and furniture. He had a sensitive, artistic, and thoughtful way that was an exciting, interesting leap from the guys I'd dated previously. A few nights later we saw a movie, and when I got home, I wrote in my diary that Scott was an "irresistible person."

At the end of February, after a couple weeks of nonstop dating, our romance was in full bloom. It became official when he was my date at a wrap party for one of the episodes at Chasen's, an old Beverly Hills restaurant on Beverly Boulevard. I remember that was an important night for us. Our hands never stopped touching each other. We skipped dessert and went to his house, where we made love for the first time. Because of the party, I had gotten permission to stay out late, and I took full advantage, turning it into a wonderful experience. I got home at four in the morning.

Then I woke up at six-thirty and drove ninety minutes out to Temple City, in the San Gabriel Valley, where I was the grand marshal in that city's annual Camellia Festival parade. I was absolutely exhausted, but in the kind of way I wanted to savor forever.

In early March *One Day* wrapped the season with a small cast party at the Beverly Wilshire Hotel. I took Scott, and, as we had before, we left early and went to his place. I eventually went to Mac's, where I'd told my parents that I planned to spend the night. I never lied to them, at least technically, about sleeping at Mac's; it was just that sometimes I slept there only for a couple hours.

A few nights later, Mac's cousin had a party. Scott and I put in an appearance before going back to his house. It's funny; someone once asked me to describe my relationship with Scott, in the context of remembering a first true love. I shrugged, offered a sheepish smile, and said, "I spent a lot of time in his bed."

But after that night's party, I returned to Mac's at five in the morning. By ten, I was at home, helping my dad paint the garage door. After months of shopping, we had moved to a new house in Los Feliz, an old L.A. neighborhood in the hills near landmarks such as Griffith Park, the Observatory, and the Greek Theater. The 1920s-era

Spanish-style home was closer to the studio and thus easier for my mom, who was still chaperoning me on the set each day.

Hoping for more independence, I turned the space above the garage into a one-bedroom apartment, with my dad's help. That satisfied me. I still ate dinner with my family and helped with the dishes afterward. On weekends I had other chores. I wasn't always easygoing and compliant about the household responsibilities, but, as was the case with my curfew, I thank my parents today for the strict boundaries they set. They kept me in line when I could have easily gone astray.

Look, I can certainly draw parallels between what could have happened to me and what has happened to some young stars today. I drove a Corvette, occasionally puffed a joint, and fooled around at my boyfriend's. I thought I knew more than I actually did. If paparazzi had followed me day and night, I'm sure that some clever tabloid writers could have papered me with scandal. If my parents hadn't been as strict, those writers might not have had to be so clever.

Then again, I wasn't *that* wild. For my seventeenth birthday, Scott and I had dinner with my parents and watched *Saturday Night Live*. A few days later we celebrated by ourselves at the beach and had what I described in my journal as "a wonderful night."

I bet.

By the standards of today's hard-partying stars, we were tame. We hit favorite restaurants like the Moustache Café (I loved the ratatouille crepes), drank Blue Nun wine, and, as I mentioned earlier, spent a lot of time in Scott's bedroom. Hey, it was true. I was fortunate. After my previous experiences, it was nice to experience the soft, caring ways a man could treat a woman.

Through those soft, caring ways, he made me feel good about myself. I don't profess to be an expert about sex, but as someone with body-image issues, I know the way a man makes a woman feel before and after sex is usually more important than the whole getting-it-on part if it's going to be memorable.

I'm sorry for the way that my mother and I communicated about my being sexually active. It would have been altogether different if we'd talked beforehand, but that wasn't the way we handled the growing-up process. As a result, we made mistakes—both of us, I'm sure—and we frustrated each other through our inability to communicate the way we should have.

One day I came home, and my mom had my diary in her hand. From the way she was looking at me, I knew she'd read it. I had put everything in that diary. I mean *everything*—all the intimate details of my life. As upset as she was, it didn't compare to the way I felt after having my most private thoughts violated.

"Oh my God," I said. "You did not—"

She interrupted me, holding up the diary like a prosecutor would evidence in a courtroom.

"What is this about?" she asked, holding the diary open to a specific page. From where I stood ten or fifteen feet away, I saw that it was one of the passages I'd written about making love to Scott. Though I don't have much of a temper, I exploded in rage.

"How dare you read my diary!" I said.

She stepped back defensively.

"Are you on the pill?"

"What?"

"It says you're on the pill."

"I can't believe you read my diary!" I screamed.

She began to say something, but I ran past her into the house and locked myself in the bathroom. She followed me inside and pounded on the door.

"Talk to me!" she yelled. "Talk to me!"

"No! I hate you," I screamed back.

Neither of us had ever spoken to the other in that manner, but, then, we'd never really talked. If I'm hammering that point about mother-daughter communication, it's for two reasons. First, it's important on many levels. Second, my mom would've had so much to say to me if she'd let herself. She knew what it was like to grow up without a mother to talk to, and consequently she'd made mistakes. She'd gotten pregnant at seventeen, the same age I was at the time, which I'm sure brought back memories.

When she read my diary and looked at me, I'm sure she got frightened. She didn't want me to make the same mistakes she had. Ultimately, I don't think she meant to scream "Talk to me," as much as she meant "I need to talk to you." In the heat of the moment, though, neither of us was thinking clearly.

It was only years later when I was pregnant with my son, Wolfie, that we began to speak openly, and I realized how much she had to say.

After a cooling-off period, life returned to normal, and, other than a few times when my dad got on me for coming home after two in the morning, no questions were asked about the time I spent with Scott, which was considerable. In June we caught the musical *Grease* at the Pantages Theater. A few weeks later we returned for *The Wiz*. We seemed to live at the theater.

Being a celebrity can spoil you, what with all the invitations to events and openings. *One Day* came along before the gift bag full of tens of thousands of dollars' worth of gifts and coupons that lures many stars to events these days. That's why some actors will go to the opening of an envelope. The perks in my day weren't that sweet. At seven-teen I thought I was hot stuff when I got my friend Karen and me into *Star Wars* for free. When I pushed it, I only embarrassed myself.

One night, as Scott and I waited in a long line at a movie theater in Westwood, I tried to cut our way into the theater early. Finding the manager, I introduced myself, as if he didn't know me, and asked if we could sneak inside, explaining that autograph seekers might mob me if I waited in line. The manager, who looked like a recent UCLA grad, was unimpressed.

"Are you being mobbed now?" he asked.

"No," I admitted.

"Then wait in line like everyone else."

Scott handled such moments gallantly. He helped me through a lot of awkward and embarrassing moments by sending me roses. I got a kick from the way the card always said "Love, The Kid." Scott had sent roses earlier in the year after Mac and I sang on a TV special star-ring game-show host Peter Marshall, Dionne Warwick, and Gladys Knight. At the time, I entertained the idea of making a record along the lines of my favorites by Linda Ronstadt and Jackson Browne. That's what teen stars did. I even took singing lessons. Then I heard Dionne during rehearsals and turned to one of the show's producers who'd also heard my run-through.

"Do you think I could ever sing as good as her?" I asked.

Without hesitating, he said, "No." Nothing more. Just "no." Blunt. Matter-of-fact. No. That was the end of my career as a singer. Scott's take on any endeavor, whether it was doing a play, a movie, or singing, was to study. His work ethic was impressive. I really admired that about him. In August I watched him tape a sitcom pilot with Ned Beatty and marveled at their skill. They were, along with Bonnie, up in that other acting league, the one I aspired to.

Scott would talk to me about acting, which he took very seriously. But I was considered a sitcom actress. What's more, I was put into the teen-star category. Every week I was in the glossy pop magazines, alongside Kristy McNichol, Leif Garrett, Willie Ames, Donny and Marie Osmond, and rock musicians Peter Frampton and the Bay City Rollers. I wasn't keen on that stuff, but it was part of the game.

Those magazines always had stories with me discussing how I handled fame, advising girls to "never steal your best friend's boyfriend," answering questions from readers ("Dear Valerie, my sister and I are both petite and like sharing the same clothes, but the problem is I'm neat and she's messy—what do I do?") and revealing "You know I'm in love when . . ."

It didn't matter that I rarely gave them interviews. They nevertheless had stories detailing what I supposedly thought about various things. I remember Scott and I sharing a laugh as I read him a piece from one story:

"You know I'm in love when I stop noticing cute guys around me."

"That's good for me," he said.

"You know I'm in love when I think about that handsome boy from the moment I wake up to the second I go to bed."

"Also good for me."

"And when I get that blank expression on my face during dinnertime, my family knows just what—*or who!*—I've got my mind on! Schoolwork? No. Watching TV? No. Talking to friends? No. Val might as well not be doing any of that because her thoughts are on H-I-M!"

"I'm glad," Scott said. "I wouldn't want it any other way."

At that moment, neither did I. But one thing about life is that things change—and depending on the choices you make, that can be good or bad.

Eight

LOVE LIES BLEEDING

Mac and I came from different worlds, but how different they were was never clearer than when I heard she'd been arrested. The news took me totally by surprise.

It was November 1977, more than five months into the shooting schedule. My parents were in the kitchen, reading the paper, when I came into the room. My mom looked up from the newspaper and said, "Something happened to Mackenzie."

I stopped and listened as she recited the details from the paper. The Los Angeles County Sheriff's Department had arrested Mac after finding her lying on the street at night in West Hollywood. They'd described her condition as "semistuporous and incoherent." A small amount of cocaine had also been found in her purse.

"What happened?" I said, dumbfounded.

"It says in the paper she was arrested and spent the night at the

USC County Medical Center," my mom said. "In the jail ward. Then she was released on $500 bond."

I shook my head.

"Oh my God."

I tried to remember what I'd been doing the night before other than hanging out with Scott.

I was upset. This was terrible, shocking, disturbing news. For a moment, I thought about work. I wondered what it was going to be like there, what people would say, if they said anything at all. But then I thought about Mac again and I got concerned for her.

I had known that she did drugs. I'd done them with her. But I knew that she was into them way worse than me. I prayed she was all right.

"What else does it say?" I asked.

My mom looked at the paper and read.

"According to Mackenzie's publicist, she stopped for coffee after a party, tripped and hit her head on the curb. A passing sheriff's car happened to see her fall, stopped, and offered to help."

What a different time it was then. These days she would've had a dozen video cameras and paparazzi filming her as she did whatever, just as they've done when Britney Spears or Lindsey Lohan has gotten into trouble. Shoot the mishap, turn it into entertainment, disregard that a human being may be in need of help.

Even in my naïveté, I knew better than to believe what my mom had read me in the paper. Mac later blamed it on a guy slipping her a pill. "Like a stupid, dumb shit, I took it," she said. "It was a Quaalude. I'd never taken one before. My knees were like jelly. I asked the guy to take me to a coffee shop, but I fell over just when a deputy came by."

Poor Mackenzie. Though we'd grown apart and in reality were

never as close as anyone believed—our worlds were simply too different—we still shared a bond, and it made me feel awful for her. I didn't know all the details of her private life, but I knew enough about Mac to understand that behind the glitz and glamour, the famous parents and celebrity friends, there was a young woman who was sad, lonely, and complicated. I said pretty much all that to my mom as we discussed her situation, though I was careful not to say much about myself.

Later that day, I wondered if anyone knew about my naughty side. I thought about the partying I'd done up at her house and hoped no one would find out. Was it a big deal that I drank and smoked pot? I didn't think so. I thought that whatever I did probably fell within the boundaries of normal experimentation. I probably drank too much Blue Nun with Scott, who wasn't into drugs, but that's as hard core as I got in those days.

But the show had created a wholesome image of me and it would've blown people away to read that I wasn't as squeaky clean as they imagined. Hell, it would've blown my parents away.

After Mac's arrest, I walked with a jittery stomach, nervous that someone might come up to me and ask, "Did you do drugs with her?"

Nothing like paranoia to keep you on the straight and narrow. And good parents. When I look back, I thank my lucky stars for parents who cared enough to set strict ground rules. Even though it bugged the crap out of me at the time, I see the benefit now. It's easy to lose your way in Hollywood. I knew as much even then. I'd seen the luck and privilege of fame turn to excess and ruin too many young stars. The difference was always found in the kid's home life, or lack of one.

Consider: After her arrest, Mac's father called her—and he wasn't pissed. "It's about time, kid," he said. "You're doing good."

Good? A few months later, Mac spent the night with Mick Jagger, who, as the story was reported in *TV Guide,* said, "I have been waiting for this since you were ten years old." In February 1978 she was put in a drug diversion program. "I'm happily diverted," she told *People* magazine. But it was a sham. She never took part in the program, she acknowledged to the *L.A. Times;* instead she was diverted by a new relationship with 34-year-old record producer Peter Asher. She also developed a drug habit that escalated from snorting coke to freebasing.

Mac was self-conscious when she returned to work after her arrest and, as far as I remember, nothing about it was officially said to the cast. I didn't know what to say to her, so I didn't say anything. After that, we drifted in very different directions. Part of me felt like I failed as a friend, but she was beyond my ability to help.

I was relieved when *One Day* wrapped in March. Instead of returning to my old high school, I traveled to London for my first movie, *The Secret of Charles Dickens,* a CBS children's special featuring me as the novelist's teenage daughter. It was a clever mix of past and present as I skateboarded through Victorian England. For my first trip abroad, I brought Dickens novels and guidebooks. I visited Big Ben, Westminster Abbey, and Buckingham Palace, and made sure to see the Abbey Road crosswalk immortalized by the Beatles.

I ran up a big phone bill keeping in touch with Scott back home. Work kept me busy. I learned to skateboard for the movie and was terrible at it. Bored, sitting in my room at night, picking the scabs on my knees that I got from falling off said board, I let myself become distracted by a cute guy—the third assistant director, who was about my age and had a charming English accent.

We hung out together a few times after work. The most we did was grab dinner. There was definitely a mutual attraction, but I resisted anything beyond the fun of a flirtation. That is, until the movie came to an end. The night before I went back to the States, he took me to a showing of *Monty Python and the Holy Grail.* We laughed through the movie, and afterward he came up to my hotel room. We started kissing. One thing led to another, and a few hours later I was staring up at the ceiling and hating myself for not having more self-control.

Ashamed and angry, I was lying next to this guy and thinking about Scott. What was I going to tell him? How was I going to tell him?

I got out of bed and walked toward the bathroom, covering myself with a sheet. It was like a scene from a bad movie.

"I'm going to take a shower," I said.

"All right," he replied, sitting up in bed.

Suddenly his English accent sounded terribly foreign and wrong to me.

"I'd really appreciate it if you weren't here when I come out." He looked hurt, confused. "I'm sorry," I added. "I'm not dealing with this well."

"It's OK," he said.

"No, it's not. I'm going to take a shower. Seriously, can you just please not be here when I'm done?"

I was a teary-eyed wreck when I got back home and told Scott what had happened and how miserable I felt about it. I know that some people would have kept the affair to themselves, but I couldn't do that. I needed my conscience clear. I trembled as I waited for Scott's reaction, which was a look of utter incomprehension.

"Are you serious?" he asked.

I nodded.

Things between us understandably fell apart for a while. I didn't see or hear from Scott for several weeks, despite my repeated calls. I was miserable not being with him, and I hated myself for being such a stupid jerk in England. As I finished high school at Hollywood Professional School, I was miserable. I didn't do heartache well and shoved food into my mouth all day long as I waited for things to shake out. When we finally got together and talked, I reiterated my feelings for him. Thankfully, Scott was willing to pick up where we'd left off—or try to.

It helped that we were distracted by my eighteenth birthday at the end of April. Scott picked me up for what I thought was going to be dinner with his father at the Universal Sheraton Hotel. Instead we walked into a ballroom where nearly one hundred friends, family, and coworkers surprised me with a birthday blowout that my parents had arranged. The night included a three-course dinner, a band, and an enormous chocolate cake that I could have eaten by myself.

Looking back, I was more ambitious than I remember or want to admit. Soon after my birthday, I jumped into the picture *C.H.O.M.P.S.,* a caper comedy about a guy who invents a crime-stopping robot dog. I read the script and told Tami that I had to have that part. I got it in my unsophisticated eighteen-year-old brain that it was going to be a huge movie and push me into a feature career. But come on, *C.H.O.M.P.S.*? All I want to say about it now is that it wasn't *Norma Rae.*

More scripts were sent to Tami afterward, but my schedule had such a small window, and by the middle of summer, I was back at work on *One Day.* Though the story lines in the show's fourth season had Barbara graduating high school and growing up, they still lagged behind the changes in my real life. In July my parents moved to Shreveport, Louisiana, where my dad went to work on a new GM plant. That was his dream: to build a plant from the ground up. With my career in full swing, I obviously couldn't go with them.

At eighteen, though, I was able to fend for myself. I bought a tri-level, two-bedroom home near the one we sold, and my younger brother David, then seventeen, stayed with me while he finished high school. Despite stardom, I was still a down-home girl. A fun night for me was watching TV with my girlfriends Karen and Marci while my cat, Tuxedo, purred nearby. Once a week I whipped up a batch of my mom's lasagna, and I kept in shape for photo shoots with racquetball and dance classes.

My parents and youngest brother, Patrick, returned for Christmas, but I traveled to Shreveport as often as possible. I fell in love with the city's small town charm, the horse races at Louisiana Downs, and, of course, the New Orleans Saints, whom I've followed from Archie Manning to Bobby Hebert to Reggie Bush.

In February, encouraged by Scott to take my career more seriously, I made a difficult decision and parted ways with Tami. I had a hard time leaving my longtime manager and mentor, but I knew it was necessary to switch to representation that focused on adults rather than children. I signed with Marty Litke for management and Jack Grossbart at the William Morris Agency.

Jack was taken aback at our first meeting. I put him to a test by asking if he'd let me do an episode of TV's *The Love Boat*. If he said yes, I knew he didn't have any long-range goals for me. If he said no, I was ready to sign.

The upshot? Jack, who later partnered with Marty, ended up managing me—and does so to this day.

After *One Day* wrapped in March 1979, I started work on *Young Love, First Love,* a coming-of-age story about a girl struggling to decide whether to sleep with her boyfriend. Timothy Hutton played my boyfriend; the movie was later shown to actor Robert Redford, who was impressed enough by Timothy's performance to cast him in his directorial debut, *Ordinary People*. The film not only captured the Oscar for Best Picture of 1980, but won Tim the Academy Award for Best Supporting Actor.

Young Love, First Love was my first real TV movie, the start of what would turn out to be a long, successful part of my career, and I prepped for the role, intending to show people that I could handle drama as well as comedy. In fact, after the first day of shooting, the movie's producer called Jack and said, "God, she's so good!" When Jack told me, I said, "Why is everyone amazed? Was I supposed to be bad?" Critics gave the movie high marks. I was glad people saw me in a role other than Barbara Cooper.

However, they probably saw too much of me around that time. I appeared on so many game shows and network specials that *One Day* director Alan Rafkin gave me a coffee mug with a caricature of myself in a track suit that said, "I've got to do *Hollywood Squares*, then *Battle of the Network Stars*, and then *The Cross-Wits*. And that's just on Sunday!" But Jack and Marty put the kibosh on doing more of those shows, explaining that if I wanted to be considered as a serious actress, I couldn't overexpose myself by appearing on so many.

There was little room in my schedule, anyway. I was pulled in every direction but Scott's, and our relationship suffered. We went through the kind of tug-of-war that Ed and I would do years later on a more serious level between our careers and the challenges of making time for each other. It was also hard for an actor as talented and serious as Scott to watch me go from project to project while he worked hard to take his career to the next level.

I wonder how it would have been if I'd been Scott Colomby's girl-friend instead of him always being seen as my boyfriend. That's what it means when people say the business isn't fair. At any rate, I was thrilled when Scott landed a role in *Caddyshack*, the classic golf comedy starring

Bill Murray, Chevy Chase, and Rodney Dangerfield. The movie shot in Florida, and Scott went there that summer. When I visited a month or so later, I got a taste of the same medicine I'd given him.

As soon as I arrived on the set, I saw sparks between Scott and actress Cindy Morgan, the kind of hot, top-heavy blonde who had always intimidated me. Between takes, she flirted with him and glanced at me for a reaction. Unable to play that game, I flew home, feeling probably as rotten as I'd made Scott feel. Our phone conversation was painful.

"You cheated first," he said to me at one point, adding, "I like Cindy. I want to see how it goes with her."

When it was clear to me that we were breaking up, I fell apart. Knowing my own stupidity was to blame made it worse. And worst of all, after Scott came back to town, which I heard through friends, we didn't see each other. I had trouble dealing with that kind of sadness and frustration. Several times I drove by his house to see if *her* car was in front of his place. When word got out, and people asked what had happened, I told the truth. Scott had been a very important part of my life. Now he was a very important part of someone else's life.

As was my way, I ate myself through the hard times. So about a year later, when Scott showed up unexpectedly to see a taping of *One Day at a Time,* I was mortified. My weight had gone up to 120 pounds from around 107. I don't know if he had any intentions beyond just visiting the set. Feeling fat and ugly, I virtually ignored him the whole night, barely saying a word to him. After the taping, a group of us went to dinner. When the two of us finally had a moment alone, Scott chastised me for not paying any attention to him. He was right, and I apologized.

I just didn't know how to tell him the truth. All I could think was, I weigh 120 pounds, and I'm sure he thinks I'm a fat pig.

Nine

DOIN' TIME

In September 1979 *One Day* began its fifth season with an emotional two-parter featuring Mackenzie's character getting married and dealing with the changes of life on her own. In real life, Mac was dealing with more serious issues.

For two years I'd watched her struggle with her drug addiction, and, sadly, it appeared she was losing the battle. She was a shadow of the beautiful young woman I'd met almost five years earlier. Her weight had dropped to under 100 pounds, and she looked worn out. One time she nodded out while rehearsing a scene with Bonnie. In other, similar incidents, she forgot her lines or showed up late.

Clearly sobriety, even after her arrest, was a battle she wasn't able to win. The show ran out of patience. In December Norman come to the set one day, and Mac left a short time later in tears. Afterward Norman gathered everyone in the green room and explained that Mac was taking a leave to rest. In March, at the end of the season, she was fired from the show. As it was explained to me, people were concerned about Mac and wanted to send her a stern message: she needed help.

Her slide was sad—and scary. No one wanted to see her die, and yet that seemed like a possibility. Those of us on the set only saw the outward signs of her addiction, her lethargy, blotchy skin, general out-of-it-ness, but she had apparently graduated from freebasing and injecting coke to heroin. She spent a fortune on drugs. She later told *Newsweek* that in the months after she was fired, she vegged out at home amid the squalor of "mirrors, razors, empty tequila bottles, and half-eaten pizzas."

I had no idea how bad off she was and was relieved to hear in November that she entered rehab. At the urging of her father, who was also in the process of kicking heroin, she checked into Fair Oaks Hospital in New Jersey and began, or so it appeared, the long, hard, and life-saving task of getting sober.

All good lessons for me. As I once said, "I learned from Mac a lot of what not to do with your life."

By comparison, my problems were less than trivial. After some heavy rains, I had leaks all over my house. All three levels were dripping water inside, like steady little waterfalls. I had buckets everywhere. When I did a photo shoot for the cover of *Good Housekeeping*—a big deal, since that was one of the magazines my mom had always kept on the coffee table—I liked the picture. Then I received a letter from a dentist who said he could fix my teeth. Till then, I'd *liked* my teeth.

"What's wrong with my teeth?" I asked my friend Marci.

"Nothing. Why?" she asked.

"This guy—a dentist—wrote me a letter and said he'd like to fix my teeth. Now I'm thinking, great, my teeth are screwed up. One more thing that's wrong with me."

"No, your teeth are fine," she said. "If anything, it's your head that's screwed up for even worrying about that."

After my brother David graduated high school, he moved out, and Marci moved in. She was in college, preparing for a semester abroad. In exchange for my helping with her French lessons, she played racquetball with me when I needed to burn off energy. We also turned weekend nights into girls-only parties by inviting our friends Karen and Shelley up for melted brie, almonds, apples, and pears.

All that girl bonding gave me the boost I needed to get back into the dating pool. For several months I went out with *Battlestar Galactica* star Dirk Benedict, whom I met on a *Network Battle of the Sexes* special. One morning I was awakened by strange, heavy-breathing sounds coming from the other side of the bedroom. Fearful of what I might see when I opened my eyes, I worked up my nerve, turned over, and saw Dirk doing push-ups in the corner. He was very into his health, which was good for me.

In February Dirk and I spent seven days in St. Thomas in the Virgin Islands. We sent a postcard to my parents, signing it jointly, and at the bottom I added a PS: "Mr. Dirk Benedict is *cute!!*"

By mid-March 1980 I was unattached again and not looking to jump into anything, when Jack called and said that Steven Spielberg wanted me to read for the female lead in his next picture, *Raiders of the Lost Ark*. Hearing that Steven Spielberg wanted you to read for him would be heady stuff for any actress. For me it was simply too much to believe. It didn't make sense.

"Steven Spielberg wants to see me?" I asked. "Why?"

"Just go in and read," said Jack, who explained this was as much about being seen as an actress on that level as it was about getting the part.

"OK, just double-checking."

Though he'd recently experienced his first semiflop, the comedy *1941,* Steven was on his way to becoming one of Hollywood's all-time great moviemakers. He'd already established his reputation by directing *Close Encounters of the Third Kind, Jaws,* and *The Sugarland Express.* After reading the script for *Raiders,* I knew he was going to add another hit. But I seemed too young for the part. It still baffled me that he wanted me to audition for it.

"Remember what I told you," my agent said.

"What's that?"

"Just go in and read."

So I did. I met Steven in his offices at Universal. I don't remember seeing any other actresses waiting to read or anyone else associated with the movie. The two of us were alone. I was impressed—and intimidated. At thirty-three, he had longish hair and a full beard that gave him the look of a dashing director. His manner was casual and confident. He seemed pleased when I told him that his 1971 TV movie *Duel* was my favorite. That put me at ease, and we had what was essentially a nice visit.

When I arrived in my *One Day* dressing room the next day, I found a large bouquet of flowers from Steven. It turned out that Steven wanted to meet with me again.

"But not about the part."

Then I got the picture. Steven wanted to go out with me. I didn't put the pieces together until later: the hotshot director, who'd recently broken up with his true love, actress Amy Irving, must have seen me as a cute face and potentially easy lay. Too cynical? Maybe. But there's truth there too. On our first date, he took me to a movie in Westwood, and he followed that up a few nights later with an invitation to a screening at his gorgeous Coldwater Canyon home.

There I found myself talking to writer-director John Milius and wondering what the hell I was doing in this crowd. I'm sure that most of Steven's friends saw me as a good old time for their pal. But that's my interpretation. Steven and his friends intimidated me without intending to. Older, smarter, more successful, powerful, they were simply in another league than I was accustomed to. I mean, good for me, but it took getting used to. Just being around Steven played into my insecurities.

One time I made a crack about my hips. Steven said that reminded him of Amy, and he told me how she gained weight between movies and then dieted and exercised like crazy to get back in shape before going to work. However, he added, as if women might be the only thing he didn't understand, she always looked beautiful to him.

I liked hearing that. It said a lot about him. It also told me that he still had a thing for Amy, whom he would marry six years later in 1985.

While I was with Steven, I wished I knew more about movies, but he was patient and tried to teach me. It was like taking algebra with Stephen Hawking. In April he invited me to attend the Oscars with him. Feeling flustered by his world, I fumbled my way through the conversation, thinking as he asked me that he'd *better* well invite me, since I was sleeping with him. But then I chastised myself for thinking like such a bitch. Even though the conversation was short and sweet, I worried after hanging up that I'd sounded presumptuous.

I replayed the whole call in my head. Was I weird? Did I have too much tone in my voice? Convinced I'd made an ass of myself, I waited a bit and then called him back.

"I'm sorry," I said. "I shouldn't have acted like you were supposed to ask me. I'm honored that you asked me. Thank you. And I'd love to go."

At Hollywood's biggest, most prestigious annual party, we had a great time celebrating as the awards went to *Kramer vs. Kramer* for Best Picture, Best Actor (Dustin Hoffman), and Best Supporting Actress (Meryl Streep). Sally Field took the Best Actress honor for *Norma Rae,* and Melvyn Douglas won Best Supporting Actor for *Being There.* Steven knew everyone. We were on an elevator on our way to the Governor's Ball, when Sally Field stepped in holding her Oscar. I so badly wanted to congratulate her, but I was too nervous to say anything.

Once again, as I had many times since meeting Steven, I asked myself, "What the heck am I doing here?"

Nevertheless, Steven opened my eyes to a rarified side of Hollywood. After the Oscars, I spent a few days with him in the desert, watching him work on some additional material for *Close Encounters.* He spoke about projects on the drawing board, including *E.T.: The Extra-Terrestrial.* I didn't care much for Steven's pet parrot, but listening to him talk about his ideas and filmmaking inspired me to keep trying to break into features.

Even though the tabloids reported that Steven and I had a "special love" and "were talking about marriage," we knew it was a fling. We had too many differences, including age, career status, and religion. I met his mother, and I knew he wasn't going to marry someone who wasn't Jewish. And there was the stuff that really matters to me: food. One night, as we made pasta for dinner, I started to chop up garlic, and Steven said, "No. Stop. No garlic."

I stopped, all right, but it wasn't because I took direction from him. I thought, Are you kidding me? I can't date a guy who won't eat garlic!

Our relationship ended early that summer when I visited my parents in Shreveport and met someone else. I called Steven in Los Angeles. Given the attention we got in the tabloids, I didn't want him to hear it from anyone but me.

The next time we crossed paths, *E.T.* was warming hearts and breaking all sorts of box office records. Steven spotted me in the commissary at Universal. On his way out, he stopped by my table to say hi. I don't know what possessed me, but I blurted out, "Boy, congratulations on *E.T.* You must be really rich now!" It was one of the few times I remember Steven being speechless.

I think I was recovering from the pressure of being with Steven when I started dating a boy my brother Patrick introduced me to when I was visiting my parents in Shreveport. Only seventeen, he was a bright high school senior who aspired to a career in law. We met that summer, as he was about to leave for an internship in Washington, DC. I met him there in July and spent a few days touring the Senate, the House, and other sites in the city.

At the time, I was shooting *The Promise of Love,* a TV movie costarring Jamison Parker and Shelley Long in which I played the young widow of a Marine killed in Vietnam. The shoot included five days at Camp Pendleton, the Marine Corps base in San Diego. I emerged from that politicized and behind Jimmy Carter for president. A few months later, I voted for him—the first time I had cast a vote in any election. Even today I still recall it as a thrilling thing to do.

In August 1980 work on *One Day*'s sixth season was interrupted by a writers' strike. The entire business—not just our series—ground to a halt. Inspired by Steven, I bought a home in Coldwater Canyon, but I couldn't take possession of it until the end of September. With time on my hands, I called my brother Drew, who worked construction, and spent a few days helping him lay roof.

The guys on his crew were surprised to see me show up in the morning. But I put down the tiles and banged with my hammer like one of the gang. Hearing that I was working construction, friends were surprised by that do-it-yourself side of me, but I'd grown up helping my dad around the house and was always handy with tools. I was probably handier than Schneider.

The part I remember most about that job was the music. As we worked, my brother put a tape of the Pretenders' first album in his car stereo and cranked the volume. When I drove home that afternoon, I noticed a tape in my own backseat that my brother David had left there a few months earlier: an eight-track of Van Halen's first album, *Van Halen*. David had said that it was insanely good, and I should check it out. Well, better late than never. I reached back and popped it into the deck.

Little did I know that I was about to hear more Van Halen than I'd ever dreamed.

Ten

FEELS SO GOOD

It's funny how decisions that you make independent of anything else can end up affecting the rest of your life. I probably would have stayed in L.A. during most of the strike, but my brother Patrick had cooked up a scheme to get into the Van Halen concert in Shreveport for free. But he needed my help.

"There's a radio station here that plays Van Halen," he says. "They're sponsoring their concert here. They know that David and I are your brothers, and said if you come out here and do this one thing, we can get backstage."

"What's this thing I have to do?"

"For free. You, me, and David."

"What's the thing I have to do?"

"Hand out M&M's to the guys in the band," he said.

"What?" I asked. "M&M's? Why M&M's?"

David explained that Van Halen specified that a bowl of M&M's

be put in their dressing room before every show, with all the brown ones removed. The infamous M&M's clause was in the safety portion of their contract. So, if they saw the brown candies, they knew that the fine print of their contract concerning safety and production hadn't been read. I didn't know if that was ridiculous or ingenious, but I laughed. That was the world of rock and roll. It was crazy.

"So all I have to do is hand out M&M's?" I asked. "I don't have to sit there and take out the brown ones, do I?"

"No. Just say yes, and then we get to go backstage."

"Fine. Yes. I'll do it."

"You should listen to some of their albums."

I went out and bought the group's newest, *Women And Children First*. It opened with "And The Cradle Will Rock . . ." I recognized the song "Everybody Wants Some!!" from the radio. As for the rest of the album, I got it when singer David Lee Roth set the band's 100-proof party tone on "Romeo Delight" by growling "I'm taking some whiskey to the party tonight," and I loved Ed's beautiful acoustic guitar work on "Could This Be Magic?"

In other words, I liked that album, even though my personal playlist tended toward Elton John and Linda Ronstadt.

"What'd you think?" asked Patrick when we spoke again.

"Pretty good."

"Just pretty good?"

He explained that David Lee Roth was a great showman, but the magic was supplied by their genius guitarist, Eddie Van Halen, who'd won *Guitar Player* magazine's annual Guitarist of the Year award three years running and was, as my brother said, an honest-to-goodness rock god.

"I'll tell you what I really liked," I said.

"What?" he asked.

"Did you see the back cover of *Women and Children First*?"

"Yeah, what about it?" Patrick asked.

"The guitar guy—Eddie. Oh my God, what a cutie!"

"Val, do me a favor," he said. "Shut up—and get your butt over here so we can see the show."

The concert was on August 29. I flew into town a few days earlier and spent time with my family. On the night of the show, I put on a long-sleeved T-shirt that covered my butt and jeans, and then I slipped into a pair of sexy black thigh-high boots for a bit of rock-and-roll flair. I wanted to look hip—and not too hippie. Then, Patrick, David, and I got to the Hirsh Memorial Arena. The promotion guys from the radio station took us backstage to a green room for guests and local VIPs.

Glancing around, I didn't see anyone from Van Halen. The radio guys handed me a few large bags of M&M's and told me to hand them to the band members when they came into the room. A photographer would capture the moment.

All of a sudden there was a small commotion. I turned and saw the band's drummer, Alex Van Halen, come into the room. He had a bounce in his step, which somehow seemed purposeful, and he was laughing about something. We chatted briefly and posed for photos as I gave him the M&M's, and then suddenly I realized he was flirting with me. Then I thought, No, he's just really friendly.

Truthfully, I didn't know what to think. Then bass player Michael Anthony came into the room, and he was also sweet and jokey as we posed for photos. I got the sense that these guys lived the lifestyle they sang about; from what I picked up, they might've already had a drink or two. We were told that Ed and Dave were prepping for the show and would say hello afterward.

When the show was about to start, my brothers and I were led into the hallway and told to wait a second before being taken out front. I was fine waiting there. The corridors and tunnels backstage were like a maze, and I had no idea where I was. I leaned back against the wall, waiting for someone to get us, when Ed peeked around the corner. He was on his way to the stage, but I bet that Al or Mike told him to check me out. Our eyes caught. He pointed at me, smiled, waved, and then disappeared.

I had to be peeled off the wall. He *was* cute—even cuter in person.

I watched the show from the side of the stage. It was adjacent to the space where Ed's guitars were set up. It looked like a mini guitar shop. His guitar tech spent the show tuning guitars and getting them ready for Ed. Each time he came over to change guitars, he flashed me a smile. He didn't seem inhibited or distracted by the roughly fifteen thousand people watching him flirt with me. He was having a good time.

Even though my concert-going experience was limited, I could tell that Ed's playing was special. He and Dave worked together on-stage in a way that was pure fun. Dave sang and scatted, and Ed echoed him with his guitar. I understood why girls fell so easily for rock stars. With a whole arena chanting *"Ed-dee! Ed-dee!"* he kept smiling at me. It was an intoxicating experience that left me giddy and wanting more.

After the show, my brothers and I went backstage again, and we were told I could give away the rest of the M&M's when the guys were back out after they cleaned up. My wait was interrupted when I was taken to a small room that was curtained off—Dave's lair. I stepped in, and he raised his eyebrows.

"You were great," I said.

"Thanks, sweetheart," he purred.

"I'm supposed to give you these," I said, handing him a bag of M&M's as the radio station's photographer leaned in and squeezed off his shots.

I think Dave made a crack about what he could give me. It was funny and full of innuendo, but that's as far as it went. Based on the few minutes we spoke, I thought he was charming if not intimidating. Then I was taken to meet Ed, who was still in the dressing room, talking to his brother. Shy and nervous, he was not what I expected after watching him prance around on stage for more than two hours.

Ed and Al made room for me in their conversation. Mike drifted in and out, as did my brothers, who chimed in from the background as they hung around, waiting for me. It was a long wait. Ed and Al were funny, and no one was in a hurry to leave. They asked what I thought of the show, and then Ed asked if I'd heard their latest album.

"Yeah, I love it," I said. "I had no idea there was all this other great music out there. I was always so closed off to anyone except Elton John."

"You like him?" asked Ed.

"Love him. My girlfriend forced me to listen to the Who. But now I love them too."

"Cool."

"I was never into that guy who plays the flute. I can't remember his name."

"Jethro Tull," one of my brothers said.

"Yeah, that's him," I said.

"Jethro Tull isn't a *him*," said the same brother. "It's the name of a group."

"See?" I said. "I don't know what I'm talking about. I just know what I like."

"That's the only thing that matters," Ed said.

I don't know how long we spent backstage talking, but the only reason we quit was because the band's road manager interrupted. He said the crowd had left and the bus was ready to take them back to the hotel. Turning to me, Ed invited me to go back with them, explaining that they were going to hang out there for a few hours before getting on the bus and driving through the night to the next city.

I said sure. I wasn't ready for the night to end, and I hoped he wasn't either.

They were at a local hotel, the kind with doors on the outside. It was quite a few rungs down the ladder from the way they travel now. The night was warm and slightly humid. We sat around the pool, drank, smoked cigarettes, and talked until they had to get on the bus and leave for Baton Rouge, the next city on their tour. By then Ed and I had moved closer and were talking just to each other. I was surprised to learn that he and Al still lived at home with their parents.

"Do rock stars do that?" I asked.

He gave me an adorable look, punctuated with a shrug. I wanted to reach over and kiss him, but I restrained myself.

"I'm staying with my parents too," I said. "Here in Shreveport."

As he got on the bus, I explained that I was going to be at my parents' house for another week and gave him my phone number. Then I went home and waited for him to call. It was a much longer wait than I expected. I was disappointed when the next day passed without a call, and then I was downright mystified when both a second and third day went by.

Finally, late that third night—I think it was slightly past midnight—while I was playing cards with my brothers, the phone rang. Though we traded looks that asked who would be calling at such a late hour, we knew. I hurried to the phone and answered. It was Ed, calling from Beaumont, Texas, where the band had finished a show.

"We're going to Norman, Oklahoma, in two days," he said. "Do you want to come?"

"What are you doing in Oklahoma?" I asked, realizing the second after I said it how stupid I was, because obviously they were playing a show.

"We're playing a festival," he said.

"Yeah, I can get on a plane," I said.

"Great. I'll see you there."

I flew in on September 3. Ed had arranged for a limousine to meet me at the airport and take me to the gig at the University of Oklahoma. The road manager met me at the backstage entrance, draped an all-access pass around my neck and took me to see Ed. I watched the show from the side of the stage again. Afterward Ed admitted that he'd been nervous playing in front of me. I was taken aback that he felt that way, considering that thousands of people had been in the audience, but it indicated something was brewing between us. From the start, we were all about each other.

When we got back to the hotel, we sat up and talked as if we were making up for lost time. Ed filled me in on some of his background. He'd been born in the Netherlands to parents who were both musicians. His Indonesian mother was a pianist, and his father had played the clarinet with the Amsterdam Concertgebouw Orchestra. Ed was seven years old when his family moved to the U.S., settling in Pasadena. A piano prodigy, Ed had won several classical music competitions. He took up the drums, but said he switched to guitar after Al took over the drum kit while he was on his paper route, earning money to pay for the drums.

Ed was extremely close to his dad. When I asked why he still lived

at home, as I had the last time we'd talked, he said in an almost embarrassed tone that although Van Halen's albums had sold millions of
copies and their shows sold out, his mother still expected him to continue with his education and figure out a career when he got the rock-
and-roll thing out of his system.

"That's why you live at home?"

"She doesn't think it's going to last," he laughed, and then added,
"We're on the road so much, like ten months a year, it's just easier."

"How'd you learn how to play like you do?" I asked.

"Like everyone else," he said. "I cut school, sat at home, and prac-
ticed."

The more Ed laughed, the harder I fell for him. He had a genuineness that I hadn't encountered before. Despite my hints that I
wanted to sleep with him, Ed said that he had gotten me my own
room. Though he made it clear that he had similar feelings, he also
said that he wanted to get to know me better first. While that was un-
expected from a rock star, I took it as a sign that both of us felt something real.

I flew home the next day and told my family about the trip. As I talked,
I made a sketch of Ed from the back cover of *Women and Children First*.
This time it didn't take as long for him to call and invite me back on
the road. I accompanied him to Lubbock, Albuquerque, and Denver,
where he sneaked a little Beethoven into one of his solos as a treat for
me. We rarely left each other's side, except at night. I still slept in my
own bunk on the bus.

The road was a unique, absolutely special place to fall in love. As
we traveled along the highway at night, staring out the windows, listening to music and talking, I was reminded of the camping trips I

used to take with my family. Sometimes Dave or Al or Mike sat with us. Other times we cuddled by ourselves. It didn't matter. The environment was safe, intimate, and isolated from the rest of the world, which is what it's like to fall in love. No matter who's around, it's just the two of you.

Traveling with him, I got to know Ed in a way that I otherwise wouldn't have. Part of him was beyond me—the virtuoso side, the guy who thrilled critics and guitar fanatics with his "vibrato moans" and "sustained harmonics." When he played, he disappeared into a world that was his. There he was most comfortable, and whatever he shared was of his choosing. This interior world would confound, anger, and frustrate me to no end later on, but early on it was seductive.

Then there was this adorable, vulnerable guy who admitted to loving his parents, loving that his father cried when he watched them play, and loving that he and his brother had been able to afford to get their father to retire and buy him a boat. What was not to like and maybe even love?

The previous April, Ed had become, at twenty-five, the youngest artist featured on the cover of *Guitar Player* magazine. He wasn't comfortable with all the accolades; it was more pressure and attention than he wanted. He was happy writing songs and, as he put it, partying on stage. Seeing how emotionally guarded Ed was, I found that these confessions drew us even closer.

After knowing him for nearly a month, I learned something else that explained why he was hesitant about jumping in the sack with me. Prior to our meeting, he'd been involved in a long-term relationship with a girl who betrayed him by sleeping with a close friend. He'd had a hard time recovering. There were other hurts in his past too. Whether or not he revealed those, I understood why the guy had trust issues and preferred talking through his music.

When I felt Ed trusted me, I found myself having thoughts about him that were much deeper than those I'd had about any other guy I'd known. I was so ready to show him how much I cared. I kept waiting for him to feel the same way.

In mid-September I left Shreveport and flew back to L.A. for a meeting concerning the show. The strike appeared to be ending. On the 15th, I met Ed in Phoenix, where Van Halen headlined the Coliseum.

After the show, we went back to the hotel, one of those places where all the rooms opened up onto a multistory atrium that featured an indoor waterfall. The sound of cascading water accompanied Ed and me as we walked hand in hand down the hall. It felt as if we were in a rain forest. Our rooms were adjoining, and we each went into our own room, but I opened the connecting door and saw Ed sitting in a chair. He looked up at me and started to cry.

"What's wrong?" I asked.

He told me that he'd just won Best Rock Guitarist award from a guitar magazine for the fourth time, and Dave had punished him for it during sound check, lashing out by telling him that he thought he was hot shit just because he won. The truth was, Ed didn't think he was hot shit. He thought he was anything but that. He wondered why he had to be so lucky. He wished the attention had gone to Dave. Then, he said, "Maybe Dave will lay off me for a while."

I wrapped my arms around him and squeezed. When I pulled back, he stared into my eyes and said, "I love you." Tears were streaming from his eyes.

"Oh, God, I love you too," I said.

We ended up in bed, making love as if we were starving for each other. I felt like I never wanted to let him go. But it was more than sex. It was as if by finally sleeping together, we were taking an oath whose words we'd already spoken.

I think Ed would agree. There was something between us, and it didn't matter if no one else understood. We knew.

Eleven

RUNNIN' WITH THE DEVIL

When I returned to work after the strike, my romance was the topic of discussion on the set. It wasn't public knowledge yet, but I wore a Van Halen pendant on a necklace. Then it went public. "TV Sweetheart's Outrageous Date" one tabloid trumpeted above a large photo of us coming out of a restaurant. The *National Enquirer* quoted me telling a friend, "He's a regular love machine."

While the *Enquirer* had made up that quote, I nodded when I read that an anonymous friend had described me as "the happiest she's ever been." It was true. Between Bonnie, the producers, and the crew, they knew me as well as I knew myself. They'd watched me grow up from a naïve fifteen-year-old to a twenty-year-old woman in love and thinking about long-term plans.

As *One Day* went into its sixth season, I was thrilled to be exploring this new role as a rock-and-roll girlfriend. I was overwhelmed by ticket requests when Van Halen played two shows at the Los Angeles

Sports Arena. Ed stayed with me at my house in Los Feliz. Somehow fans found out he was there, and cars honked all night.

"*Ed-dee! Ed-dee!*" a couple guys chanted.

"Is he here?" asked some girls who rang the doorbell.

"Who?"

"Eddie Van Halen."

"No!"

The two-night stand wore me out. In mid-October Ed came back to L.A. during a break in the touring schedule and moved into my new Coldwater Canyon home, which I was in the process of moving into myself. *Bionic Woman* star Lindsay Wagner lived next door. We picked up his stuff at his Pasadena home, where I met his parents, both of whom were sweet to me. His father insisted on teaching me some Dutch phrases, and his mother was a feisty character who made spicy Indonesian food that was as good as any restaurant's.

I enjoyed walking around his childhood home. I tried to picture Ed as a kid, roaming the house with his guitar, learning Eric Clapton's solo from Cream's "Crossroads" note for note, as he'd told me he'd done, until he knew it perfectly. There was a part of Ed I couldn't picture, however. That was the twelve-year-old whose dad had given him a drink and a cigarette, and the fifteen-year-old who played guitar all afternoon while working his way through a six-pack of Schlitz malt liquor.

In mid-November Van Halen wrapped up the first leg of their world tour. Until they went out the following May, Ed and I had a block of uninterrupted time together, the first extended period we shared at home. After handling an unpleasant legal issue—Ed had to deal with a paternity suit filed by a girl from his past, which turned out to be false—we settled into a domesticity that was easy and comfortable.

Ed put all of his music equipment in the back bedroom, and I set up an office in a room off the kitchen. We shared the living room and large master bedroom. My brother Drew and his girlfriend Michelle occupied the guest house, an arrangement that was made prior to my meeting Ed, who got along with my brother, though I remember coming home a couple times and finding them punching the heck out of each other in the ivy.

After Ed moved in, I developed a new appreciation for the large gate in front, which kept groupies from ringing the doorbell. I couldn't do anything about the honking or yelling *"Ed-dee! Ed-dee!"* We didn't have a lot of land, but the acreage we did have, plus large trees and full hedges, afforded plenty of seclusion.

I raised the idea of marriage first. Even though we had been together for only a short time, it felt right. After I brought it up, Ed adopted it as if it had been his idea. He was a real guy. "Wouldn't it be great to get married?" he asked. You could look in our eyes and see we'd drunk the same Kool-Aid. In November we visited a jewelry store at a mall in Champaign, Illinois. A month later, we went to another jewelry store at a mall in Northridge, California, where I found a diamond ring that I loved.

"You really like it?" Ed asked, inspecting the ring.

I nodded. The jeweler measured my finger.

"This ring?" he asked, still holding it.

I nodded again.

"OK, we'll think about it," Ed said, giving it back to the salesman.

I don't know what made me think that Ed had purchased the ring, but later that day I asked if he had picked it up without my knowledge. He said no and was so convincing that I believed him. If it had been a car or a piece of guitar equipment, I wouldn't have believed him. But

I already knew him well enough to know that if it didn't involve one of those items, he probably hadn't paid attention.

Then as we were getting ready for bed, about to turn on the TV, Ed went into another room and returned holding a small jewelry box. He got down on one knee and said, "By the way, I bought the ring. Will you marry me?"

"Oh my God," I said. "Honey . . ."

We were beginning to celebrate when someone buzzed from the gate. It was the runner from *One Day*, delivering the changes in the script for the next day. I let him in, and both Ed and I answered the door. The runner was upset.

"Did you hear?" he asked.

"No," Ed and I said. "What happened?"

"John Lennon was killed."

"What?" Ed asked.

"Yeah, John Lennon's dead. I heard it on the radio. Some guy shot him."

"Holy shit!" I exclaimed.

"Where?"

"In New York. In front of the place where he lived."

That was one of those benchmark moments you don't ever forget. The three of us stood there, talking about Lennon, the Beatles, and their music. Ed and I continued to discuss it as we climbed back into bed and watched the news. I went to sleep thinking about all the crazies who followed Ed. On a personal level, it made me wonder what I'd gotten into with this guy. The tragedy of John Lennon's death, like the music he made, was bigger than the individual.

I felt like all of us lost something that night. Apparently love wasn't all you needed.

* * *

When Ed and I first started going out and he told his father about me, Mr. Van Halen disapproved. "What the hell are you doing?" he said. "She's only fifteen." Ed laughed. "Dad, you're watching reruns. She's twenty." But I may as well have been fifteen; that's how mature I was behaving by insisting we get married quickly. What the hell was I thinking? What the hell were *we* thinking?

Both of us were hell bent on marrying.

Only our crazy schedules slowed us down. After a brief pause in January when I won a Golden Globe for Best Supporting Actress in Comedy (as I accepted my award, I looked out and saw Steven Spielberg in the front and thought, Hmm, *that's* interesting and awkward). I finished *One Day* and went directly into preproduction on a slate of TV movies. Ed started writing songs for Van Halen's next album. I don't know why we thought we could or should get married when our biggest challenge was finding time for each other.

We needed an efficiency expert, not a wedding planner. While my job had regular hours, Ed typically worked all night in the back bedroom where he'd set up his equipment or at a studio in Hollywood. He sat there with his engineer and tinkered with ideas until he either got them the way he wanted or ran out of booze, coke, energy, inspiration, or all of the above.

He put tremendous pressure on himself to create, and the band added even more stress. Even though he wrote like a machine, he always said that he had to come up with another song: something better, something catchier, something Dave approved of, something the record company liked, something that everyone—from the band to the execs in the record company boardroom—thought was a hit.

I'm biased toward *Women and Children First* because Ed and I fell in love while he was on that tour. Two earlier songs, "Dance the Night Away" and "Ain't Talkin' 'bout Love," were fun to watch live, because the guys played with fiery passion. They always delivered two hours of rock and roll, and you knew they meant it.

Ed and I meant it, too. We were punch-drunk in love—and just plain punch-drunk. We drank Southern Comfort and vodka tonics. He also drank his Schlitz malt liquor. I tried to keep up with Ed's partying as best I could and as much as my body let me. I remember too many times when I heard the birds start to chirp and thought, God, what are we still doing up?

The answer was simple. Partying with Ed was my way of trying to fit into his world. I wanted to be with him. He was almost totally nocturnal, and if I hadn't stayed up drinking and doing coke with him, we would have been on completely different schedules. Other than when we passed each other by the bathroom in the morning, we wouldn't have seen each other.

Somehow, after only four and a half months together—most of which had been spent on the road and in hotel rooms—we found ourselves planning a wedding. That was the craziest part of our relationship. We should have still been getting to know each other instead of debating invitations, flowers, caterers, and guest lists. We needed to take a breath, slow down, and see if we were compatible; see if we were actually friends. We needed to get close. The guys in Ed's band warned him to slow down, though they went about it the wrong way. Ed claimed it was more like all or nothing; that they wanted him to call it off. Dave especially pressured him to reconsider. Ed apparently overheard him say, "That fucking little prick, not only is he winning all the guitar awards, he's also the first to marry a movie star."

I appreciated the upgrade. We only had a small window in which to schedule the wedding. After *One Day*, I went straight into the TV movie *The Princess and the Cabbie*, which was shot in San Francisco; then, starting in May, Ed was to tour for the rest of 1981. The stress of planning the wedding got to both of us. I remember Ed snapping, "God, can't you just leave me alone?"

I don't blame him. Not for nothing was *Fair Warning* Van Halen's darkest effort. Ed told me that I'd inspired the song "Sunday Afternoon in the Park," a heavy, grinding instrumental. He said it was us fighting all the time.

"I'm so glad I inspire cheerful songs," I said.

We set the date for April 11, 1981. I cringe at how we prepared. The priest we tapped to perform the ceremony gave us questionnaires so he could get to know us better and offer more personal words. As we filled out the forms at home, we each held a little vial of coke. If you ask me, those aren't two people who should be making decisions about the rest of their lives.

Not only did we make decisions, though, we slogged through all the issues that make you wonder if elopement isn't a better idea. First there were problems getting the bridesmaids' dresses ready, and then I didn't want to hurt the feelings of my best friends, Marci and Karen, or my cousins by picking one over the other as my maid of honor, so I compromised by choosing singer Nicolette Larson, who we knew through Van Halen's producer, Ted Templeman. Ed's feelings were hurt when Dave turned down his invitation to be a groomsman. Then it was decided that Van Halen wouldn't play a song at the reception. I didn't get it, since Dave had sung at Michael Anthony's wedding a month earlier.

In the meantime, our guest list got so out of hand that we said screw it and solved everyone's concerns about who to invite by inviting everyone—more than four hundred people. In fact, on the weekend of our wedding, we had forty guests camped out in our 2000-square-foot, three bedroom home. Fortunately there was ample room at St. Paul the Apostle Church in Westwood, where my dad guided me down the aisle and gave me away to Ed, who looked dashing in his tux. Holding red roses, I wore a traditional white gown with a lace mesh across my chest and up to my neck. Both of us looked very loving and serious during the ceremony. Finally, after Nicolette sang a beautiful French love song, Ed and I kissed, and everyone burst into applause.

A party followed at the same Beverly Hills mansion that was used in the movie *A Star Is Born*. Guests dined on all types of seafood, Italian pastas, and meats that we hoped reflected the different backgrounds in both of our families. Our wedding cake was an architectural feat that spanned a long table. I put the top tier in our freezer, but we forgot to eat it on our first anniversary, and it ended up staying there for ten years. By that time, I thought it would be bad luck to throw it out.

By the end of the evening, there was no doubt that every one of the thirty-five thousand dollars we had spent on the festivities had been put to good use. It was a great party, and we were great partiers. Ed and I finished the night with champagne at the Beverly Hills Hotel, where we eventually stumbled into a private bungalow. Our wedding night—well, it wasn't one of our best, but it was typical: I passed out on the bed in my gown, and Ed fell asleep in the bathroom.

Twelve

FAIR WARNING

We didn't slow down unless we were forced to, and the first and only time I remember that happening was the weekend after our wedding. While driving to Santa Barbara, California, for a honeymoon weekend, Ed and I were pulled over by a cop on the 101 Freeway just past Camarillo. The cop immediately recognized Ed. Then his eyes landed on the open champagne bottle between the seats. Ed explained that we'd just gotten married and the cop let us off with a warning.

"Just slow down," he said.

Not possible. In May Ed left on the *Fair Warning* tour, a five-month zigzag across the U.S, and I returned to *One Day* in June. That in a nutshell summed up our first year. He moved into writing and touring, and I was working. We didn't spend time together—at least not enough time. When we did, we were doing drugs and drinking. How are you supposed to get close when neither of you is there?

We thought we worked it out by talking throughout the day and never letting more than two or three weeks go by without seeing each other. That usually meant that I hopped on a plane Friday night to wherever the band was playing, spent a virtually sleepless weekend on the tour bus, and flew home Sunday night so I could be at work on Monday. If my schedule allowed, I stayed out longer. Although it was draining, I enjoyed the excitement of the road. I worked out by running the arena steps during sound check, then went back to the hotel and showered, ate, and returned to the arena to watch the show. The night typically ended at the hotel bar.

On July 17 Van Halen headlined their biggest gig of the tour, Madison Square Garden in New York City, which had sold out immediately, signaling that Van Halen, after years of working their way up from clubs, were at the top of their field. I flew in to be with Ed. A girl called our room. I could've sworn that she said her name was Christie Brinkley. I thought that was strange. Why would she be calling Ed's room? Perhaps, like so many celebrities, she called to get on the guest list.

For some reason, I didn't worry about Ed and groupies or infidelity—not like I would years later. Ed put my concerns to rest every time I heard him tell someone that getting married was the best thing he'd done, and he said it frequently. Don't get me wrong, though, the groupies still drove me crazy. I was infuriated by the way they threw themselves at these guys even knowing they were married or in relationships. They didn't care; anything for their one night.

But what is that saying—the things that bother you the most in other people are the things you hate about yourself? Maybe that's part of it. When I was sixteen, I went to a club with Mackenzie, and I spent the evening backstage necking with Rick Springfield, who, whether you liked his music or not, was a hottie. I would have done anything that night—except that I looked at my watch, saw the time, and exclaimed, "Oh, shit, I've got to get home. My dad's going to kill me!"

The *Fair Warning* tour ended in October, and soon after I found a groupie in our home. She'd broken in—or "wandered in," as she claimed—wearing a haltertop and miniskirt. I found her in the hallway.

"Who the hell are you?" I asked.

"I came to see Ed," she said.

"Get out of my house," I said.

"He's not here?" she asked.

I couldn't believe her chutzpah.

"Leave! Right now!"

We also left. Following the *Fair Warning* tour, all the guys went on much-needed vacations. Dave was into exotic adventures then, like rafting down rivers in South America and traipsing through the African jungles. Ed and I opted for a trip to Mexico, where it rained for nearly a week without letup, the power went out, and Ed got sick. Relieved to get home, I went back to work. In November Mac made a celebrated return to the show for the first time since getting fired. We'd been out of contact since then, so I was happy to see her looking good. Her eyes were alive again.

On the series, her departure had been explained by having a newly married Julie move away from home. For her return, she knocked on the door with news: she was leaving her husband—and she was pregnant. The two-part story line was pure Mac—high drama, laughs, and headlines.

Likewise, in real life, she'd continue to struggle with her addiction for more than a decade. She went with me the next time Van Halen played L.A., and then spent the night at our house. That was interesting; we talked late into the night. I told her how jealous I'd been of her. She said that she hadn't been as secure as I'd imagined; in fact, she'd envied my secure family. Other secrets and regrets came out, and for the first time I felt like I had a sister.

The only other people I had ever opened up to that intimately were Bonnie and Ed, who was going through a frustrating time with Van Halen. After the band recorded a version of Roy Orbison's "(Oh) Pretty Woman" in January 1982, the record company pressured them to get an album together quickly—their fifth LP in as many years. Despite Ed's abundance of new songs and ideas, and his intention of writing more, Dave and producer Ted Templeman insisted on turning *Diver Down* into an album of mostly covers. As Ed groused to a journalist, Dave thought that reworking a proven hit virtually guaranteed another hit. Although "(Oh) Pretty Woman" shot to number 12 on the charts and *Diver Down* outsold its four predecessors, Ed would have rather failed with original material. Angry, he turned to me for support, and then he turned to his booze for relief.

That album was one frustration after another for Ed, who'd started to write on keyboard as well as guitar. He had a great original song composed mostly on the synthesizer that Dave and Ted put in the background of "Dancing in the Street," the Martha and the Vandellas Motown classic. Ed was furious. Another time he complained that Dave didn't want him playing keyboards; he was to stick to guitar heroics. OK, so that's what it meant to be in Van Halen. You needed chops *and* skin like armor.

That's just what I saw and heard. So much more happened between those guys that I didn't want to see or hear. I resented them, and especially Dave, for making Ed so unhappy, which in turn made my life unhappy. As far as I was concerned, Ed took such unnecessary hits. He'd emerge from the studio dazed and distraught, and it wasn't from the booze and drugs he'd ingested as part of his creative process.

Ed internalized everything. He was like an honorary Bertinelli in that way. He kept all his emotion inside until he couldn't take it anymore and blew up. He'd traded blows with my brother, and I'd seen him go at it with his brother Al. What with Dave and record company execs at him all the time, I marveled that he functioned at such a high level creatively.

Ed wasn't good at fighting back either—or communicating. That made sense when I reminded myself that he didn't speak English when he moved to California from Holland, and that as a child, he spent hours every day sharpening his skills as a piano prodigy. Instead he retreated into himself and into whatever bottle was nearest him. My instinct was to protect him.

Did he need me to do that?

Hell, no. Ed was a big boy and able to take care of himself. That was merely the dynamic I created to rationalize our complicated relationship as it gradually evolved from lovers to one that resembled a mother and son or a brother and sister.

When I saw the final script for the movie *I Was a Mail Order Bride,* a steamy romance about a reporter investigating relationships through personal ads, I went into a panic over a scene that called for me to wear a revealing red bathing suit. The problem? I was terrified of exposing what I still thought of as my big Italian child-bearing hips.

Ed did his best to boost my self-confidence, but my body image issues were too deeply tied to emotions beyond my control, and his. Compliments and a few good nights in bed with my husband, who was a wonderful lover when he was available, didn't alleviate my anxieties. What anxieties? I think deep down inside I knew my life wasn't turning out the way I wanted. But I didn't want to admit it. It was the old Bertinelli way—you just deal.

Instead I obsessed about my body. Even though I weighed just 115 pounds, I thought I was fat. Looking back, I see that I would have been unhappy no matter what I weighed because I was unhappy with myself.

It all came out in terms of looking good in that swimsuit. Having put myself on numerous diets over the years, I knew what worked and what didn't, and I headed straight for the weight-loss aid that I knew curtailed my appetite: cocaine. Instead of limiting my eating to just grapefruit or protein, I tooted a couple lines whenever I got hungry, and the craving disappeared. It was much simpler than any of the other diets I'd tried over the years—and we had plenty of coke around. They called it Bolivian marching powder. I could do my ten thousand steps through my nose! And I didn't need to work out. The pounds melted off me. By the time I had to slip into the one-piece swimsuit, my weight had dropped to 106 pounds. (Actually, I was even lighter, but that's what I told people so they wouldn't worry about me.) A photo from the movie scene ran in *Time* magazine's "People" section, and everyone said I looked great. I agreed.

When I look at those pictures now, though, I see that I was actually too *thin*. The frightening thing is that I kept getting thinner. The weight loss was like a drug, more addictive in a way than the drug I used to facilitate it. I enjoyed looking in the mirror every day and seeing the pounds disappear. It was a control thing, and I was the only one to whom it mattered. Ed had found me attractive at 115. I didn't get it.

Nor did I see the drastic change in me. When I went back to *One Day at a Time* later that summer, my weight was down to 98 pounds—the lowest I'd ever got. My normal energy was gone, and I didn't actually feel good, but I ignored that, because, when I got on the scale, I felt like I'd accomplished something. I liked fitting into the smaller sizes. But I obsessed about the fact that I still had an ass—or so I thought. Looking back, my perception was distorted. My ass was nothing but bone.

I might have kept losing and gotten into serious trouble if Ed hadn't intervened when I hit that 98 pounds. He thought I was too skinny. Knowing I was using coke to diet, he said, "That's enough. I can feel the bones in your back. I don't care what you think; it's not beautiful."

He then walked me to the car and drove me to Carney's, a hot dog stand down the hill from our house, where I had a chili cheese dog and fries. After having barely eaten anything for months, it tasted phenomenally good. Again, my love of food—and my husband—saved me from a serious eating disorder.

In mid-January I got two weeks off from *One Day* and went to South America with Ed and the band for a series of concerts in Caracas, São Paulo, and Rio de Janeiro. My weight was back up to 109, and I looked forward to having fun. I even packed that red bathing suit to wear in Rio. We were advised to leave all our jewelry at home, so I replaced my diamond wedding ring with a cheap gold band from one of my movies. I felt naked without a ring on that finger.

On the trip, I hung out with Al's fiancée, Valeri, a sweet, pretty, rock-and-roll chick. We were opposites. I barely wore any makeup and dressed in jeans and T-shirts, while she had big, eighties-style blonde frosted hair, and wore off-the-shoulder shirts and leggings. I mention this because of what happened one evening in Rio. The four of us had just had drinks in the bar. We were headed back to our rooms, walking across the lobby, but at the elevator, the attendant watched as Ed and Al stepped aside to let Valeri and me get on first. As I followed

Valeri into the elevator, the attendant put up his hand and blocked my path, saying something in Portuguese.

"What the hell?" I said, perplexed.

In the midst of more explanation, the attendant pointed to the stupid ring I had on. Al and Ed, seeming to get the gist of his explanation, tried not to laugh while letting me suffer this mysterious indignity. Pissed off, I argued that we were registered guests, and I put up enough of a fuss that an English-speaking assistant manager hurried over. After conferring with the elevator guy, he stared at me.

"What's the problem?" I demanded. "I want to go up to my room. We are guests in this hotel."

He nodded toward Valeri.

"You may go up to the room," he said, adding similar nods to the guys. "I'm sorry for any inconvenience."

"What about me?" I snapped.

He shook his head.

"You are familiar with the rules."

I raised my eyebrows. "What rules?"

"We do not allow prostitutes in the rooms in this hotel," he said.

"What?" I snapped and pointed at Ed. "I am married to him. This is my wedding ring."

The assistant manager smiled.

"We see that all the time from the professional women."

As I was about to clobber that guy, Ed and Al, laughing like a couple of twelve-year-olds, intervened. I got in the elevator as the embarassed hotel employees apologized profusely. It didn't matter. I was flabbergasted. That night we got a good laugh out of it, though, had a few drinks, and passed out.

Thirteen

AFTERSHOCK

On May 29, 1983, Ed and I were in a helicopter on our way to Glen Helen Regional Park in San Bernardino, California, the site of the US Festival, a three-day rock extravaganza cooked up by Apple Computer cofounder Steve Wozniak, who was using his personal fortune to the tune of about $20 million to bankroll this modern-day Woodstock.

From three thousand feet in the air, I felt like I could see it all. If I could've seen into the future I probably would never have gotten out of the helicopter.

The Woz had agreed to pay Van Halen $1 million—then a record for a single performance—to headline the all-hard-rock day 2, whose opening acts included Motley Crue, Ozzy Osbourne, Quiet Riot, and the Scorpions. The previous day's new wave bill had featured the Clash and Oingo Boingo, and the following day was all classic rock, with David Bowie, U2, and the Pretenders on stage.

As we hovered over the crowd of four hundred thousand people,

Ed and I smiled at each other. This was the big time. I pictured a similar scene in the movie *A Star Is Born,* but this was way better; it was actually happening.

Ed and the guys were extremely nervous and jittery; they always got butterflies before important shows. To let Ed get settled, I left and wandered around the backstage VIP area, where I met Wozniak. Only ten years older than I am, he looked to be having the time of his life, living out some kind of rock fantasy in megazillionaire fashion. I asked him about Apple computers, thinking I could finagle one for free, but no such offer materialized. Wozniak had to pay the band so much money that I'm sure he thought I could buy my own damn computer.

As night took over the sky, and temperatures cooled, the performers backstage crowed with machismo and rock bravado. Motley Crue's Vince Neil memorably called it "the day new wave died and rock and roll took over," and, though I missed the confrontation, Dave and the Clash's Joe Strummer went jaw to jaw. I made sure I got my spot on the side of the stage next to Ed's guitars as the guys, introduced over a booming PA system as "the mighty Van Halen," opened up with a version of "Romeo Delight" that showed all of them, and especially Ed and Dave, at the top of their game.

Dave had fired himself up with plenty of Jack Daniel's. "I forgot the fucking words!" he crowed in the middle of the opening song— and the crowd loved it.

I beamed as I watched Ed, in a red shirt and pants that matched his signature Frankenstein guitar design, blaze through hits like "Jamie's Cryin'," "So This Is Love?" "Dance the Night Away," "Everybody Wants Some!!," and "Ain't Talkin' 'bout Love." His interplay with Dave was hot, and I saw how he really did speak with the notes he played. I toasted him with my drink in the middle of a song, and he winked at me in return. I was incredibly proud of him.

. . .

Prior to the show, Ed had stood among a few select friends and played a tape of a brand new song he'd written, later to be called "Jump." Dave had yet to add lyrics, so it was just a catchy instrumental, written on a portable keyboard in the hall outside our bedroom. On the tape, you could hear me in the background shouting from the bedroom, "Goddamnit, keep it down! I have to get up early!"

Nice supportive wife, huh?

But that was a constant issue. We were on two different schedules, and though we lived under the same roof, we were in two different worlds. Ultimately we were two different people who, though we loved each other, refused to take time out to figure out how to make that love work in a way that would last.

We motored ahead with blinders and bruises. In April we celebrated our second anniversary with a trip to Holland. Ed showed me where he'd grown up and told stories about his family. I relished those moments when he opened up—like the times we made love—wonderful but too infrequent.

We also visited Anne Frank's house, attended the symphony (Chopin entranced me; I fell asleep during Bartók), and shopped at charming outdoor markets. The pièce de résistance was a long, romantic boat trip down the canals.

When we got home after the wonderful trip, Ed and I decided to tear down the guesthouse in back and build a combination recording studio–racquetball court. We were such homebodies that we joked we might not ever have to leave the property once we had a place for him to work and me to exercise. Though my brother Drew took charge of construction, Ed and I demolished the structure by ourselves, taking turns driving a little Caterpillar tractor into the place.

After the structure was finished, Ed moved in his equipment and

dubbed his new studio 5150—the police code for the criminally insane. He moved straight into work on the band's next record, *1984*.
The studio made Ed a happier man but also a busier one. He spent less
time driving to the studio, but just because he worked at home didn't
mean I saw him more often. Other people were always around, too:
engineers, techs, and producers.

By spring, I wanted a place where we could go to be by ourselves,
so we rented composer Marvin Hamlisch's house in Carbon Beach, a
small patch of paradise in Malibu. Our long weekends there turned
into longer rejuvenating, relaxing getaways where we spent time on
the same schedule. That seemed to solve one problem for a while. At
least when Ed was working, I was sitting next to him, staring out at
the surf.

But the beach presented other problems. I nearly drowned over
Fourth of July weekend. We were barbecuing with my hairstylists
Jimmy and Phil, who also did Ed's hair. One minute I was standing on
the deck, looking out at the surf, and exclaiming, "Boy, the waves are
great!" The next minute I ran into the water, Ed warning me to be
careful of riptides. He'd heard a report on the news warning swimmers, and he'd noted it because he wasn't a strong swimmer.

"I'm fine," I said, as Jimmy followed me into the surf.

A few minutes later, we were out too far. The waves were strong.
Every time we got knocked down, we were pulled under and out. We
were caught in a riptide. Ed noticed us in trouble, jumped onto the
sand from the deck, and screamed at me to swim to the side. I couldn't
hear him. I was too far out and struggling too hard. He sprinted over
to some guys playing volleyball nearby and got them to help. The
three of them ran into the water. The two volleyballers turned out to
be strong swimmers. Leaving Ed behind, they passed Jimmy, who'd
gotten himself out and collapsed on the sand, and battled the surf

until they reached me. As they pulled me out, we passed poor Ed, who was still flailing in the shallower water.

"Honey, I'm OK!" I yelled between spitting out water.

The two of us struggled out of the water and hugged.

While at the beach, Ed wrote several songs for my most recent movie, *The Seduction of Gina,* the story of a young woman with a gambling addiction. We laughed together about the network execs' reaction to that picture. Though they loved the movie, they hated its original title, *Another High Roller,* which, they said, sounded like a gambling movie. But it *was* a gambling movie, we said. They responded by saying that gambling movies didn't do well and then coming up with a title that sounded like a sexy romance.

We enjoyed the beach so much that I wanted to buy Marvin's house, but his asking price of $2.2 million was way too steep for us. We found another home nearby, but negotiations were thwarted after the *National Enquirer* ran a story on how much Ed and I were worth (untrue and inflated, of course), causing the seller suddenly to raise his asking price. Finally we found a cozy Cape Cod–style home north of Malibu.

But damn those tabloids for the problems they created. The stories that appeared every few months claiming we were on the verge of a breakup were a pain in the ass—more like an irritation under the skin. They didn't run stories about us laughing at Disneyland or holding hands as we took in a performance of the musical *Dreamgirls.* Only the hint of disaster interested them. Though we had our share of fights, we'd never gone to that dire place where we spoke about splitting, as the tabloids suggested. And yet if you read it often enough, or if others read it often enough and call to ask if it's true, as they did, it pollutes the air.

But Ed and I were fighters. The more we heard or read that we were splitting up, the more committed we felt to each other, no matter what. There were, however, other breakups ahead of us.

In August 1983 I went back to work on *One Day,* knowing it was going to be the last season of the show. After nine years, CBS had decided to pull the plug. When Mac had returned, there'd been talk of a spin-off featuring the two of us, but those rumors faded over time.

Creatively, the show was finished, and everyone associated with the series agreed that we'd plumbed all the relevant topical story lines and that continuing the show would only damage the credibility and spirit we wanted to preserve. Critics never embraced *One Day* the way they did Norman's other series, but it spoke to issues, and the public picked up on it, watching us grow and change and following our lives off screen the same way I'd watched the kids on *The Brady Bunch.*

Selfishly, I wanted Bonnie to continue doing the show for another year without me. I saw myself taking a year off and then coming back. But Bonnie needed a break as much as I did. She didn't want to re-up. We were finished.

I still had to come to terms with leaving the show, which had been such a major part of my life. The people involved in it had become like family; our routines had become comfortable. The last episode felt like graduating from college and starting life on your own. The air was filled with both joy and sadness. In the final show, Ann moves out of the apartment. Near the end of the taping, as Bonnie, Mac, and I stood in the alcove together, the place where it had all started, I flashed back to that moment where I'd said to myself, "Wow, my life is about to change." Then I added a new thought that brought tears to my eyes: after tonight, I told myself, I'm never going to be here again.

Bonnie looked over at me. "Don't cry," she said.

"I'm not," I said. But of course I was.

All of us were. Aside from Pat's jokes, it was a big girly sobfest for the rest of the night as we moved from the set to a farewell party. I took some clothes from my dressing room, but no other mementoes other than great memories. And ahead of me? Both the best and worst of times.

Six months earlier, Ed had recorded a blistering guitar solo on Michael Jackson's song "Beat It," a contribution that earned him a lot of fanfare. It's been said that wedding hard-rock guitar to the Gloved One's modern rhythm & blues almost singlehandedly integrated MTV. I remember Ed talking about doing that part (in just one take), but it wasn't a big deal to him. And despite the fact that "Beat It" went to number one and won Michael two Grammy Awards, Ed never saw a dime; nor do I believe he ever thought to ask to get paid. That was Ed. I was also thanked on Michael's album, even though I hadn't met him yet.

That happened a year later when Ed played with Michael at a concert in Texas. After the show, we went back to Michael's hotel room. He'd converted it into a dance room with wood floors and mirrors. Michael seemed frail. When I hugged him, he felt like he was going to break.

Ed mimicked Michael's high voice. I laughed when he repeated the remark Michael had made to him in the studio. "I really like that high, fast stuff you do."

Ed was at the peak of his artistry as he worked on songs for the *1984* album. But Dave made life hard for the band's resident genius. He seemed to be pissed at Ed for venturing beyond the band by doing "Beat It," and to have thought it a distraction.

I would get so mad at the way Dave and Ed interlaced, but then Ed would tell me it had been like that from the band's earliest days when Ed was a shy guitar genius plagued by low self-esteem, while Dave was this big ball of gorgeous machismo who knew people loved him and knew he had the talent to back it up. Ed once told me that an L.A. newspaper had singled him out as the band's key member before their first album had come out. Ed thought Dave was jealous since the lead singer was supposed to get all the attention.

Ed didn't know how to react then—and he still didn't six albums later. Did he play too well? Should he play worse? As much as he thought about songs, he also thought about what would please Dave. Theirs was a fragile, difficult, combustible relationship; that was the bottom line.

"What Eddie and I do is, we argue," Dave once said. "Somehow we reach a compromise. No one is ever happy except the public."

One needed only to look at and listen to Ed and Dave's collaboration on the nine songs comprising *1984*. An instant rock classic upon its January 1 release, it raised the band to new heights with "Jump," the band's first number one single, as well as the future hits "Panama," "Hot for Teacher," and "I'll Wait." *Rolling Stone* magazine called it the "album that brings all of Van Halen's talent into focus" and added, "Every song hits harder than expected, until by album's end you're convinced that, despite all the bluster, Van Halen is one of the smartest, toughest bands in rock & roll."

I loved the video for "Jump." It was perfect in its simplicity: just the four of them playing on a stage against a white backdrop. It was a moment to capture, and remember. By the time they embarked on the *1984* tour in mid-January, Ed and Dave had basically had enough of each other. Onstage there was nothing but respect, but offstage they were like warring countries, unable to communicate.

As far as Ed was concerned, Dave made his life miserable, as he always had, only now the stage was bigger. Devoted to his music, Ed saw Dave glamming it up with a smarmy Vegas style that didn't feel like rock to him. After seeing Al's wife, Kelly, behind the drum riser, Dave banned any blondes other than him onstage or among the crew. Then he issued an edict banning wives backstage before shows. Then he stipulated that the women permitted to watch from the side of the stage had to wear black jumpsuits. It was endless.

I didn't know whether I was welcome or not. For instance, I was allowed on the set of "Hot for Teacher" the day Ed shot his solo walking across the desks and I was even asked by Dave's production partner, Pete, to sit behind Ed while he played piano on "Panama." Other than those times, I felt so uncomfortable that I hung out with Ed in his tuning room.

Unfortunately all the ego jousting spilled onto the stage and you could see it during their 1984 tour, which had everyone doing long solos. In other words, the fun and camaraderie was gone. The party-time spirit was over.

I kept trying to figure out how to stay in tune with Ed. As a child, he was content to practice a single piece of music all year in preparation for piano competition. Even as an adult, he was most comfortable when he was playing music. Ed's inner life was richer and safer than the stuff going on outside. Between the creative demands on him, his fights with Dave, and his natural tendencies to work compulsively in the studio, it wasn't like he was interested in playing Yahtzee and Uno with me.

His drinking, which worsened along with the tension in the band, made it even tougher to reach him. I tried hanging out with him in the studio, which was fun. He laid down tracks of songs that I liked, and we sang them together. One night we stayed up till three or four in the morning singing "Leather and Lace." We weren't Stevie Nicks and Don Henley, but we entertained ourselves. Another time I tried amusing him by playing the piano, though it was a brief performance—since my entire repertoire consisted of the first three bars of "Stairway to Heaven" and "Für Elise."

But I didn't have the stamina or the schedule to party with him till four and five in the morning day after day. By this time, I was done with coke. I didn't like the way coke made me feel or the people involved with acquiring it. Ed and his engineer sometimes worked in marathon sessions for two or three days in a row without sleeping.

On tour, Ed had changed. He would break down physically, suffering headaches and stomach problems from all the fighting, and from the stress and pressure he felt. Off the road, he sealed himself in the studio. Whenever I asked if he planned on coming to bed soon, I always got the same response: "after I get this idea down." I spent too many nights sitting in the living room with our hairstylists Jimmy and Phil, playing Uno and trying to stay awake until Ed finished. I can still see those guys turning to me with their sleepy eyes and asking, "Can we go yet?"

Eventually I went to bed too—alone. I knew when I was whipped. I couldn't compete for Ed against the more alluring combination of music, booze, and cocaine. When Dave recorded his *Crazy from the Heat* solo EP at the end of 1984, I thought it would relieve some of the feuding and strain, and maybe all of us could get back to the way things had been when I first came into the picture.

I was naïve.

Fourteen

SUNDAY AFTERNOON IN THE PARK

In an interview, I told the *L.A. Times* that I wasn't that committed to my career. That wasn't altogether true. While I was something of a slug and preferred, as my own mom once said, to play Suzie Homemaker, I really wanted to land a role in a feature film. But it was difficult to do, which accounted for my comment to the *Times*.

I came close with *The Big Chill* when I auditioned for the part of Chloe, the melancholy outsider whose dead boyfriend Alex (Kevin Costner, whose scenes were deleted) gives the group of college friends a reason to reunite. It was the best script I'd seen since *Raiders of the Lost Ark*, and I read with Jeff Goldblum, who was funny and brilliant, with an aura of security around him that I envied.

I didn't think I had a chance in hell of getting the job, and I was right. The part went to Meg Tilly, who played Chloe with an ethereal sadness that was beyond me then. At that time, I wasn't able to get myself to that vulnerable place—I was too busy covering it up. I lost out on *Footloose* and the movie *The Sure Thing* for the same reasons.

Jack would put off giving me bad news about my auditions. Whenever he did say something, I either got quiet or found a way to criticize myself and make it my fault. It was only after I went up for *Adventures in Babysitting* and the casting director told Jack that Elisabeth Shue got the part that he and I had a real talk that hit home. Jack told me that the casting director had been surprised by me. He'd expected a warm, happy-go-lucky young woman. Instead he thought I came across as mean and angry.

Angry? Hmmm. *Wow.* That comment rattled me.

Without realizing it, I *was* angry. I didn't think of myself that way, but I was so blocked off from any other emotion that I had no joy. Had I changed that much without knowing it? Apparently so, and this insight made me examine myself more than I had previously, though I wouldn't say by any means that I said, "Oh my God, I have to change."

But it made sense that I was angry and unhappy. Though Ed and I vehemently denied rumors of trouble, we really were having problems after, at this point, five years of marriage. It wasn't one thing or another as much as it was everything together. There was a lot going on: Ed's fights with Dave, Ed's drinking and coke, his obsessive work habits. We just did not communicate as effectively as we should have if we really loved each other as much as we professed. I reacted by becoming angry, and Ed—well, he seemed to be falling for another woman: rocker Patty Smyth.

And that's when the shit hit the fan.

It took time before we reached a boiling point. I was actually responsible for Patty entering our lives. An enthusiastic fan of her group,

Scandal, I also watched MTV, and their video was in heavy rotation. When I saw that they were playing in L.A., I asked Ed to take me. After the show, we went backstage and struck up a friendship. We had such a good time together that we ended up on their tour bus for a couple days, singing, talking, and hanging out. Then we flew home.

A while later, Patty visited us in L.A., and we saw her in New York. At the time, she was pregnant but going through a hard time with her husband, rocker and poet Richard Hell. The three of us hit it off. Looking back I see that both of them gravitated to each other through their mutual experiences in music.

I had such trust in Patty that I had no qualms about her staying at our house with Ed when I went out of town. Likewise, he palled around with her on an occasion when he was in New York. Eventually I heard him talk about Patty did this or Patty said that or Patty likes this designer one too many times, so that I asked if anything was going on between them. He said no.

In February 1985 I spent three weeks costarring in the play *Vanities* in Santa Barbara, which was a wonderful experience. The instant positive feedback of a live audience every night raised my spirits and took my mind off of Ed, Patty, Van Halen, and the whole lot. But when I came back after three weeks, Ed was in a dark—make that darker— place. Dave, buoyed by the success of his EP and its two hits ("Just a Gigolo/I Ain't Got Nobody" and "California Girls"—both of them remakes, interestingly), had quit the band. He would make a formal announcement with a thudding finality on April 1, 1985—April Fool's Day—but even before that Ed looked totally defeated and bleaker than I'd ever seen.

"Dave doesn't want to come back," he said. "I don't know what the hell I'm going to do."

The really unfortunate part in terms of our relationship was that his bad news came down at a time that I had a lot going on that I couldn't reschedule. I had off one week between the close of *Vanities* and the beginning of a feature film, *Ordinary Heroes,* which would shoot in Salt Lake City. My time was filled with wardrobe fittings, appointments with my acting coach, and various other meetings. Even though I was supportive, I didn't have time to offer much solace.

In May, after only a week off following *Ordinary Heroes,* I spent a month in Pittsburgh making *Silent Witness.* During that production, I started to gain weight because I spent all my free time noshing to calm my anxiety. It was the first time I'd ever put on weight while working.

When I returned home after production, I found Ed campaigning to have Patty take Dave's place in Van Halen. The other guys vetoed that idea, but it didn't end Ed's friendship with Patty. His infatuation with her seemed to intensify after she had her baby, and soon I was listening to him compare my hair or makeup to Patty's. For the first time, I felt as if I was losing control of our relationship—and, unsurprisingly, I lost control of myself.

It was around this time that we went to Shreveport to hear a band my brother Patrick liked called Private Life. Led by a dynamite girl singer named Kelly, they played a spicy New Orleans–style rock. Patrick had a crush on their keyboardist, a pretty brunette named Jennifer, and I talked Ed into getting them a record deal and producing their album. Unfortunately, it gave Ed one more excuse to spend more time in the studio. Another unforeseen twist born out of that arrangement was that, from spending time with the band, I developed a crush on the drummer, Craig.

Remembering this episode fills me with disappointment in myself. I knew better. The fact that I developed a crush on him, or that Ed had let himself become taken with Patty, should have been a big red flag that we had trouble at home. But we ignored it, and, in fact, barreled ahead in the opposite direction.

In August Private Life had an opportunity to make some money by playing a few gigs in Japan. Patrick wanted to go in order to spend time with Jennifer, and he convinced me to go too. Since I'd wanted to visit Japan, I didn't require much persuasion. That, and I knew damn well I was going to be with Craig.

We ended up in Osaka for nearly a week at a hostel—not even a nice hotel. Patrick made a play for Jennifer, who only wanted his friendship, and I let Craig know what I had in mind. He wasn't even the type of guy I was normally attracted to, but I desperately needed to have someone pay attention to me. I was convinced my husband was into another woman, and he was obsessed with his work, and my self-esteem couldn't handle that. At twenty-five years old, I wanted to feel desirable. So one thing led to another, and, without going into the sordid details, I messed up.

When I look back at the way things unfolded, I see that a part of me knew exactly what I was doing. I was putting myself in a situation where I knew I was going to fuck up. Yet I still did it. Why? Did I want to hurt Ed? I knew what it was like to hurt a man by sleeping with someone else. This was my husband, not my boyfriend. What was I thinking?

The long flight back from Japan seemed interminable as I wrestled with my guilty conscience. The idea of going back home paralyzed me. As soon as I walked in the front door, I stopped and nearly had a panic attack. The reality of what I'd done hit me full force. As I stood there, I might have even exclaimed, "Oh, crap, what did I do?" Indeed. How was I going to handle it? Was I going to tell Ed? How was I going to live with the secret? *Could* I live with it?

Looking back, I should have faced my problems with Ed, which were making me so angry and unhappy, rather than run to Japan and put myself in a situation where I knew I wasn't going to have any self-control. Or I should have admitted I was miserable and broken up with Ed. Even then, in my confused state, I knew I should have behaved a hell of a lot better than I had.

In the end, I chose not to tell Ed. I wanted to see if I could put the affair behind me. Don't they say time heals all wounds? It didn't heal mine. Five years into my marriage, I wasn't happy, but my powers of denial were way too strong for me to have been frank enough to admit that it wasn't working the way I wanted.

But I was hurting, and I dealt with it by continuing to eat anything and everything. Food was my drug. That September I left L.A. to shoot the movie *Rockabye* in New York and Toronto. I used to wolf down salami and cheese, whole pizzas, and hot fudge sundaes. I didn't know how much weight I put on. After passing 125 pounds, I stopped getting on the scale. But I remember having to wear a tank top and being struck by the change in my arms. They didn't look good. The producers called Jack and wanted to know what to do.

"What do you mean?" he asked. "Do about what?"

"She's so big," they said. "She got fat."

I remember Jack calling and trying to mention subtly that he'd seen the dailies and noticed for the first time that I'd put on weight.

"Yeah, I saw my arms in that friggin' orange tank top," I said.

"And?"

"I just went, 'Oh, crap.' What can I do?"

The movie ended up number one for its week, but a lot of good that did me. After returning to L.A., I had to do pickup shots for *Silent Witness*, and, much to my dismay, I couldn't fit into any of the clothes I'd worn seven months earlier. Of course I couldn't; I wasn't the same person anymore. That other person I'd been had gone into hiding inside that weight.

It was October, and when I finally stepped back on the scale I saw that I'd gained 20 pounds since April. I weighed 132. My disappearing act had begun.

I thought I looked as bad as I felt, and yet I ended up on *Penthouse* magazine's list of Hollywood's ten sexiest actresses, something David Letterman pointed out when I promoted *Silent Witness* on his show. With Ed sitting in with the band, I pointed out that I was listed at number nine, between Sophia Loren and Pia Zadora.

"Yeah, I'm real proud to be on *that* list," I said to Dave, tongue firmly in cheek. "Ed calls me *number nine*."

I bombed on Letterman. I barely smiled. Nervous and insecure, I kept turning away from Dave, who winced at several of my comments, making me even more uncomfortable. He also acknowledged my brief relationship with bandleader Paul Shaffer, pointing out that I'd been sixteen when I dated the then twenty-seven-year-old musician-actor. "We were just good friends," said Paul, who looked as awkward as I felt at rehashing those days. Instead of leaving it alone, I tried to get a laugh by saying he dumped me when his girlfriend called.

"That's because you were number two," he quipped cleverly.

"Touché," I said as sweat dripped down my back.

I just wanted to get out of there. Dave must have felt the same way, since he's never had me back on the show.

Bidding goodbye to his own Dave problem, Ed finally found a new lead singer in former Montrose singer and solo artist Sammy Hagar. After getting Sam's number from a mechanic who worked on their sports cars, Ed invited him to the studio for a series of jam sessions that led naturally to songs. They clicked immediately and put pedal to the metal on a new Van Halen album.

Sammy's arrival helped me push the Craig thing into the background as Ed became completely occupied by work. Recording of Van Halen's *5150* album filled our driveway with Lamborghinis and Ferraris and the studio with music. I enjoyed the harmonious atmosphere as the guys began referring to themselves as "the real Van Halen" and devouring chips and beer and cigarettes all hours of the day and night as if they were a troop of grown-up Boy Scout dropouts.

Things were so friendly that Sammy bought a beach house a couple doors up from ours. One day he pulled up our driveway in his Ferrari while Al was taking up a collection for beer.

"Hey, Sam, did you get a speeding ticket today?" Al asked.

"No," Sammy said.

"Great!" said Al, grinning. "One day in a row!"

Sammy brought to the band a maturity and stability that I welcomed. He was older than the other guys, had been married seventeen years, and had two sons, one sixteen and the other under two. Mike and his wife, Sue, going on five years of marriage, had an infant daughter. Al and Kelly were on their second year. Both Ed and I seemed to forget about our extracurricular interests and got along. I raised the idea of starting a family, something we'd talked about early on in our marriage but rather wisely had put aside. Now I told him that I wanted to try to have a baby, and he agreed the time was right.

In January, after about a month of trying, I experienced that odd, queasy feeling that women instantly recognize and that makes us run straight to the pharmacy to pick up a home pregnancy kit, which I did. As I expected, mine came back positive. Ed and I were extremely happy. Though we agreed not to tell anyone for three months, I still went out and bought a stack of pregnancy books.

A month later I began to spot, and from then on I had trouble. In March, after experiencing some severe pains, I went to the doctor. After a brief exam, he told me that my pregnancy was no longer viable, doctor-speak for miscarriage. I'd lost the baby.

There was nothing wrong with me physically. The pregnancy just didn't take. I went through the necessary procedures and, at home, Ed brought me tea and soup while I recuperated in bed. He was very sweet and tender. Although my body bounced back, my mood didn't. What's more, I was unable to tell anyone, most painfully Ed, the real reason I remained depressed: I was convinced that God had taken the baby as punishment for my affair in Japan.

I'm sure it wasn't coincidental that, soon after, I began suffering asthma attacks. One afternoon Ed rushed me to the emergency room in Malibu. It was strange. I'd never had asthma before. A few weeks later I had another attack. Out of the blue. I was choking emotionally. I had too much to think about, and I didn't want to think about any of it. As we returned from the emergency room that first time, the phone rang. I was still trembling from the asthmatic episode. The person on the other end of the phone identified himself as a reporter, said I'd been spotted at the emergency room, and wanted to know if I was pregnant.

"No, I'm not pregnant," I snapped, angrily. "I just had a miscarriage. Thanks for asking."

Click.

That same month, March 1986, Van Halen's album *5150* was released and did just fine with Sammy, who opened the album with a slurpy "Helloooooooo, baby!" The LP shot to number one three weeks after its release, the band's first-ever chart topper. Fueled by the hits "Why Can't This Be Love," "Dreams," and "Love Walks In," as well as high-octane rockers like "Get Up" and "5150," Van Halen fans who'd felt that *1984* was the band's best ever suddenly had a debate on their hands.

Ed felt vindicated, and I relished that he had emerged from years of tension and turmoil with a monster success. In May the band arrived at the Alpine Valley Music Theatre, in East Troy, Michigan. They were two months into a nine-month tour, and all was great. Sammy and Mike traveled with their families in a bus they dubbed Toys "R" Bus, and fans greeted them with signs saying "David Lee Who?" Backstage, Sammy's love of gourmet food and fine wines made his area the place to hang out before and after shows.

But the celebration was short-lived: before the second of two sold-out shows, Ed and Al got word that their father had suffered a heart attack. Ed's face turned gray.

After that show, we got on a private jet and flew back to L.A. Ed and Al went straight to the hospital to check on their dad. Both of them were devoted to him, especially Ed, who worshipped his father. But it had been a severe heart attack, and Mr. Van Halen, who smoked and drank heavily, never fully recovered. For the next seven months, he was in and out of the hospital. The tour ended in November, and the guys were able to spend time with their dad, who passed away, at age sixty-six, that December.

When the doctor made a point of saying that alcohol had contributed to Mr. Van Halen's weakened health, my thoughts had naturally turned to Ed and his health. After his father's death, every day seemed to become more and more of a battle, whether we were fighting each other or just battling the sadness of life.

As we said good-bye to his dad with a lovely service on a boat off Malibu's Point Dume, I worried whether Ed would be OK—and whether I could handle it if he wasn't. And mostly I worried about us. Were we going to be OK?

Fifteen

AIN'T TALKIN' 'BOUT LOVE

Dirt. My life was full of it.

It was early 1987, and if I looked out the back door of our house and past the recording studio I saw a huge hole and a mountain of dirt. A year and a half earlier, Ed and I, wanting a larger home and more backyard, had bought the house next to ours from actress Lindsay Wagner, whom I knew from calls she understandably made in the middle of the night to remind Ed that he had left the studio door open, and it sounded like Van Halen were rehearsing in her living room.

We'd torn down her place and hired an architect to create our dream home, an 10,000-square-foot Tudor mansion, with a gym, huge closets in the master bedroom, and four bedrooms for the four children (two boys and two girls) we wanted. But progress was excruciatingly slow, thanks to one delay after another. As it turned out, the house turned into a metaphor reflecting our marriage. Despite the best plans and intentions, nothing was easy.

Following his father's passing, I wracked my brain for ways to bring joy into Ed's life, but he retreated into his comfort zones: work and alcohol. So when I was offered the juicy miniseries, *I'll Take Manhattan,* I jumped at the chance to play Maxi Amberville, a thrice-married publishing heiress and one of the most delicious characters of my career. Miniseries were the marquee events on the TV landscape at the time, and I wanted to be part of that business. All the major TV actresses did them. At eight hours long, *I'll Take Manhattan* promised to be one of the biggest to date.

For my first meeting with Judith Krantz, who'd written the novel and the screenplay, I colored my hair and added a white streak just like Maxi in the book. I wanted Judith to see that I could pull off this sexy part even though I didn't think of myself that way. But I wanted that part. I knew the excess and drama would be perfect therapy for me.

As a novelist, Judith's powers of perception were strong. With one look, she must have seen that I was going through problems. But she made only one comment, and conveyed it gently and indirectly. During my fittings, the woman in charge of wardrobe, a friend of Judith's, smiled sweetly after fussing with the fit of a dress around my hips and butt, and said, "Wouldn't it be nice if you were just a size smaller?"

The implication was clear. I needed to lose weight.

I exercised daily, biking and jogging along the trails in the Malibu hills. Although I enjoyed working out, it was always difficult to get started and keep the momentum without seeing immediate or dramatic results. As I pushed myself up and down those hills, I actually battled my conscience more than my appetite, but every week I worried about my meetings with the wardrobe woman. I knew she'd get on the phone to Judith as soon as I left and tell her whether I was any thinner. One time I got badly sunburned while on a six-mile bike ride, and I used that as an excuse to postpone the meeting and get in a couple extra days of dieting.

By the time shooting began, I hadn't lost as much weight as the producers wanted, although no one said anything. But a photo of me taking a break in Manhattan's Washington Square Park ran in a tabloid, along with a headline that said something like "Valerie Bertinelli Takes Five—and Has Put On Another Five." Someone might have planted that as a message to me, yet I ruled that out after it was clear that the production, which shot in New York and Toronto, was all about having fun.

I was intimidated whenever Judith was on the set, but I liked her and she boosted my self-confidence by telling people I was a perfect Maxi. After seeing me in a gold beaded gown from Neiman-Marcus that was slit up to my waist, she complimented my legs. I loved her for that. In fact, from the knees down, they are great. They're the only skinny part of my body.

The best times on *Manhattan* were sitting around with costars Jane Kaczmarek and Julianne Moore, making up "sniglets," words that describe things that don't have words. I admired Jane's quickness and wit; also her intelligence. As she sounded off about the way women were portrayed in the media, or the messages they were fed about having to sacrifice their own needs to make their men happy, or how they were pressured to look a certain way rather than be themselves, I'd think, Oh my God, she's brilliant. I hope she doesn't notice I'm not as smart.

Instead of listening to what she had to say, however, once again I felt "less than" and dwelled on what I perceived as my shortcomings. I was extremely hard on myself. Way too hard. Where did that come from? Why did I have to be like that? Why couldn't I just enjoy or accept myself?

Simple answer: I was hiding from my problems—and myself. Until I faced them, I would never feel comfortable in my own skin.

When I got home, Ed was helping Sammy finish a solo album. They worked in L.A. and Mill Valley. I flew up north to hang out with them, but ended up spending most of the time by myself. I saw an acupuncturist who put something in my ear to help me control my appetite. That worked for about three days. The spell was broken on one of the long, daily walks I took from the hotel to the studio.

There was a burger and fish stand on the road I followed. It smelled like heaven. I swear they fired up the grill every time I passed by. I obsessed about those burgers and fish tacos until finally I gave in to temptation and bought three different entrees—fish and chips, a burger, and clam strips—plus onion rings and french fries, and took everything back to my room and pigged out. Afterward, feeling stuffed and sick, I hid the wrappers in the trash, making sure no one saw.

It was almost as if I'd had an affair with the food. Indeed, I felt as if I'd cheated. Isn't that one of the worst feelings when dieting?

Like Ed and his drinking, I turned to food as a solution to problems. It had the opposite effect, right? Even my mother told *People* magazine that I "could probably work on watching [my] weight a little more." But, hey, when the going got rough, I wanted to eat. I ran to the fridge. Occasionally I complained to friends about my weight and my struggle to control my appetite, which I now see could have been a subtle invitation for someone to ask me what else was bothering me. Think about it: why couldn't I control my appetite? If I'd mentioned being unable to shake a cough or a sore throat, someone would have said, "Val, what's going on?"

In my case, weight was no different. It was a symptom of something wrong. But I didn't dwell on it. You wouldn't have heard me harping on it. I had a hard enough time drawing any attention to my body, fat or thin. Actress Ally Sheedy, who I met at the beach, did give me a food scale for my birthday. She also worked out with me. It helped to have a workout partner—and a friend. I got in the best shape of my life riding bikes and running with her.

Ed didn't have anyone to help keep his drinking in check. After his dad's passing, I think he relied more heavily on alcohol than before, even compared with the bust-up with Dave. His drinking made me feel like a failure. My job, as I saw it, was to take care of him, and that summer, as he drifted into the dark, remote place that alcohol took him, I knew that I wasn't doing my job very well.

We fought way too often about his drinking and the lack of time we spent together. I made so many mistakes back then, from the classic one of thinking that he'd quit if he loved me, to the simple one of trying to force him to do something (to make time for me) because I wanted him to. What's that old saying—you can lead a horse to water, but you can't make him drink? I had the opposite problem. I couldn't lead my horse to water, but he drank way too much.

Anyway, one day that fall I was about to walk in the studio when I stopped just outside the door. I overheard Ed in the studio on the phone saying that he wanted out of the marriage. I thought it was Patty. I shook my head. Just a few months earlier, I'd complimented Patty in a magazine for taking care of Ed in New York City when I wasn't around. Could I have felt like a bigger idiot?

Two decades later I ran into Patty in New York City. By then she'd been married to former tennis star John McEnroe for several years. We hugged, and I made some crack about "the woman who my husband had a crush on," which made her cringe. I have a habit of doing that to people. But she explained that there was nothing beyond friendship, and knowing what she knew and where she was coming from at the time, her intention was only to help Ed get off the booze. I believe her.

As I thought back to that time, I realized that Ed had responded to her, and that had made me feel like even more of a failure as a wife. Didn't he need me? And wasn't it sad that our marriage had hit that point, where I thought my only value as a wife was whether or not I kept him sober?

As a result, Ed and I split up. It was our first separation. I stayed in the house, and he moved into the studio and wherever else he landed. To be honest, I don't really know where he went, but it wasn't like I'd seen him that much before.

I breathed easier after I presented at the Emmy Awards, and no one asked about Ed. Somehow our separation stayed out of the press. It lasted only three weeks, but I made it clear to Ed and those closest to him, including Al and the band's manager, that I didn't want to continue to live like I had been. I should have left it at that and said, "See ya, I'm out of here—permanently. I need to take care of myself, since I'm as miserable as you." I should have focused on changing myself instead of Ed, but I needed another fourteen years before I reached that point. (Hey, I *told* you I was a procrastinator.)

Instead I insisted that Ed get rid of his coke dealer and quit drinking. Period. As I told everyone—and this was justified—I worried that Ed was going to kill himself with these habits. I pointed out that he stayed in the studio for days in a row, drinking and doing coke. That wasn't normal or healthy. At one point after I complained, Ed said, "It's not like I'm going to bars and screwing around. I'm working."

"You call it work," I snapped. "I think you're killing yourself."

I ended up staging an intervention with a few others who were closest to Ed. It was intensely emotional and most of us there had trouble sharing our emotions on a good day, which this wasn't. However, despite tempers and through all the tears, it was clear that we were united in our concern for Ed and wanted him to get help. In the end, we obtained the desired result. Ed left that day for the Betty Ford Center in Rancho Mirage, California.

A few days later, I checked into a nearby hotel so I could be there for the weekly family-day meetings. While he underwent treatment, I worked out. I figured we'd both get in shape at the same time. I remember going back to my hotel room after long walks, cooling off and showering, and then relaxing with a wine cooler in the late afternoon. One time I visited Ed with wine cooler still on my breath.

"Have you been drinking?" he asked right after we kissed.

"No," I lied, wondering how I could be so inconsiderate and stupid.

After thirty days of treatment, Ed returned home and dived into work on Van Halen's next album, *OU812*. At first, his sobriety lightened the mood at home, but as time passed, I saw it get more difficult for him, and I remember having the sense of walking on eggshells. I also remember knowing that the question wasn't will he stay sober but how long will he stay sober?

I poured my energies into the new house and trying to get our crew to push past the dirt-moving stage and on to actual construction. I was ready to strap on a tool belt and help with the framing. Entire shopping centers were built faster than our house. But it was a massive undertaking, and the way I obsessed over details didn't speed things up. For instance, I spent months searching solely for used brick that I liked, finally settling on some from a newly razed building in Chicago. People thought I was insane.

That winter Ed and I vacationed in Aspen, Colorado, the first of what would become an annual ski trip. It was a good, healthy escape for us. However, by spring Ed was drinking again. Even though I tried to put a positive spin on my disappointment by telling myself that at least he wasn't drinking heavily, I was really pissed off and frustrated. We couldn't seem to break out of the old patterns.

In April we went to Turtle Island, in Fiji, for a long vacation before Van Halen released their next album and hit the road. We called the eight-day getaway the honeymoon we never took. Other than the mosquitoes, it was paradise. Our thatched-roof villa overlooked the turquoise blue water. We sunbathed on private beaches, canoed and swam. One morning we woke up to wild horses grazing outside our window. Another afternoon I read a book to Ed as we relaxed on the sand. It was one of the most romantic times I remember the two of us sharing.

But beneath the surface I was still angry and resentful toward him. I didn't realize how strong those feelings were until we'd been home for two days, and Ed woke up in agony. I heard him groaning in bed, and then suddenly he sat up and projectile vomited all over the wall. The poor guy. Instead of asking, "Are you OK, honey?" or "What's wrong, honey?" the first words out of my mouth were "What the fuck did you take this time?"

Nice, huh?

It turned out that Ed had to spend three days in the hospital with dengue fever. That's how compassionate and sweet I was.

In May 1988, as Van Halen's *OU812* album rocketed to number one and they set out on a new tour, I got in shape for my next movie, *Poncho Barnes*, the true story of the female aviator and adventurer who beat the speed record held by Amelia Earhart and later operated the Happy Bottom Riding Club, a bar that was a second home for Chuck Yeager and the other test pilots with the "right stuff" from Edwards Air Force Base.

As I began the workout regimen, I looked at myself in the mirror and thought, Here we go again, back on the merry-go-round.

After training my ass off, I got down to a fit 112 pounds. I felt terrific and good about myself. Was there a connection between that and not being at home? Probably. But I also needed to be in that kind of shape for the two and a half months I spent on location in Irving, Texas, riding horses, running, and flying in 1930s-style airplanes. It was the most fun I'd ever had on a set.

Early on, as I was riding a horse, I pulled the reins too hard and went flying over the horse's head. After that, I spent every weekend with an instructor, learning to ride cutting horses at a nearby ranch. I got to the point where I was riding while they filmed me from a truck going thirty-five miles per hour.

I discovered a little daredevil inside me. During production I spent lunch breaks zipping through the sky. The stunt pilot would take me up in his open-cockpit biplane. By itself, that was exhilarating. But he'd fly it straight up and then cut the engine. We'd topple over and twirl until he pulled out of it. I screamed through practically the entire flight. The crew on the ground could hear me. After one such flight, I remember telling a reporter it was better than sex. I don't know if it was *that* good, but it was at the time—since I wasn't getting any.

When I returned to L.A. after production ended, I tried to keep up my workout routine and periodic facials that I'd treated myself to during the shoot. Ed was on the road, and I wanted to stay fit and firm and feeling good. Poncho Barnes used to say, "When faced with a choice, choose happy," and not only did I agree, I said yes—and to this day, that's the choice I try to make.

That fall was a good time for me. I'd gotten through the rough patches of my miscarriage, Ed's father's death, our separation, and Ed's struggle with sobriety. I thought of that grind as *my* Sunday afternoon walk in the park, and though I felt good about myself at the moment, I recognized that all those experiences had changed me. I saw it. At a photo session for the cover of *Us* magazine, I picked up the test shot. Ordinarily I'd give that a glance, trusting the photographer. But this Polaroid stopped me. Something was different about it, about the way I looked.

I looked like a grown woman.

Holy crap, I said to myself. How did that happen?

My newfound maturity was admired by no less than Warren Beatty, who asked to meet with me about a role in *Dick Tracy,* his movie adaptation of the comic strip character. Apparently he wanted to consider me for the part of Tess Trueheart. It was arranged that I'd go to Warren's house, which was about a mile up the road from ours. As I drove there, I kept telling myself that I was too young for the part and wondering if there was another reason he wanted to meet me.

At the door, I was told that Warren was in the shower. He appeared moments later, looking fresh in a white shirt and jeans. He made a great entrance, that's for sure. He was taller than I imagined but just as handsome. I noticed a playful glint in his eye as we shook hands, and he said, "Hi, I'm Warren."

Indeed he was. We sat in the kitchen and talked. Warren told me that I had beautiful teeth. I thought, OK, that's nice. He already had me at "Hi, I'm Warren." What was next?

Next he told a story about himself and Dustin Hoffman shooting their ill-fated movie *Ishtar.* He described an idle moment the two of them had in the desert when they asked each other what beautiful woman they would have sex with if they could have their choice.

"Isn't it funny," Warren said, "that your name came up on both lists?"

I chuckled while running a hand through my hair, as I did whenever I got nervous or felt myself blush. Part of me enjoyed the compliment, or tried to, since I never thought of myself as sexy or desirable in *that* way that guys—hell, major movie stars—might discuss. Another part of me, which was by now much savvier about men, thought he was so full of shit. And that part also wondered how many times he'd used that story.

At the end of a couple hours, nothing sordid or steamy had been entertained by either of us, and I knew I wasn't getting the part. As I was leaving, I mentioned I was going to meet Ed in New York, and Warren said he planned on being there too, and would call. He followed through as promised, and he, Ed, and I met for lunch at one of the swanky hotels. Jack Nicholson joined us. He was exactly as he seemed: mischievous, smart, charming, fun, entertaining, and cool.

But I wasn't all that comfortable when hanging out with the boys in Hollywood's big leagues. The last time I saw Warren was at a 1992 fundraiser for Bill Clinton at a big mansion in the hills. Magnetic, funny James Woods was on the bus that took my group there, and I saw why he is so attractive to women. Once at the party, I noticed Steven Spielberg, who seemed to avoid me, and his second wife, actress Kate Capshaw. I shook hands with Hillary Clinton and got a sense of her warmth and genuineness that ended up being the reason I voted for Bill that year. Then I bumped into Warren, who, before introducing me to his wife, Annette Bening, whispered in my ear, "Don't say anything."

About *what*? I had nothing to tell because nothing had happened. But his comment caused Annette, who sat atop the list of actresses I admired, and who looked gloriously beautiful and glowing that night, to give me an odd look; a cross between curious and not amused. She and Warren had just gotten married. I was completely rattled, and when I'm like that I have no idea what will come out of my mouth. As a result, I said, "I'm a huge fan," and then added half-jokingly, "and I didn't sleep with your husband."

As the words came out, I saw Annette's expression change. It was as if she was asking which crack pipe I'd smoked. I was such an idiot. I really had to get my act together if I wanted to be a grown-up.

Sixteen

BEST OF BOTH WORLDS

"Pritikin."

That's what I said to Ed when we returned from Japan in February 1989. I'd gone there to be with him for the end of Van Halen's *OU812* tour, and as soon as we got back home, I stepped on the scale for what I knew would be depressing news—and it was. I was 20 pounds heavier than when I'd whipped my ass into shape for *Poncho Barnes* six months earlier. I weighed 131 pounds.

"I need to go to the Pritikin Center," I said forlornly, referring to the Santa Monica weight-loss clinic where you checked in and ate three low-calorie meals a day based on the famous Pritikin low-fat, high-fiber diet.

Before putting myself on that strict regimen, we went to Aspen for a brief indulgence. Once we were back, there was no question in my mind that I needed help not just losing weight but curtailing my intake of food. Still, it was April when I finally checked in. Ed went with me, saying that maybe he'd quit drinking. I liked the sound of that, but my hopes were dashed when I saw him bring a six-pack of Schlitz into the room. I overlooked that in favor of his company while I put myself through the rigors of the program and focused on getting results. After two weeks, I dropped 7 pounds and went home weighing 124.

It was a good period. Ed and I were getting along. Van Halen had received three American Music Award nominations and then won at the MTV awards. Their song "Feels So Good" was in heavy play on radio. While watching Ed accept his award on stage, I thought, Well done. He'd worked hard, made great music, and earned the accolades. I hoped he found satisfaction in it. Such moments sometimes didn't register with workaholics like Ed.

They didn't register for long with me, either. Even though I had tranquil domestic moments when I worked in the garden, planting flowers while our Dalmatian puppy dug them up, or stood in the grocery store checkout sorting through my coupons, I wasn't able to get myself together—or rather, keep myself together. I had both a Stairmaster and a Lifecycle at home, and spent a lot of time on both machines before starting my next movie, *Taken Away*. Whenever a movie came up, I devoted myself to losing weight. Right or wrong, the business creates pressure to be thinner. No one ever says *how* thin, but it's understood that thinner is better. And my weight was never the same. I was always struggling to change.

I stressed badly as soon as Jack Grossbart scheduled any wardrobe fittings for me. It wasn't just that I hated being fat. I also worried that the wardrobe people were going to see that I was fat. I know the normal response is, so what if they did? Well, first, I disliked the idea that people might be whispering about me behind my back. And now, looking back, I see something deeper was also going on. I think I was scared that someone might look at me and see the truth, as that one casting director had a few years before when he'd told Jack that I'd come across as angry.

By the start of *Taken Away,* the story of a woman who loses her child after being deemed an unfit mother, I was down to 120. After another two months of taxing myself—and my tear ducts—in the emotional role, I lost another 4 pounds. In September I was lured back to weekly television in *Sydney,* a new CBS sitcom that paired me with the brilliant young actors Matthew Perry, Craig Bierko, and Daniel Baldwin.

My then agent Marc Schwartz had me meet with the show's co-creator Michael Wilson, whose energy and humor convinced me the show could be a hit. You'd think my journal from that time would reveal my excitement about the pilot, but no, all it contains is my weight: 116 pounds. Once again, how strange is it that I remember every big moment of my life by my weight?

But what a cast! I fell in love with Matthew, who at nineteen was such a burst of fresh, fast-talking comedic genius that Craig dubbed him "Doogie," after TV boy genius–doctor Doogie Howser. Nothing was more entertaining than sitting with Michael, along with Craig and Matthew, while they riffed on the show. They wrote entire episodes in front of my eyes. I tossed in a line every so often, but they were hilarious.

Work was good. The pilot was a hit with network executives, and *Taken Away* brought in both strong reviews and ratings in November. But those sorts of things had a way of being overtaken by personal problems.

It started in mid-December with an asthma attack, always a sign of tension building inside me. Those attacks were like an early warning system. On the home front, the summer's bliss was gone. Both of us were on different schedules, and Ed was drinking heavily. The holidays added stress. I scalded my legs with hot soup while recuperating from my asthma attack and had to be taken back to the emergency room with third-degree burns.

As Gilda Radner's *Saturday Night Live* character Roseanne Roseannadanna said, "It's always somethin'. If it's not one thing, it's somethin' else." That something else was bad.

It was New Year's Eve, and we spent it at the beach with my parents. Ed was drinking Jägermeisters and getting progressively drunker and angrier for no apparent reason. Pissed off at everyone, he decided that he wanted to leave. Everyone knew that he was too wasted to drive—everyone, that is, except for Ed. As he got up, I grabbed the car keys, and the two of us tussled as he tried to pry them from my hands. My dad stepped forward and yelled at Ed to take his hands off of me.

"Daddy, I'm OK," I said.

"Stop it, Ed," my dad ordered.

"Daddy, he's not hurting me," I said. "Don't worry about it. I'm just going to hide the keys."

Suddenly Ed lunged for the keys though it appeared he was going for me, and *boom,* he collided with my dad's fist. Or vice versa. It didn't matter. My dad had been imploring him to stop, stop, stop, but then he threw a right that landed squarely on Ed's cheek. My dad had boxed as a younger man and knew what he was doing when he threw a punch. Later, as Ed got over the sting, he blew his nose, and the whole side of his face blew up. His cheekbone was cracked.

I took him to the emergency room. After examining him and hearing an explanation of what had happened, the doctor told Ed that he'd be all right physically, but added, "You might want to check yourself in someplace and get help."

On January 1, 1990, Ed checked into the hospital, staying for the next twenty-eight days. On the 2nd I began work on *Sydney*. Caught between the best and worst of our worlds, during the day I was a comedic actress, and at night a woman trying to save my husband and my marriage. At work, Michael, Matthew, and Craig would sometimes notice my faraway looks and ask if I was OK. Compared to when we had shot the pilot, something was obviously bothering me, and it was impossible to hide. But I always said, "I'm fine. It's fine. Everything's fine."

I tried my hardest to make it that way. After work I drove to the hospital and spent time with Ed. On Wednesday nights, following our run-through of the week's episode, I sped to the hospital for couples group. I would constantly check my watch on those nights, because I couldn't be late. Following therapy, I tried to exercise for forty minutes. Then I added Al-Anon meetings, which I hated. Supposedly anonymous, there was nothing anonymous about those meetings for me, and I feared people would talk about Ed and me. After a couple meetings, I stopped going.

At the end of January, about the time Ed left the hospital, I signed up for Overeaters Anonymous meetings. I told Jack that I was tired of the constant up and downs. I wanted a way to stabilize. At the time, I weighed 123 pounds, and thought I was fat. Looking back, it's so transparent: I really wanted help controlling my life, not my weight. But the OA meetings were beneficial. I related to them much better than Al-Anon, perhaps because they were about me and my problems rather than Ed and his.

Unfortunately my sponsor made me uncomfortable. She demanded more daily contact and personal info than I wanted to give. When I balked, she pushed back hard. Though I liked the meetings, I left because of her.

But Ed's and my personal work paid off. By spring we were making a nice connection with each other. The proof was in the bedroom. We made love more over a month than we had in the past year, but even more important than the frequency was the intimacy I enjoyed with my husband. It had been absent far too long. We may not have had the wild life in the sack people imagined, but Ed was a tender, caring lover. That's what made it so painful when he was off in his own world.

He provided much-needed support when I battled network executives about *Sydney*. When the sitcom debuted in March, CBS gave it a Wednesday night time slot behind Moon Unit and Dweezil Zappa's show, *Normal Life*. Despite positive reviews from the critics, we knew Wednesday night was a slow but certain death. I tried using my clout as the star and executive producer to get the network to move the show to a better spot on its more popular Monday night, which was anchored by the hit *Murphy Brown*.

Network battles aside, we had fun making the show. We were shooting *Sydney* in April when I turned thirty. The guys gave me a satin-sleeved jacket from my beloved New Orleans Saints. I remember Craig saying, "It's stupid. You're never going to wear it." He was wrong. I still have it. Ed gave me a classic white Jaguar XJE. I pulled into my parking spot at the studio the next day as Michael, Doogie, and Craig were walking by, and their heads whipped around.

I grinned. As the daughter of a GM exec, I'd always been a car freak. My favorite car of all time was a '74 Chevy Nova. It still is. Ed bought me one shortly after I got used to driving the Jag; it was bright orange and all tricked out. The problem with both the Jag and the Nova was that neither was reliable. What I liked was one thing, but what I needed was a car that started in the morning when I turned the key.

Not that I had anyplace I needed to be. In the second week of May, as we shot the last of the thirteen episodes, the network canceled *Sydney*. I turned to Jack and Marc the night after we shot that episode, knowing that the business slowed during the summer, and said, "Now would be a good time for me to get pregnant." Everyone assumed there were fertility problems, since we'd gone ten years without having children. But, no, there weren't fertility problems. We just hadn't been having sex.

That changed. I told Ed that I was ready to take on a new, more personal project. Instead of TV, movies, or construction crews, I explained that this one involved diapers, cribs, and formula. I figured we'd gone through the tough parts of marriage, a miscarriage, so why not finally get to the good stuff and have a baby? He agreed. It was time for us to start a family.

After several months of peace in our home, trying to have a baby allowed us closeness and joy. It was a nice change, which I credited to sharing the same goal. I couldn't remember a time since before we were married when we thought about ourselves as a couple this way. Life got fun. In May we saw Madonna's Blonde Ambition tour at the Forum and a week later we heard Sinéad O'Connor at a smaller venue. In June we went to Big Sur, followed by a trip to Mississippi, where Ed made a personal appearance on behalf of a guitar company.

When we checked into the hotel in Mississippi, I gave my bags to the bellman and whispered to Ed that he had a job to do, and he knew what I meant. All of our activities were planned around my ovulation schedule. I was obsessive about keeping track of when I was ovulating. You could have set your clock by me. During those months, Ed learned more about a woman's reproductive system than he ever cared to know.

Back home, I spent a week starring with Judd Nelson at Beverly Hills' Canon Theater in the play *Love Letters*. I was already pregnant then (a few days) but didn't know it yet. I used to put a little dash on the calendar on the day I was supposed to get my period, and then turned it into an *X* when that annoying time of the month arrived. But the dash at the end of June wasn't x-ed over on time. That sent me to the doctor, who confirmed the happy news that I already suspected: "You're pregnant."

Those were the happiest words I'd ever heard. At home, I jumped up on Ed and gave him a hug. He was over the moon too—as he should have been. Between our careers, the dream house we were building, and now a baby, we were incredibly blessed. I hoped Ed would be able to use that as motivation to keep himself healthy. It seemed he might. In the early stages of my pregnancy, he was nearly as excited as I was and pretty much stayed off the booze.

I was strong as an ox until the fifth or sixth week, when the nausea hit me like the front line of the Saints' defense. Mornings were toughest. After waking up, I struggled to get myself to the sofa. Sucking on lemons helped with the nausea. Oddly, after Wolfie was born, the color yellow, which I'd never really cared for, became my favorite. Early on, I actually lost weight from being so sick to my stomach. Then I figured out that I wasn't nauseous when I ate, so, like many women, I ate all day long: peanut butter sandwiches, turkey sandwiches on white bread with mayo, crackers. Later my cravings included Japanese apple-pears and my mom's famous Italian submarine sandwiches. What did I care? I was pregnant.

In fact, for the first time in my adult life, I let myself eat without worrying about my weight. Funny enough, that c'est la vie attitude carried into the rest of my life. In August I saw *Phantom of the Opera* with my friend Marci, and then went again the next month with Ed, who took me to dinner a few nights later at Café Four Oaks, a romantic hideaway in Beverly Glen Canyon. Driving home, I rested my hand atop Ed's as he navigated the dark roads. He turned up the music on the stereo to make sure the baby inside me could hear it.

The night air felt good. Ed revved the engine as he took the turns on Mulholland Drive. It seemed like we might have finally gotten our life together in gear.

Seventeen

AND THE CRADLE WILL ROCK

In mid-November 1990 Ed and I moved into the new house, even though it wasn't completely finished and still didn't have electricity. We didn't care. We'd broken ground four years earlier; with the baby kicking inside me, I'd decided it was time to move in. I was excited. With or without electricity, it looked magnificent, like a fairy-tale castle, and I was ready for my fairy tale to begin. Within a week, the power was turned on and Ed and I celebrated by watching TV. There was something incredible to me about being thirty years old, pregnant, and living in this mansion that we'd built.

The home took some getting used to despite the fact that all we did was move across the yard. Clearly I'd over-compensated for having shared a closet and bathroom with Ed for so many years. The library, my favorite room, was cavernous; the den, where we put the big screen TV, was stupid big; *my* closet alone was bigger than my present kitchen; you couldn't yell from one end of the house to the other, which is how most people communicate; Ed and I had to phone each other.

Luckily, though, after my nausea had passed, I turned into one of those pregnant women with boundless energy. Not only could I scoot from one end of the house to the other without losing my breath, I also gladly undertook Thanksgiving dinner for both Ed's and my side of the family. Our kitchen was a pine-accented Mecca for food. I whipped up Dutch-Indonesian fried noodles, or *bahmi goring*, one of Mrs. Van Halen's specialties, and I followed my mom's recipe for traditional turkey and fixings. With the football games on the TV as I cooked, it felt like home.

As I moved into the last trimester, comments about my belly got to be old. I was even sensitive about getting on the scale at the doctor's office, but would grudgingly do it because I wanted to know that the baby was healthy. I didn't need to know how much I was enjoying myself. By December, though, I'd gained almost 45 pounds. I'd add another 15 pounds by March, the last month, and weighed slightly more than 180 pounds. But I felt great. I exercised regularly and walked daily.

Choosing not to find out the baby's sex beforehand, Ed and I picked names for both a boy and a girl. If we had a girl, I liked the names Wilhelmina, Gracie, Tallulah, and Sophie, but none of them sounded good with Van Halen. For a boy, we agreed on Wolfgang. There was never a question. Ed's favorite composer was Mozart, and I loved the way Elizabeth Berridge said "Wolfie" in the movie *Amadeus*.

My pregnancy was perfect in every way except for one: about three-quarters of the way through, Ed began drinking. I'm sure it had something to do with the fact that he'd gone back to writing songs for Van Halen's *For Unlawful Carnal Knowledge* album. As soon as that button was pressed, he went back to his old habits and patterns, using them to get into the zone where he came up with hits like "Right Here" and "Top of the World."

By January I knew he was back on the bottle. He met me at Lamaze classes smelling of liquor and behaving in ways that drew stares from the other couples. Those sessions could be horribly embarrassing because I knew people were wondering what I'd gotten myself into. Yet Ed also doted on me with presents and jewelry. He has exceptional taste, but I would have traded all of that for a sober week of his time.

It got so that I hated the sound of his guitar. If I heard him play piano, especially late at night, my shoulders tightened with tension: it meant he was drinking, and I wouldn't see him until the morning, if then. At nine months pregnant, you don't generally want to start examining the state of your marriage, especially if you've already been married ten years and have come to accept even the shittiest moments simply as the way life is, which was where my head was at. There were so many questions I could have asked, but the reality was that all the answers came back to the same source, me, and I wasn't ready to face that.

At that point, Ed was secondary to the more pressing matter of giving birth. My March 3 due date came and went with nary a rumble down under. That bummed me out. My feet were swollen, my back ached, and I had pains down my legs from the baby pushing on nerves. On my doctor's advice, I spent two weeks on my side in bed, watching TV. That was torture. Nothing was on but news about the LAPD's beating of an African-American man named Rodney King. It was like a loop. I got sick of it.

Normally I have ample patience, but it ran out somewhere between Rodney on TV and Ed coming in and playing guitar to my stomach. I was *that* uncomfortable.

· · ·

A week and a half later, my mom suggested drinking root beer and castor oil. She told me the story of how she'd done that herself when I had been late.

"My doctor said it would either get the baby out or give me the most godawful diarrhea," she said.

"And what happened?" I asked, though I quickly changed my mind. "Don't tell me. I'll do anything."

Amused by the forty-year-old home remedy, my doctor gave me the go-ahead to try it, though she suggested substituting orange juice for root beer to get some vitamin C. She also wished me luck. Let's just say that after I drank the mixture, everything but the baby came out of me. Then I was back visiting the doctor. My water was low, and she wanted me to check into the hospital that night or first thing the next day, after which she wanted to induce labor.

"Thank God," I said.

I spent the rest of that afternoon at home with my parents. We opened a bottle of 1972 Chateau Montelena cabernet, which I'd bought after my doctor said I could relax with a glass of wine. Ed, who, to my annoyance, had gone to Riverside to buy cars, came home later that night with a souped-up Chevy Nomad for me. Fittingly, its license plate read SHESMAD. It should have said SHESREADY. Later that night, he took me to Saint John's hospital in Santa Monica. After settling in, we ate a grilled cheese sandwich with tomatoes in the cafeteria. It was my last meal for what seemed like eternity.

The next morning my doctor induced labor with a Pitocin drip, and I was by myself when it hit me. The nurse walked into my room and found me sitting up in bed, crying from being by myself and in pain. But that was temporary. At ten, Ed showed up. Then my parents arrived, followed by my brothers. Then Al and his wife came. By the

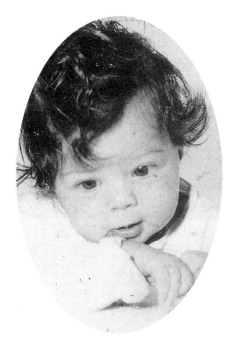

Me, hair and all, at five weeks old.

My grandparents, Angeline and Nazzareno Bertinelli,
at twenty-two and thirty-two, in 1930.

My Rita Hayworth mom, at seventeen—she was gorgeous, and still is.

Don't mess with my dad, also at seventeen.

Just married—and still married.

My parents at Fort Jackson, South Carolina.

The Bertinelli kids in 1967.

Moving day, 1974.

Zuma Beach, California, in 1976. This is what I thought were child-bearing hips. Crazy!

Mac and me hanging out at my house one weekend.

Signing autographs at
Universal Studios in 1976.

Meeting The Who's Roger
Daltry, though my T-shirt
proves my loyalty remained
with Elton John (I made
that T-shirt, too).

At twenty, getting married, done up and clueless.

I now pronounce you . . .

Our wedding was a family affair.

Mr. Van Halen thought I was fifteen until Ed said, "Dad, you're watching reruns."

That cake was so delicious—and *so* not Jenny.

The Bertinelli clan, plus Ed and Bud (the dog), in Shreveport, Louisiana

Three generations of Bertinelli women and Wolfie.

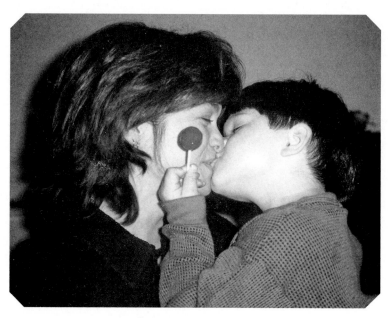

Look at how Wolfie is helping me diet.

My book group gals on our tenth anniversary together, Suzanne, Julie, me, Julie, Alyson, Kathy, Debb and Jessica. Sharing our love of books and our lives.

Tom and me at a wine-tasting the day after we met (with my sister-in-law Stacy, my brother Pat, and friends Kellee and Gina).

Jenny Craig and me—yes, the actual Jenny Craig—
in the Winner's Circle where we belong. Isn't she beautiful?

Tom and me shortly after we met.

My first martini after I lost 25 pounds . . . yum!

Wolfie and me in Halifax, both of us pretending we're Captain Jack Sparrow.

That's me, with my favorite groupie.

"At least we got that right," Ed said of Wolfie backstage before the Charlotte gig, and he was right.

My son, the rock god, 2007.

Golfing after the gig in Charlotte, Ed and Wolfie lost twenty-two balls between them and Tom didn't do much better, but we had fun.

Backstage on Van Halen's 2004 tour, this is the first time I'd seen Wolfie in two weeks.

Tom and me in the Louisiana Superdome. Heaven for me!

In the beginning, the skies parted, the sun shone, and God said, "Hey, give her a kiss!"

time I went into heavy labor, the whole gang were taking pictures and pointing their video cameras.

I didn't care. All of my modesty disappeared as the pain worsened. Inspired by my Lamaze coach, I was adamant about giving birth naturally, without drugs, and staying in the moment in order to experience everything. However, when I got to about six centimeters, I thought, Screw the inspiration! I turned to the nurse and asked, "Where is the guy with the drugs?"

"I'll get him," she said.

"Find him quickly," I said. "Because I'm done with this shit. I want the epidural right now!"

I needed a double dose; the first epidural shot took only on one side. There's a break in my memory as the drugs took effect and I fell asleep for an hour. I slept through transition, the most difficult part of labor. My doctor woke me, and after a quick check said, "I think it's time to push." After a bit of pushing, she gave me a puzzled look.

"I thought you said you had massive diarrhea a couple days ago?"

"Hey, I've eaten since then," I said unapologetically.

God bless Ed, who was busy cleaning and comforting me. But I smelled peanuts on his breath and I was starving.

"Are you serious?" I asked.

"What?" Ed replied, perplexed.

"You had a Payday bar, didn't you?" That was one of my favorite candy bars. "And you were eating it while I was sleeping, weren't you?"

He stepped back from the bed. I think my tone scared him.

"I ate it outside," he admitted. "While you were sleeping after the second epidural."

"But I can smell it now," I said. "I can smell the caramel and the peanuts."

"Honey, I was so hungry. I'm sorry."

"Well, I'm hungry too."

After ten hours of labor and one and a half hours of pushing, I heard a sharp cry. Then I heard the doctor say it was a boy.

"Wolfie's here," I said to the crowd.

He checked in at 7 pounds, 15 ounces, and 21 inches long. When I first held him, he didn't look like a Wolfie to me. I grew concerned.

"What does he look like?" Ed asked.

"I don't know," I said. "He looks like a baby. The most beautiful baby in the world."

I'd read someplace that newborns were sensitive to smells, so every time Wolfie was brought into my room for a feeding, I jumped out of bed, ran into the bathroom, brushed my teeth, and gargled with Scope. Only then did I pronounce myself ready to nurse the baby. I thought that kind of attention to detail was going to make me a great mom. I know how nutty and silly that was, but maybe it shows how badly I wanted to succeed in my new role.

I felt a good kind of nervous when Ed and I took Wolfie home. I sat with our baby in the backseat, staring at his tiny head covered in black hair poking out of the car seat. He slept for six hours the first night, which was six more than I slept. I spent the night checking on him, making sure he was breathing and cross-checking in my baby books to see if it was normal for a newborn to sleep that long.

My mom came over to help. One day I yelled for her to come into the baby's room. I was sobbing. From the sound of my voice, she thought something was wrong. But I greeted her with a dirty diaper—Wolfie's first.

"Look, he pooed!" I said. "He's healthy."

My mom shook her head. "Honey, calm down," she said. "He's normal."

"I know! Isn't it great!" I said.

Ed was also eager to learn new daddy skills. He paid close attention as my mom tutored us in the art of changing diapers. Sometimes I caught Ed staring at Wolfie with a look of disbelief, as if he couldn't have helped create something that miraculous. It was good he felt that way. When I was laid up with a breast infection, he took over feeding Wolfie using milk that I'd pumped ahead of time and put in the freezer because Ed sometimes liked to feed him in the middle of the night when I was too tired and he was wide awake. He even kept a bottle heater by his side of the bed.

Even with all the information I got from my mom, friends, and books, I was dogged by my own insecurities about this new responsibility. Each time I walked down our spiral staircase holding Wolfie, I was gripped by a fear of falling down and blood splattering everywhere. I could have used more perspective to get me through my worries. Just as God gives women almost ten months to get used to the idea of a new life growing inside them, God also gives you a lifetime being a parent. The worries don't get easier, but they change. In my head, I can still see myself freaking out at Wolfie's first cold and fever, but, damn, if that doesn't seem tame now, compared to letting him go out on a rock tour!

In any event, for those first two months, I kept things simple and focused on Wolfie. The two of us camped out on the L-shaped sofa in the den, where I fussed over him while my mom looked after me. Pretty soon I started to exercise again. Mindful that I'd eventually have to go back to work, I began with long walks and then added racquetball. I tried to cut down on the fattening foods I'd eaten while pregnant, but my mom pushed snacks like toasted white bread with butter and cinnamon sugar in front of me, insisting that I needn't worry because breast feeding burned calories.

Maybe so, but it didn't burn enough—and my ass was proof.

Seven weeks after bringing Wolfie home, I put myself together for the premiere of Madonna's documentary *Truth or Dare*. Normally I wouldn't have dreamed of walking a red carpet weighing as much as I did (the mid-140s), except everyone knew that I'd recently had a baby. But they wouldn't be as forgiving when I returned to work on a miniseries in September. That summer, serious about losing weight, I hired Anthony Cortés, the trainer who'd helped Linda Hamilton sculpt her body into incredible shape for *Terminator 2: Judgment Day*. Like every other woman, I'd been blown away when I saw Linda in that film.

A few days later, I showed Anthony into our gym for the first time and gave him simple instructions. I told him to kick my ass. And he did. Every day he came out and put me through a hard workout. He also started me on a high-protein, low-carb diet that had my metabolism firing like a blast furnace. By August I was 10 pounds lighter. The weight hadn't come off as easily as in the past, but I was pleased.

Then a few more pounds came off before I finally had to leave for the North Carolina location of my next project, *In a Child's Name*, a successful CBS miniseries. I put off flying there for as long as possible. Because I was a relatively new mom, they moved the schedule so I was able to arrive twelve days after shooting had started. Wolfie and my mom came with me, and the three of us settled into a beautiful rented home on a golf course.

One of the reasons I took the project was because the main character was pregnant through half the movie. They were going to have to pad me. So the weight I still carried didn't matter as much. It also had a good, gripping script: a chilling true story based on a Peter Maas book about a woman who fights for custody of her dead sister's child after learning that her sociopath husband murdered her. But I got off to a rough start. It rained my first day of work. With the humidity, the heat index was 112 degrees. For my first scene, they dressed me in pregnancy padding under a wool pantsuit and a wool sweater, and I got so hot and uncomfortable that I started to cry. It was more like I started to wilt.

"How do I get off this movie?" I whined. "I can't do this. It's too hard."

That's when director Tom McLoughlin put a comforting arm around me, and we began a friendship that, over the course of the movie, would extend to include his wife and children. Actor Chris Meloni costarred, and the two of us played racquetball on our off days. As it turned out, though, the movie was even more suspenseful off camera. The entire cast and crew went into hiding as Hurricane Bob rolled onto land from the Atlantic and then headed north, where its winds of 100-plus miles per hour, rain, and heavy surf caused major damage and the loss of ten lives.

I should have stayed in hiding considering what happened when Ed visited. Like the hurricane, that too was a disaster that left lasting scars.

Eighteen

HEAR ABOUT IT LATER

Curled up on the floor of the home we had in North Carolina, I held my head in my hands as I cried my eyes out. All I could think was, How could he? We had a baby. But clearly things hadn't changed with Ed, who had come into town for a visit during a short break from Van Halen's new tour and proceeded to drink his way through the entire time we spent together. Worse, the four of us had gone out one night, and Ed had exploded in a rage. He yelled at my mom and then destroyed our rental car, breaking the windshield and kicking the rear until it dented. My poor mother was traumatized by Ed's verbal assault, while my emotions ran from embarrassment at having to call the producers and lie about what had happened to the car, to hurt, outrage, and anger.

I couldn't wait for him to leave, which wasn't a good way to feel about your husband, but the relief I felt after he'd gone was real. The shock of the incident stayed with me for days and made me ask myself, What the hell had happened? What the hell was going on? What the hell should I do?

So many questions, but there were no clear or simple answers, since I never went to the place where divorce was an option, especially now that we had Wolfie. Why? I didn't want to admit that our marriage might have been a mistake and then have to address the reasons I was unhappy. I'd invested too much. Ed struggled with his own issues, too. Every so often, he would fly out a girl to meet him on tour. Everyone knew but me. Looking back, I think that explains his behavior in North Carolina, but it doesn't excuse it.

I want to say that I pulled back from our relationship, but there wasn't much to pull back from. Relieved to have him on tour, I focused on Wolfie, who gave me immense joy and satisfaction. Work was also an unexpectedly welcome diversion. I'd envisioned spending more time at home with Wolfie. But a few weeks after getting back from North Carolina, I went to Pittsburgh and started the NBC movie *What She Doesn't Know*. I felt bad for Ed, who'd missed out on Wolfie's first tooth in North Carolina and then missed out again when he laughed out loud for the first time in Pittsburgh.

But you know what? I also felt worse for myself that I didn't have Ed around to share in these tiny miracles.

Thankfully, I was able to stay at home for my next project, *Murder of Innocence*. Although shot locally, it took me as far away from myself as I'd ever been. The character I played, Laurie Wade, was a newlywed whose childhood traumas trigger a series of psychotic breaks that lead her to shoot at schoolchildren. She then commits suicide.

Though the project let me work with director Tom McLoughlin again, I didn't for one minute like climbing into the skin of this woman. I had the feeling that the ghost of Laurie Wade didn't like it either. One day Tom and I were walking down a tree-lined street in a residential neighborhood, going over a scene in which Laurie is in a manic state, when suddenly we heard an ear-splitting squawk that I swear to God sounded like someone saying "Fuck off!"

Both of us looked up and saw two giant ravens sailing toward each other, like two planes on a collision course. We didn't see them hit, but suddenly one bird fell from the sky, hitting tree branches on its way down and landing with a thud at my feet. I looked down and saw blood dripping from its mouth.

Unnerved, I quickly stepped backward and turned to Tom. His eyes were wide, but not as wide as mine.

"I don't want to be this woman anymore," I said.

As the weeks progressed, I broke out in hives and rashes. The makeup artist advised me to calm down. They had dermatologists visit the set. Nothing worked. Something about that part got under my skin and triggered a reaction. I'm sure good old Laurie stirred the pot of anxieties and insecurities I'd locked in my own Pandora's box. My job was all about showing emotions, yet in real life I went to great lengths to avoid them, which put me in conflict with myself.

That's why I couldn't wait for that movie to end. I wanted Laurie to leave me alone.

After that movie, I wanted normalcy and routine in my life. I met girlfriends for lunch, played racquetball, worked out in our gym, and sat at Mommy & Me and Gymboree. I had so much going for me, yet something was missing. At a friend's urging, I made an appointment with a therapist. Although I'd thought about therapy many times in the past, for one reason or another I'd never gone. My therapist appeared to be only about ten years older than I was. She began therapy with a simple question. She asked why I was there.

I sat quietly for a moment, gathering my thoughts. I found myself overwhelmed by reasons. I tried to gather them into a single encompassing response. Then it dawned on me, and suddenly I burst into tears.

"I don't want to be angry anymore," I said. "I'm really, really tired of being angry. And I don't know why I'm so angry."

We spent months working on that response, until I started to understand that my anger was a response to fear and grief: the fear I had that my marriage wasn't working and the grieving I did for all of the mistakes Ed and I had made the past twelve years. Confronting issues like this was very un-Bertinelli-like. I had no idea what I was getting into. I just knew I needed help.

As much as it interested me, it frightened Ed. He looked terrified as I said good-bye before my appointments. I'm sure he worried about what I was telling her and whether she would tell me to leave him. When I returned, I usually found him waiting for me in the driveway or puttering around on a car, eager to hear what I'd said and how it had gone.

The truth was, she gave me information and insights without telling me what to do. Mostly, I just cried.

In mid-1993, with Wolfie in his terrific twos, I looked for a project that would let me stay home and be a mom. That's when I signed on to star in *Cafe Americain,* a sitcom about an American who serves food and advice to a bunch of eccentric characters at a café in Paris. The talented writer-producer Peter Noah came up with the idea, and NBC, aware of his success with the Jamie Lee Curtis sitcom *Anything but Love,* went for it, hoping the series could round out the hour following *The John Larroquette Show.*

Cafe Americain ranks as one of my favorite projects if for no other reason than the three days we spent in Paris shooting the opening credits. How can you not love Paris? On top of being a beautiful city, there's the food. After two and a half days of phenomenal eating, the Parisian crew celebrated our last night together by taking us out to dinner at a fancy restaurant with a breathtaking view of the city. From my seat, I looked toward the Eiffel Tower. But foremost was the food. The wait staff brought one course after another. Somehow I found more room each time.

For one course, they served tiny bowls filled with what looked like miniature white buffalo mozzarella balls, which I love. I excitedly popped one in my mouth and turned to the person next to me, poised to remark on this latest course, when suddenly I cringed after biting down.

"These buffalo mozzarella don't taste right," I said.

"They are not mozzarella," he said.

"What are they?" I asked, a look of worry painted across my face.

"They are calf brains," he said.

I still had the half-chewed white thing tucked into the side of my mouth. I'd been trying to be polite. But hearing that I had a calf brain in my mouth, I thought, Screw it, and I spit the gross food into my napkin.

A waiter saw me.

"Is everything all right, madame?" he asked.

"Yes, I'm just done," I said. "I think I'll just enjoy the view for the rest of the night."

The series proved once more how fortunate I was in my working life. The great comedy director James Burrows was in the driver's seat behind the camera, and I got to work with wonderful actors like Maurice Godin, who played my love interest and gave me Margaret Atwood's collection *Bluebeard's Egg.* (Two of my favorite books are *The Blind Assassin* and *Alias Grace,* so I'm grateful to Maurice for opening my eyes to such a talented writer.) Although I was unaware of it, my wardrobe choices were the source of an inside joke on the set. If I felt good about myself, I tucked in my shirt. If I left the shirttail out, I was feeling heavy and out of sorts.

I didn't find this out until later. But let's just say that from week to week, it was never the same, even if my weight didn't change.

Those reasons were my secret. One day, in early 1994, as *Cafe Americain* was nearing the end of its run, I overheard Ed talking on his phone in his bathroom, a space he used as his private office. He spent hours in there. Our dysfunction was such that there were times when he called me from the bathroom while I was downstairs. We had some of our best conversations like that.

But the conversation I overheard was beyond belief. Speaking in a stern tone of voice, Ed was telling a woman—I assumed it was a woman—that he was through paying her to keep her mouth shut. He was tired of being blackmailed, and if she wanted to go to the press and sell photos that proved they'd slept together, that was her decision. He'd given her enough money over the years.

What?

My heart raced as I made sense out of the fragments of conversation I'd heard: another woman . . . they'd slept together . . . money . . . blackmail . . . years . . .

Intent on keeping myself together until I knew more, I went downstairs to wait for Ed. As I waited, I kept my cool by thinking of Wolfie. I had to stay strong for him.

Ed finally came downstairs, and what ensued was an extremely unpleasant confrontation. He confirmed what I now knew: that there was another woman. He quickly clarified: there *had been* another woman. He also explained the situation I'd overheard. I can't begin to detail the conversation other than to say it was painful and loud. What emerged was that Ed had brought this woman into our bedroom. She'd taken pictures. Then she had threatened to sell them to the tabloids if he didn't pay her. For more than a year, he'd sent her money. Now he wanted to stop.

First I had to get through the idea that he'd had another woman in our bedroom. What man brings another woman into the bed he shares with his wife? Even worse, what kind of woman wants to go there?

"That bitch!" I fumed, and, after taking a deep breath, added, "I just hope it never makes it into the rags."

I went into a self-protective shut-down mode. Even though Ed assured me the affair was long finished, there was no way I was going back into our bedroom. The thought disgusted me. Needing to calm down, I followed my instinct to get away. Taking Wolfie, I moved in with my friend Jane Leeves, who I knew through my dear friend actress Faith Ford, who talked me through many arguments with Ed.

After a few days of cooling off, however, I returned home. Once again, I decided that I wanted Wolfie to have an intact family, but I didn't know how to repair the damage between me and Ed. The most practical solution was therapy. He started seeing my therapist on his own, and then we also went together. For weeks we rehashed everything, every little detail concerning his infidelity. At some point, Ed, who felt awful, came clean about other affairs, including the wife of a guitar company executive, another woman in St. Louis—and other women.

That floored me. I knew what went on out on the road and about the code of silence those guys had, almost as if they were a band first and husbands second. But I'd never wanted to believe it about Ed, because what would that say about me? Wasn't I pretty enough? Sexy enough? After I digested his admission, I said to myself, Well, shit, if he's going to be that honest, I should be too. Truth be told, I hadn't been perfect either. So I said, "Ed, listen, don't feel so bad. Remember back about ten years ago when I went to Japan?"

After confessing my affair with Craig, I felt better. Although weird, it felt cleansing. But Ed flipped out.

"What?" he said.

I went through the story in detail, just as he'd done with his affairs. It was strange, though. He couldn't accept my admission. There was a double standard stamped in his brain. I'll never forget it. With the utmost seriousness, he maintained that he'd never done anything that bad to me. Ultimately, though, we came out of therapy with the desire to stay married. "Look," I told Ed. "You fucked up. I fucked up. Let's just get this behind us."

That's what we tried to do. In Orlando, Florida, where Van Halen prepared for a swing through North America, Ed quit drinking again, while I devoted myself to Wolfie. As was our pattern following a rough patch, we paid more attention to each other. We had several fun weeks together there—though Ed and Sammy were at odds for reasons I didn't pay attention to. After celebrating Wolfie's fourth birthday at Disney World, Ed and the band went on tour, while Wolfie and I returned home.

I didn't want it to be back to normal, though. A yearning for something more than my own petty concerns led me to start thinking about the bigger picture of God and faith and the role they played or didn't play in my life. Hey, I had problems, and I was looking for solutions in all directions. Why not God? For a brief time as a child, I'd attended Catholic school, and my family had gone to church. But I wasn't affiliated with an organized religion. I'd played a nun, albeit a fallen one, but I hadn't spent much time recently around nuns or any other clergy.

But I believed in God and the value of a relationship with a spiritual side of life, though even more I think I was looking to bring faith into my life. Looking back, I see that Wolfie had deepened my investment in life, yet I hadn't done anything to nourish that feeling of being part of something bigger than myself. If indeed I was part of a bigger picture, what was I doing to understand it and contribute? I think a relationship with God, whether it's through organized religion or some other way, gives you a center of gravity, and I needed that.

Through a friend, I attended several of Marianne Williamson's "A Course in Miracles" seminars. In her lectures, she spoke about making paradigm shifts in your life. I liked the sound of that. First I had to look up the word *paradigm* ("a model of how ideas relate to one other; a conceptual framework"). But that led me to start examining the ideas I relied on to make decisions. I took Wolfie to a day camp at the Self-Realization Fellowship Center, a ten-acre oasis of gardens near the ocean, where a portion of Gandhi's ashes had been placed in a peace memorial by the lake. While he was in camp, I attended lectures by visiting spiritual teachers, dutifully writing down aphorisms that touched me.

- May I spread mental sunshine!
- Tune out the junk, tune in the good.
- If we love God with all our heart, he wipes out bad karma.
- Fear works against willpower.
- Live each moment completely, and the future will take care of itself.
- Love is stronger than fear.

Today when I look back through the notebooks in which I wrote those lines, I see that they sound trite, particularly in the context of what I was looking for in my life when I attended those lectures. But they opened the door for the healing I was able to do later. The truths I heard, whether uttered by priests or yogis, were the truths I wanted and, in fact, *needed* to find in myself. You have to start somewhere. Enlightenment, like change (or even weight loss), doesn't happen overnight.

If change had been easy, I wouldn't have made one of the truly stupid choices of my career. Around this time, I was asked to come in and discuss playing Ross's pregnant ex-wife Carol on NBC's hit *Friends.* It should have been a no-brainer. I adored Matthew Perry, and I'd recently worked with the show's director, Jimmy Burrows, on *Cafe Americain.* Plus, I loved the show.

But I didn't even go in for the meeting. My reason was pathetic. I felt too fat to stand next to Jennifer Aniston, Courteney Cox, and Lisa Kudrow, all three of whom are drop-dead gorgeous on top of being brilliant actresses. I didn't even want to risk being offered the part. Consider this: One day I pulled into a McDonald's and spotted "Doogie." But rather than say hello, I hid. I didn't want him to see me looking heavy. If I did that, how was I going to go to work every day with Jennifer, Courteney, and Lisa?

Instead, in the summer of 1995 I went to London for *The Haunting of Helen Walker,* a remake of the Henry James novel *Turn of the Screw.* I portrayed Helen Walker, a nanny who's put in charge of two parentless children and finds them haunted by spirits from their past. The movie paired me again with director Tom McLoughlin. Wolfie and I and the McLoughlins spent two weeks outside of London in a beautiful bed-and-breakfast that I think had once belonged to Pink Floyd's David Gilmour; the pool was shaped like a guitar.

The house was divided into a new part and an old part. Wolfie and

I stayed in the new part, and the McLoughlins set up in the old part, which they loved after hearing rumors that it was haunted. The high point of their year was Halloween, so it was perfect for them. I felt I had enough ghosts in my life already, especially after what happened after Ed visited us in London. It was the end of June, and Van Halen were on tour, supporting Bon Jovi. Ed's hip had started to cause him a lot of pain, so much so that he walked with a cane. I went to the show at Wembley Stadium and afterward picked up the phone back at my room. It was a business associate of Ed's.

"Your husband is fucking my wife!"

"What?" I said, shocked.

The guy went off on me like a loaded gun. After a minute or two, I interrupted.

"Excuse me. You're going off on *me?* Keep your fucking wife in check. She's the one who's apparently going to Ed's room."

"But he came on to her."

"And she went to his room!"

Talk about your insane situations. We were fighting about our spouses screwing each other. What was the point? To this day, I'm more pissed off at her than I am at Ed, who, like a lot of men, was weak. Like most women, she should have known better. We're wired differently. We need to act differently.

A few days later, Ed called with a problem. The woman who'd black-mailed him had finally sold the photos of her in our bedroom to a tabloid. I let out a groan.

"Call Jack," I said.

Ed then called my manager and said we had a problem. It was the first that Jack had heard about Ed's affair. Embarrassed by it, I'd never said anything about it to anyone, including Jack.

"What were you thinking when you let her take pictures?" he asked.

"I'd had a couple beers," Ed replied.

"But you're posing naked with a guitar. And you're smiling!"

Ed sighed.

"I'll call Heidi in the morning," Jack said.

Heidi Schaeffer was my longtime publicist as well as a dear friend. By the time Jack got a hold of her in the morning, the tabloid had already contacted her, and she'd called me in London. There was no stopping publication, she told me. She asked if I wanted to give a comment. I wanted to say plenty of things, but nothing was appropriate to share with the public.

I sat down on the bed, shaking with anger. Then came the tears. I felt the same intense pain that I had a year earlier when I'd first learned of the affair and the photos, except this time I anticipated the public embarrassment. Once those photos were out, everyone would know about it. Look what I wrote in my date book:

> Ugly, ugly, ugly things went down today. This morning
> Ed's little friend sold her story to the Globe. I'm going to
> get a nice dousing of public humiliation next week.

Indeed. On July 4 the story broke. I forced myself to go to work. I was quiet and withdrawn on the set. I'd become close with Tom and his family; after he couldn't get me to open up, he called his wife, Nancy, who came to the set and consoled me. Their kindness pulled me through the ordeal. That night we had dinner in Windsor and afterward took our kids to a carnival in a nearby little town. Again, I credited my responsibility to Wolfie for preventing me from sinking into a depression. If he hadn't been with me, I wouldn't have gone to the carnival. Once there, I had a blast. I went on the free-fall tower over and over again. It got everything out of me.

It's the hardest I've laughed in a long time. I had a lot of fun. I needed it.

Nineteen

YOU STILL NEED WORK

At the end of September 1995, I went to work on the movie *A Case for Life,* a dramatic look at the abortion issue through the eyes of two sisters, one prochoice and the other against it. I liked the idea of doing an issue-oriented project.

It came along at a time when I was angered by news reports of bombings and protests outside women's health clinics. Understanding that there are two sides of the issue, I was against violence, intimidation, or pressuring women inside or outside of these places no matter what. How could those who followed the Bible turn that vicious? I got particularly upset when I saw women attacking other women.

The movie enabled me to explore the issue and bring attention to it. Instead of playing the prochoice sister, who was closer to my personal feelings—that role went to Mel Harris—I chose the role of the fundamentalist sister. I wanted to get inside the head of a woman who refused to get an abortion even when told she would likely die and leave her other children motherless if she didn't. It was an interesting journey that left me confounded by zealotry and confused by people who claimed to act in the name of God but seemed to me to behave in the opposite way that I understood God.

The really interesting part of this time of my life was watching me juggle my various roles without losing my mind. During a typical week, I arranged playdates for Wolfie, led an antiabortion protest in a movie, drove real-life carpools, and lay in a hospital bed while doctors tried to convince my character that I'd die if I didn't abort my pregnancy. Normal stuff. In between all that, I was glued to the O. J. Simpson trial. Closing arguments were in October. The entire cast and crew gathered around TV sets during our breaks.

Let me just say that I was irate when the verdict came in. I didn't understand how the jury could arrive at such a decision. Everyone I knew, including me, had come to the opposite conclusion. I surprised myself by caring so fervently and took it as more proof that, at thirty-five years old, I was maturing and caring about things other than myself. I looked forward to my next movie, *Two Mothers for Zachary,* a true story for ABC about Sharon Bottoms, a Virginia woman who lost custody of her little boy when her own mother sued for custody, claiming that Sharon's being a lesbian made her an unfit mother—and the Virginia courts agreed.

When I met Sharon, I embraced her for having endured such a nightmare. She and her partner were sweet, kind, cool women and very much in love with their little boy. Even though she'd come through the ordeal, it had left her sad. I found myself blurting out "how fucked up were the courts to do that to you!"

The five-week production, which began in spring 1996, gave me the privilege of working with Vanessa Redgrave, who played my mother. I was in awe of her as a smart, talented, independent, political, outspoken woman. And she opened her arms to me and made it seem as if the work wasn't beneath her. We went out for margaritas one night and had a great time. Her passion for life and her work impressed me.

I had a scene in which I had to give my on-screen partner, Colleen Flynn, a romantic kiss. A same-sex kiss was still considered controversial, even though that ground had been broken on TV on *L.A. Law, Roseanne,* and *Melrose Place.* Even Chandler and Joey had kissed on *Friends.* I approached it with a sense of humor. Right before we shot it, I winked at Colleen and said, "Get ready. I'm going to shove my tongue so far down your throat you might gag."

She gave me a nervous look.

"Just kidding," I laughed.

Later that night, I was surprised by the memory that scene stirred up. Though I'd forgotten about it, years earlier I'd shared a passionate kiss with another woman. It was 1981, during my first year of marriage, and I had had an actress friend of mine over for dinner. I'd been having a difficult time with Ed's drinking and our lack of time together, a foreshadowing of the years ahead. After a couple glasses of wine, I opened up to her. It was one of the rare moments when I took an honest look at reality and wondered if I'd made a mistake. The conversation got very personal, and she also told me about issues in her life. When she got up to leave, I walked her to the door to say good-bye, and before I knew it we were locked in a deep, passionate kiss.

Though I don't know about her, I had thoughts of going further. But I pulled back. It wasn't because I was weirded out by the feelings

I had for her. That still doesn't bother me. She was a beautiful woman, and I think she was attracted to me too. I only stopped because I didn't want to cheat on Ed.

The funny thing is that I'd never told anyone about that until recently when I mentioned it to my boyfriend. You should have seen Tom's eyes widen. Normally he's a sensitive, conservative man, but the thought of me with another woman made him grin. He jokingly asked if there were pictures or if that made me gay or bisexual. I had the sense I disappointed him by answering no on all counts.

"But could you have done it with her?" he asked.

"I don't know. Maybe," I said. "It would've been different. But not a big deal."

"Not a big deal?" he exclaimed. "Valerie Bertinelli doing another woman—*that's* a big deal!"

"Oh, shut up," I said. "I was aching for some kind of contact, compassion, affection, connection . . . anything. But it didn't happen. And it's not going to happen. End of story."

And end of fantasy.

As for *Two Mothers for Zachary,* I was proud of the attention I brought to the story and its theme about the devastating effects of prejudice. At the Emmy Awards, which took place a few weeks before the movie's September 23 airdate, Holly Hunter, who I have admired since *Raising Arizona* (I love saying "Get me that bay-bee") and *Broadcast News,* tapped me on my shoulder. She'd seen me talking about my movie on *Larry King Live* on CNN, and said I'd been eloquent. That I was getting a compliment from Holly Hunter—you could have knocked me over with a feather. I couldn't believe she even knew who I was.

· · ·

While I was making *Two Mothers,* Ed and Sammy were in the midst of three months of falling out of favor with each other. They came off the road ravaged. Al had back and neck problems. Ed was hampered by severe hip pain. Sammy's marriage had ended after twenty-three years. In addition to rest, they needed time away from one another. But Ed and Al dived into working on the song "Humans Being" for director Jan De Bont's movie *Twister* and then moved on to preparing the band's first greatest hits album. Both projects resulted in Ed and Sammy's going at each other until they parted ways. It was probably one bad phone call too many. Whatever the details of their falling out, I remember thinking that Ed's points were valid. In fact, one day he hung up and told me that Sammy had the same problem as Dave: LSD.

"Huh?" I said.

"Lead singer disease," he said, shaking his head. "It's all about them. Not the band."

In the aftermath, Ed and Sammy had totally different versions of what had transpired between them. Ed maintained Sammy quit to pursue a solo career again, and Sammy claimed he was forced out. I didn't follow the soap opera enough to weigh in. It was enough that it consumed Ed's life. As the relationship unraveled, he drank heavily again. Even though Ed tended to most of his Van Halen business in the studio, it still filtered into the house.

By the time of Sam's departure, the atmosphere at home had thickened with tension. One weekend I arranged for Wolfie to sleep at a friend's and took off with my girlfriend Alyson for some pampering at the Ojai Valley Ranch. On my last day there, Ed called and informed me that our cat Draco had killed Sally the hamster. On my way home, I picked up Wolfie, and we had a funeral that night.

Soon after, Dave reappeared in our lives. I knew that Ed had spoken to him a few times on the phone about the forthcoming greatest hits album. One talk had gone so well, Ed told me, that they'd apologized for some crap they'd said to each other when they were younger. After a meeting at Dave's house, he came over to ours to work on two new cuts Ed wanted on the album.

I liked seeing Dave again. He looked great, and I got a laugh when he sat down on a chair in the library, and I pointed out that it was Wolfie's "time out" chair. "When he's behaving badly, I make him sit there," I said. As quick as ever, Dave made some clever wisecrack about it being an appropriate seat for him. After eleven years, I forgot whatever grudges I had toward Dave. My problems with him had all stemmed from the friction in his relationship with Ed. Otherwise I liked Dave—and still do.

There was no doubt that Ed and Dave had a special chemistry. A couple times, I went into the studio while they worked on new songs, and the music I heard impressed me. Unfortunately, the reunion got only as far as the MTV Awards in September. Their egos got in each other's way as they gave interviews after presenting an award to Beck. It was too bad. Ed was angry and depressed when he got home. When I asked what had transpired, he simply said that Dave had turned back into Dave.

After starting Wolfie in kindergarten, I went to Park City, Utah, to make *Night Sins,* a movie based on a bestselling book about the kidnapping of a small boy. I played police investigator Megan O'Malley, whose work on the case in small-town Minnesota also unearths twenty years' worth of mysteries. Harry Hamlin played the local police chief whose turf jealousies are usurped by his attraction to Megan, and

Mariska Hargitay was a bigtime reporter. The book's author, Tami Hoag, provided a taut script.

The story of the kidnapped boy, though, made me go through Wolfie withdrawal. Going from driving carpools and volunteering in his classroom to being away for two months was a harder transition than I'd thought it would be. Ed and our housekeeper, Lettie, took over while I was gone. But I missed my son and my main job of being a mom. I called Wolfie three times a day. During downtime on the set, I needlepointed him a Christmas stocking.

At least I knew a couple of Park City residents: my brother David and some of his friends, who were good for a couple dinners each week and some skiing when time allowed. I burst into tears one day when I received one of Wolfie's school drawings in the mail. The kids had been asked to draw a picture illustrating where they'd fly if they had wings. Most of the kids drew themselves flying to the North Pole to meet Santa Claus or to the candy store. Wolfie had drawn a picture of himself over a mountain, and his teacher had included the note, "Wolfie wants to fly to be with his mama." That ripped my heart out. When I got on the phone with Ed the next time, I sounded like Holly Hunter in *Raising Arizona,* saying, "Bring me my bay-bee."

I tried to stay busy. I also worked out nonstop during production. I started the movie at 130 pounds, and I was in the low 120s after a month. I got to work in the snow, which I loved. Ever since I was a little girl, something about the snow and starting the day with the ground blanketed in white gave me a lift.

At night, I enjoyed myself with some of the crew and Mariska, who had us laughing so hard we were crying. When she mentioned that she hated the place that had been rented for her, I had her move into my four-bedroom condo. We celebrated Harry's birthday at a local sushi restaurant. The next night was Halloween, and Ed called after taking Wolfie out trick-or-treating. The poor guy sounded wiped out from daddy duty.

In November I flew home for a three-day fix of Wolfie, who kept me up the whole first night with a stomachache and diarrhea. As tired as I was, I couldn't have been happier. My son needed me, and I was there to help him. I also tried to cram in as much of my normal everyday life as possible. I drove Wolfie to school, stopped by Faith Ford's house to give her a hug, and got my gray roots colored.

I hated leaving home again a few days later. My frustration came out when I got a flat tire while driving to meet my brother David. As I was jacking up the car, two big, strong guys walked by and they stopped to look.

"Oh, you got a flat?" one asked.

"Yeah," I replied, thinking they might help.

"Bummer," he said.

"Yeah, too bad," his pal added, and they kept walking.

"Assholes," I muttered. "Thanks for the help."

I brightened considerably when my parents, Ed, and Wolfie flew into town for Thanksgiving. We had an old-fashioned family dinner and enjoyed a couple days of skiing and snowman building before everyone left. After such a good time, I was thrilled to be headed home when the movie finally wrapped a few weeks later. I'd been as lonely as I'd ever been during a movie and wanted to reconnect with Ed to see if I could once again breathe new life into our marriage.

Absence had made my heart grow fonder, but my daily workouts had gotten me in great shape, and I felt good about my body. For the first time in my life, I had the abs I'd wanted. A thousand sit-ups a day had paid off. As far as I was concerned, I looked as good as I ever did in my twenties. But I wanted Ed's opinion too.

On my way home, I concocted a whole seduction fantasy that I thought was a sure bet to rekindle the passion we'd had in the early days of our relationship. I'd gone months without making love and was eager to cuddle up to my husband. I recalled old memories of when we had made love with the passion and zeal of people still discovering each other, and I missed that Ed. I figured it was normal for couples married as long as we had been to have their ups and downs in the bedroom, but I was ready for the ups again. Feeling and looking as I did, I thought if there was ever a time to reclaim my place in Ed's heart—and pants—this was it.

After catching a flight in Salt Lake City, I arrived home around eleven o'clock at night, and, in what I should have taken as a sign from above, I couldn't find my house keys. I fumbled around in the dark, then banged on the front door. After Ed didn't answer—knowing what a deep sleeper he was—I walked around until I found an open door.

Even though I found Ed asleep, I slipped into a pair of black panties and wife beater, then got into bed and tried to get him interested. Hey, I'd watched my share of afternoon talk shows; that was supposed to work on men, right? I didn't give up at the first "not now," but eventually I uttered a frustrated "all right" and got out of bed. As I walked toward the door, Ed said, "Val, you look good. You still need to work on your ass. But you look great."

That was harsh. I ended up in the kitchen, where I fumed through the night, wondering why I even bothered, while picking my way through jars of olives and bags of chips and other assorted foods. It was as if I'd risked exposing myself for the first time since packing on the weight after my affair a decade earlier, and after the rejection, it was as if I needed to disappear again.

The next night I got my belly button pierced. I'd gotten the thought earlier during production when Sandy, the director of photography from *Night Sins*, had lit my abs in a close-up—and I was actually proud of them.

Thinking that might get Ed's attention, I decided to do it. First we went to Lucy's El Adobe restaurant for a couple shots of tequila, and then Sandy took me to a nearby tattoo parlor. The place looked reputable. Buoyed by the tequila, I hopped on the table and pulled up my shirt. But as soon as the guy jammed a giant awl-like tool through the skin around my belly button I screamed, *"Whoa, shit!"*

I needed a couple deep breaths before I could speak. Then I turned to Sandy.

"What the hell am I doing?"

It was a good question.

Twenty

FINISH WHAT YA STARTED

In early 1997 I decided to pull back from work. I called Jack and told him that I didn't want to take on any jobs for a while. As my longtime manager, he understood the effect that being away from Wolfie for two months had had on me. He'd calmed me down on the phone after I'd opened Wolfie's drawing. After more than fifteen movies and three TV series, I wanted to focus on motherhood, and he supported my decision.

Other things had influenced that decision. In January Ed's mom had moved in with us after breaking her pelvic bone the previous Christmas Eve. In her eighties, Mrs. Van Halen was still a feisty character. Over the years she had given me delicious traditional Dutch-Indonesian recipes and taught me how to cook them. She was a hoot when she'd go to the grocery store with me, picking items off the shelf and complaining in her accented voice, "Fifty-nine cents for this?

That's a rip-off, Valerie!" She was also typically the first one to mention that I'd gained weight.

One afternoon after Mrs. Van Halen had moved in, I had a girlfriend over who asked Ma how she felt.

"How the hell do you think I'm feeling?" Mrs. Van Halen said. "I
broke a bone."

For months, Ed and I were hands-on nurses. We fed her, moved
her from room to room, and even bathed her. That was intense; the
two of us taking off her clothes and washing her. Interestingly, Ed and
I functioned best in family situations like this. Looking back, I see that
we were better suited to a brother-sister type relationship than we
were as husband and wife. And eventually, Mrs. Van Halen thankfully
healed and was able to return to her home.

I found the fulfillment I needed and another type of intimacy in
close friendships with Wolfie's friends' moms, women who were raising children, helping at school, and basically concerned about the
same issues that occupied me: bringing down a fever at night, knowing the good teachers at school, figuring out where to sign up for karate classes, soccer, and T-ball.

This was a whole new, eye-opening, comforting, growth-inspir-
ing experience for me. On movies and TV shows, people were divided
into two groups. You were either above the line or you were below the
line. Talent and producers were above it, and crew was below it. I
hated that demarcation. It was as if some people were more important
than others. Which is ridiculous. With these moms, we were all the
same. There were no false lines dividing us. Rich, middle-class, famous, not famous, divorced, married—whatever—it didn't matter.
All of us were special because we were trying to be great moms. I
could call them if I needed the name of a doctor. Or they called me to

sub in carpool. Or someone mentioned a recipe she'd seen in a magazine that looked delicious, and we arranged a dinner.

Simple stuff, yes. But one day I had a profound realization that,
through these friends, I'd acquired something that had been missing
from my life since I'd started leaving school to go on auditions; maybe
even since elementary school. I fit in. I had a group of people who
were there for me whether I was grouchy or good humored, fat or
thin, late or early.

That was most true in my book club. It started randomly one day
when I dropped Wolfie's friend Zach off at his house after picking the
boys up from school. Zach's mom, Suzanne, came out to say hi, and I
noticed she was holding Wally Lamb's novel *She's Come Undone*. I was
reading that book too. It had been Oprah's pick for her TV book club.
Both of us immediately rattled on about the brilliance of this story of
a colorful, lusty, fat woman who, as she turns forty, describes an amazing life of ups and downs, culminating in her reinvention.

"Isn't it amazing that it was written by a man and he can speak so
well in a woman's voice?" I remarked.

Suzanne agreed, and we found ourselves full of comments about
this wonderful character Wally Lamb had created and her continuous
battles against adversity and her search for love.

"You know what? We should start a book group," she said. "How
fun would it be to get together with other friends of ours and talk
about all the great books we're reading?"

Fun but nerve wracking. I'd always been insecure about not having gone to college; in fact, I ended two classes shy of getting my high
school diploma. Privately, I'd compensated by turning myself into a
voracious reader and an appreciator of words by tackling the crossword puzzle every day.

But that book group became a crucial part of my life. Our first group met at my house, and we read *Angela's Ashes,* Frank McCourt's brilliant memoir in which he somehow made his impoverished Irish upbringing not only tolerable by the way he wrote it in a child's innocent voice but also inspirational. He showed that hope can nourish the soul through any misfortune—and I really related to that.

I had the opposite reaction when we read Nicholas Sparks's best seller *The Notebook.* Despite admiring the cleverness of his construction, I took offense at the dewy notion of love and romance he presented. I didn't realize how much of my own baggage I brought to that opinion, but no one in the group seemed impressed with the book, in spite of its place on the bestseller list. Not that it mattered. We had the most amazing conversation that night. Inspired by the book, we talked about Alzheimer's disease, then got on the topic of abortion, and from there went to politics and whether or not we believed in God.

The friendships from those nights around the table sustained and inspired me in a way that my marriage didn't. I appreciated the little moments that were giving meaning to my life, like spring cleaning in May 1998, Wolfie's first big hit in Little League that summer, and even the new place mats I bought to go with the chicken marbella I prepared from the *Silver Palate Cookbook* that Suzanne had given me. The regularity of the meetings, the dependability of their presence, the desire to come together and share our lives—sadly, I didn't have that with Ed.

In the spring; while in New Zealand with Ed for a Van Halen tour, I read Niall Williams's *Four Letters of Love,* turning the pages at night while Wolfie played Nintendo 64 in the hotel room. The Irish novel was about a son's effort to figure out his father, who'd abandoned his job and family after hearing God tell him to paint. As I read, I found

myself substituting Ed as the father, Wolfie as the boy, and me abandoned in the home. I brought up the similarities at the next book
club.

I kept one disappointment to myself: though Ed and I had talked
about wanting four children, I was coming to terms with the idea that
I wasn't going to have any more due to the circumstances of our relationship. That was a tough pill to swallow. One year turned into two,
then four, and then six—and the bedrooms we'd planned for children
remained empty. But I was practical. Aside from the fact that we
needed to have sex in order to have more children, I didn't want more
kids without an active, interested partner.

I told myself that I had enough on my hands as it was. I also told
myself that Wolfie and I were such special buds that I couldn't possi-
bly love another child as much. I lost track of all the excuses I came up
with for my disappointment. Ed suffered for it indirectly. Whenever
he showed interest in helping with Wolfie, I became territorial and
resentful of the fact he was invading my space. He had his studio in
the back, while motherhood was my domain.

Then I started to have a hard time with Wolfie. His behavior toward me for a while was awful, angry. At one point, I think I even
described him as a troll. He may have been reacting to his dad's not
being around much, and when he was around, we fought. But Wolfie
may have just been going through a phase. One day when he was
eight, we were hiking with some friends, and he made a joke about the
size of my butt. Although he was playing around and, as I realized
later, merely aping one of the many off-hand remarks I frequently
made about the size of my ass, I was hurt—and I got angry with him.

I shot him an angry look, then walked off in a huff. A moment
later, a woman's voice was in my ear: "Girlfriend, that's not how you
deal with an eight-year-old." I turned. My friend Julie, who'd also

been Wolfie's kindergarten teacher, had jogged up alongside me. She doled out a brief lesson on dealing with children and advised me not to take every comment personally.

"He doesn't understand he hurt your feelings," she said.

"So what you're saying," I replied, running my hand through my hair, "is that *I'm* the one who needs a time out?"

"Parents aren't always perfect," she said.

"Don't tell that to Wolfie," I laughed. "Or Ed."

Through much of 1998 and '99, Ed was occupied by Van Halen's latest album, *Van Halen III*, and a tour featuring new lead singer Gary Cherone. Gary impressed me as pleasant, talented, and intelligent, with a good, patient attitude. I watched him throw a baseball with Wolfie one afternoon while waiting for Ed to wake up from a nap. He also liked to talk about the Bible. We had many feisty arguments that proved his superior knowledge about the Bible. I delighted in debating the subject, even though I had nothing but instinct and passion to back it up.

But at this point I wasn't as involved or as interested in the band as in years past. There were too many difficulties, egos, and dysfunctions. It was Ed's thing. He went off and did it.

With the help of my therapist, I came to terms with Ed's drinking. I accepted as much as I could that nagging, pleading, getting mad, and crying weren't going to get him to quit. Not that I was perfect at keeping my mouth shut. My temper flared regularly and sharply. It was hard when I saw the drinking intrude into Wolfie's life. But I understood that Ed had to make that decision on his own. Only he could come to terms with why he drank and whether he wanted to quit.

When Gary left the band in November 1999, I didn't care to know why. The drama didn't interest me anymore; I wasn't invested as I'd been with Dave or Sammy. At least Gary parted on decent terms. Ed still referred to him as a "brother." From what I observed, the band's manager, Ray Daniels, simply wasn't able to handle the roaring egos within Van Halen. They needed a lion tamer, not a manager.

They also needed doctors. Although Al had healed after injuring his arm on tour in Europe, Ed's hip was so bad that he needed an operation. When his hip first began bothering him in 1994, doctors thought it might be gout. By 1995 we knew it was a degenerative condition brought on from years of jumping up and down on stage, as well as punishing his body with alcohol and cigarettes.

Ed had postponed a scheduled operation in December 1996. Despite warnings from doctors, he continued to put it off until he reached the point where he could no longer manage the pain by drinking or doing whatever else he did. I offered little help with his discomfort and less sympathy. First he had to help himself. I used to say, not so jokingly, that my capacity for compassion was degenerative too.

Life had made me battle weary, and sometimes remote and difficult even for friends to reach. Mackenzie Phillips, who battled drug addiction through the eighties and nineties without hearing a word from me, began leaving me messages every six months starting in 1992. I hadn't returned a single call. I knew that she wanted to make amends for anything she did that might have hurt me in the past. From Ed's stints in rehab, I knew that was part of her recovery program. But the idea of hearing Mac apologize for something that had happened so long ago, especially when I didn't feel like she'd done anything to me, made me uncomfortable. I also simply had enough on my plate and didn't want to add her remorse.

Truth be told, I feared that talking to Mac would make me face guilt that I always felt for having done drugs with her without anyone knowing, while she took the heat as *One Day*'s resident druggie. Unlike Mac, I never arrived to the show late, missed rehearsals, forgot my lines, or had any of the other problems that resulted in her termination. But I wasn't as squeaky clean as people thought.

It was all more than I wanted to go into when Mac began leaving messages. Then, as the years went by, I felt bad for not being able to be there for her. The talk may have benefited me too. But I was simply a crappy friend.

Then one day I was at the beach house, and I decided to call her. I have no idea why I chose then to pick up the phone, but that's me. Sometimes I get these little hairs up my butt and think, OK, it's time. I don't know where it comes from or why I suddenly feel I have the energy and interest to do something, but that's what happened with Mac. I shut the office door and called.

I was glad that I did. We had a nice conversation. I stopped her as she tried to apologize for whatever she might have felt she'd done in the past, saying it wasn't necessary. We quickly moved on to catching up with each other's lives. Both of us had sons; hers was already a teenager. Mac's voice sounded good, as did her spirit. As we hung up, my heart was full for her.

It was shortly after that conversation that Ed checked into Saint John's hospital for surgery on his hip. He'd made the decision after talking to a friend who'd undergone the same operation and assured him it was the best decision he'd ever made. The operation was a success, though Ed initially had doubts when he woke up in severe pain. He complained that the morphine they gave him made him high but didn't relieve the pain.

But he recovered quickly. On his third day in the hospital, he was up and walking. The next day he went home. Ed, who always walked around with small bags of stuff and rings full of keys, entered the house carrying something new: a little plastic bag containing his old hip bone. He put it in the freezer. Because I often had a ham hock or two in there for making soup or beans, first he wrapped the bag with tape, and in large, bold letters he wrote:

MY HIP BONE—DO NOT COOK!

Fair warning. But Ed was still about to land in hot water—and unfortunately both of us would feel the burn.

Twenty-one

HOUSE OF PAIN

As we opened presents next to our towering Christmas tree, Ed and I grinned while watching Wolfie play with his new toys. The living room floor was layered with wrapping paper that he'd dispatched after tearing open his presents. It was a happy picture, and then the picture got even brighter when Ed handed me a small gift-wrapped box. Inside I found an absolutely beautiful cabochon ruby ring set in silver. It was my taste exactly: antique, small, and delicate.

After admiring the ring on my finger, I wrapped my arms around Ed and gave him a kiss. He couldn't see it, but I had a tear in the corner of my eye. My joy was bittersweet. The new ring was another treasure to put alongside my other gorgeous pieces of jewelry, fancy cars, and our beach house. But none of those things mattered if we weren't happy. Part of me wanted to keep kissing Ed, and part of me wanted to wring his neck and scream, "Don't you get it?"

My efforts at creating normalcy in our marriage ranged from putting Wolfie in a good school, to cheering him on the soccer field, to shopping at the grocery store, to scheduling time when Ed and I could watch TV together. I repeatedly said that nothing was as important to me as family, and I meant it. I remember too many nights when I cooked our favorite dinners (lasagna, roasted chicken, quesadillas, turkey meatball soup), and Wolfie and I waited at the table for Ed to come in from the studio. Eventually we gave up, said grace, ate, and played video games.

In January 2000 Ed went to the dentist for a checkup and cleaning. He had bad teeth and bit his tongue frequently when he ate. It was painful to watch. The dentist thought that Ed's tongue looked funny where the scar tissue had developed over the permanent gash. He suggested getting it checked by a specialist.

We went to the specialist at UCLA Medical Center, who cut out a section of Ed's tongue and had it biopsied. Cancer. The specialist saw that it didn't look good and cut out a slightly larger piece, probably to make sure he got as close to the margins as he could. After he was finished, he called me into the room and said he wanted both of us there at the same time so Ed and I could hear him at the same time.

"I don't want either of you to misunderstand me," he said. "I want to make this very clear. Ed, you are never to smoke again. Never. I don't know if I can be any more clear. You are never to smoke again. If you do, this will return."

Though still groggy, Ed nodded. I was a basket case. I was choking back the tears until I finally lost it as I stared at Ed.

"Don't you ever smoke again," I said, shaking my fist at him. "Because if that doesn't kill you, like the doctor says it will, I will kill you."

Did he listen? No.

Within a month or two, if that long, Ed began to smoke again. At first he tried to hide it from me. But then I smelled cigarettes on his breath. I was like, Ugh, are you kidding me? I didn't confront him about it, though. I was tired of being on this treadmill of confrontations. That's probably when he started to light up in the open. I couldn't believe it when I saw him puffing away. I didn't want to believe it. Was he insane? He'd heard the doctor's warning: the cancer would return. Even if he didn't care about his own life, what about me and Wolfie—most of all Wolfie?

Once, in the heat of an argument, I snapped, "Why don't you have another cigarette and get some more of your tongue cut off? Keep it up. Soon you won't be able to talk."

There was no justification for speaking to someone that way. But Ed's refusal to take care of himself finally pushed me past my boiling point. After years of competing—and not very successfully—with music, I simply ran out of patience when cigarettes and cancer moved ahead of me too.

I was tired of fighting with Ed. I didn't want to be that person anymore. I didn't want to live in a house filled with so much anger. It was enough already. Marriage is work and a challenge but it shouldn't be as difficult as we made it. Ed and I were terrible examples of what a husband and wife should be. Frankly, I'd said that to myself before, but this time I said it knowing that it wasn't just about us. Wolfie deserved better.

That spring would have been a perfect time for an honest self-evaluation. I was about to turn forty years old. Even if I didn't want to think about issues like my marriage, Ed's cancer, and my state of mind, my girlfriends and family asked how I felt about reaching the big four-oh often enough that I was rarely without the opportunity to examine the significance of the occasion.

But I couldn't focus on anything other than my weight. I didn't see that it was an expression of the disappointment I felt inside. I just saw fat.

"One hundred and fifty-eight pounds," I said while staring at myself in the mirror. "Why? What the hell have I done with my life?"

Rather than tackle the big issues and make real changes, I issued myself a challenge: to get under 140 pounds by my birthday. Failing that, I told myself that since I was turning forty, getting into the 140s would be good enough. I was already compromising and preparing myself for failure. I went on both the Atkins diet and Weight Watchers, without committing to either. Each morning I resolved to eat better. By nighttime I was popping Jordan almonds as if they were pain pills and promising myself that I'd try harder the next day.

By my birthday, I was still in the 150s. And I was still utterly clueless that my weight-loss battle would continue to be futile until I dealt with the reasons why I ate and understood the behavior patterns that drove me into the kitchen. But I set that aside for the moment. It was party time. For my birthday, I planned a girls-only soiree in Las Vegas. This gave me an excuse not to have Ed there (although I amended the girls-only policy to include my dad and two of my brothers).

Before I left for Vegas, Ed made dinner reservations at Il Tiramisù, our favorite restaurant. He arranged with the owner for us to dine before the restaurant opened, so that we could have the place to ourselves. That upset me, because it meant that the people who worked there had to show up earlier, and I didn't want to put them out like that. Ed was so sweet, but we were on different wavelengths. In my state of mind, I found fault with everything he did. Ed stayed calm and pleasant. Nothing upset him. I kept thinking, Why are you being so nice? I need to figure out how to leave you.

I was confused. I wanted us to be married forever, but our marriage was becoming unbearable, which is why I'd begun pulling away. It was really a process. Like a wall of switches. One had been flipped when he'd turned me down in the bedroom. Another was flipped when he began smoking again. Then it was my birthday dinner. All the lights weren't off yet, but they were dimming.

I was relieved to finally land in Vegas. My birthday celebration began with a tour of Bellagio owner Steve Wynn's gallery of multimillion-dollar paintings by Picasso, Matisse, and van Gogh. Then came a feast for about twenty-five people on the outdoor patio at the Bellagio hotel's Prime Steakhouse restaurant. The hotel's elaborate dancing fountains and light show played in the background, while Andrea Bocelli's beautiful singing wafted from hidden speakers. My mother, several cousins, and about twenty girlfriends, including Mac, helped me whoop it up. Finally I led those with an appetite for risk into the casino, and we played blackjack until the wee hours. Everyone made fun of me because I kept saying, "I'm so happy. I'm so happy."

A month later I was in New York with Ed, who'd arranged to meet with a doctor about alternative cancer treatments. I don't know how he found this so-called expert, whether it was through a recommendation or from the internet. But the doctor definitely seemed like a quack. He arrived at our hotel room smoking a cigarette and carrying a bottle of wine.

"That's the doctor who's going to help you?" I said after watching the two of them smoke and drink through the initial meeting.

However, Ed was of the belief that his cancer had been caused not by cigarettes and alcohol but from a reaction between the metal in his artificial hip and a metal guitar pick he bit on during rehearsals and performances. There were fans online that elaborated on his theory, citing as possible causes electromagnetic waves, radiation attracted by the pick, and even the nickel-plating in his guitar strings that rubbed off his fingertips and into his mouth.

There were also people who wouldn't have blinked twice if Ed claimed he could turn water into wine. But he's been cancer free since his operation while continuing to smoke and drink, so who knows?

I chose to go back to work and signed on to the CBS movie *Personally Yours,* a comedy in which two kids set about fixing up their divorced dad with his perfect match: his ex-wife.

We used Vancouver, British Columbia, as a substitute for the story's Alaska location. I began working out before going up there, taking Tae Bo classes from Billy Blanks. But I really applied myself like an athlete to spinning classes led by Debbie Rocker, which were much better for my self-esteem than standing next to a tall and toned albeit very sweet Brooke Shields in Tae Bo.

In Vancouver I set up a bike on the balcony of my apartment, which had a view of the waterway and snow-capped mountains. I pedaled for an hour every morning while watching planes take off and land on the water; it was glorious. Sometimes I hit the bike again at night. By June I was down to 140, and feeling good. When Wolfie got out of school, Ed brought him up to hang out with me.

Ed didn't stay long, but one night we went to dinner with Mackenzie, who was in town shooting her Disney Channel series *So Weird.* As we walked to the restaurant, I noticed he was checking me out. I had on a tight T-shirt and Chinese pajama-style pants.

"What?" I asked.

"Nothing," he said. "It's just that you look nice tonight."

That made me feel good. Ed left soon after, leaving Wolfie with me until work on the project finished several weeks later. We had a couple of adventures before returning home. Then Ed and I went back to our separate routines, back to the same old underlying tension that wore on both of us and created pressure that built up until something happened that brought it to a head.

In early 2001 Ed had another cancer scare. I was adamant: enough with the alternative clinic crap; go to the best doctors in L.A. Fortunately, tests by a trio of oncologists at Cedars-Sinai Medical Center came out clean, and Ed was given a clean bill of health—as well as a stern warning about what was necessary to stay cancer free. Despite the good news, I didn't react well. Ed's continued smoking and drinking frustrated me, and I was unable to stay calm and grateful. It was like I loved him so much that I wanted to kill him before he put us both through hell by killing himself.

We got in a big fight, and I fled to our beach house, where I unloaded on my brother Drew and his wife. Just yada yada yada. Finally Drew put up his hand, like a traffic cop ordering a driver to stop. We were quiet for a moment while the air settled.

"Why don't you just divorce him?" Drew said. "I mean, enough."

I shook my head as always.

"No, Val," he said. "Listen. Why live like this? It's not fair to either of you. Have you ever thought about it?"

I looked at my brother as if hearing him for the first time.

"Yeah, I've thought about it," I said. Then, after a long pause, I added, "But I'm not going to do it."

That was true. Even with all the ups and downs, the frustrations, lies, battles, and arguments, I wasn't going to leave Ed. Never mind that he was my love story, and I'd promised to love him for better or worse. We had a son. In my mind, it was that simple. I wanted my son to have a two-parent family no matter the cost to me. But I was beginning to realize that there might be a cost to Wolfie too, from being surrounded by constant friction and unhappiness. And I noticed that I was asking myself more frequently, Well, what if I *did* leave him?

In the past, I'd done my share of thinking and threatening to leave, but even during our few separations, I always knew we'd get back together. However, Drew's comment put a crack in the wall that I had built to keep me in the marriage. Next I went from asking, Well, what if I did leave him, to telling myself, Maybe that's what I need to do. Unfortunately, there was no easy, clear, or right answer. And so, as one of the world's great procrastinators, I didn't do anything.

I let life happen. And it did.

Twenty-two

WHERE HAVE ALL THE GOOD TIMES GONE!

In spring 2001 my managers Jack and Marc received a call from the casting director for *Touched by an Angel,* asking if I was available to guest on an episode or two of the heart-warming CBS series starring Roma Downey, Della Reese, and John Dye. Jack and Marc had received similar calls from the same casting director for the past couple years, but they'd always turned him down for one reason or another.

"I know the answer is no," the casting director said. "But I'm making my annual call."

Marc, who had taken the call, paused.

"Are you sitting down?" he asked.

"What?" the surprised executive asked. "You *aren't* saying no?"

"I'm not," Marc said, laughing slightly. "I think it's a strong possibility."

My managers had seen an opportunity for me and seized it. I don't know that I would have made the same decision without them, but it was a good one. The TV movie business that had been my bread and butter for years had dried up. Almost overnight the jobs that had allowed me to work when I wanted disappeared, and the leading female roles that were available in TV movies were now being offered to movie stars. The reality of Hollywood is that careers change; they don't wait for you.

The show's Salt Lake City location also appealed to me on a personal level. We had a small home there. If I were to split from Ed, I had to be able to earn a living. I wasn't going to ask him to pay for my decision. Like any woman considering leaving her marriage, I worried whether I'd be able to survive on my own.

What if I could support Wolfie and myself? If I could give him a different life? Not a better life, but a different life, one not so full of chaos and discord?

Well, that would cross one more question off my list.

Touched by an Angel's creator, Martha Williamson, proposed working me into the last two episodes of the 2000–2001 season, the show's seventh, and then, if it worked out, bringing me on full-time the next season. Since taking baby steps into the series also allowed me to ease into the idea of commuting between home and Salt Lake City, Jack and Marc were able to work out a deal easily.

Without telling Ed everything on my mind, I talked with him about the pros and cons of taking the job. Considering my lack of compassion lately, I laughed to myself as I explained that I was about to become an angel. It was a promotion, I'll say that much, though I don't know if it was deserved.

Ed, bless him, encouraged me to take the job if I wanted it and said he would handle weekly responsibility for Wolfie. Our beloved housekeeper, Lettie, would help too. In reality, we knew the first two episodes in April weren't a problem. But if the network picked me up, I'd be in Utah for eight months starting in August.

"I'm going to come back and forth," I said apologetically. "If I fly in and out of Burbank, it's basically an hour and twenty minutes away. Wolfie can stay there with me on weekends."

"Sure, OK, go for it," he said.

The two shows in the spring breezed by before I was able to miss home. I called Wolfie daily and saw my brother David who lived in Park City, near the small house Ed and I had bought a few years earlier. Even with the work, I felt like it was almost a vacation.

Going back a few months later to begin my first full season was much harder. Ed and Wolfie eased my initial homesickness until school started, but after they left for L.A., I was hit by a rash of emotions ranging from guilt to loneliness to confusion and anxiety about my life. I called in to my book club one night and talked about how much I missed all of them. I didn't even mention the book, which I'd dutifully read.

The consolation was being in Park City. It was a thirty-minute commute from there to the *Touched* set, and worth every second of the drive to live amid the beauty of the small mountain village.

Roma welcomed me to the set with open arms. Someone had warned me that I might detect some tension from her because I was told the network had used my signing as a hardball tactic when she'd renegotiated her contract, but I didn't feel anything but loveliness from her. Aside from being so beautiful, Roma had a warm, generous spirit that made me like her instantly.

There was only one reason to dislike her: she had a perfect little figure. She was gorgeous. I was sure she'd never had a weight issue in her life.

Della was tougher. On my first morning, she looked me over

without cracking a smile. My efforts to warm her up throughout the day didn't work. I figured it was a turf issue. So at some point that first week, I coinfronted her. I made it clear that I felt some tension between us, and I didn't understand or want it.

"I'm not here for Roma's job," I told her. "I'm here to make her life easier. I don't know what you heard, but I don't want her job. It's her show."

Della raised an eyebrow.

"And your show."

She cracked a joke that softened the mood. I hoped she believed me. Just like when I'd started *One Day,* I wanted to be liked—that was all.

Knowing I was going to be on location for eight months, I started off having a harder time being away from home than the previous spring. Trying to have one foot in each place, I flew home for the long Labor Day weekend and stayed for Wolfie's first day of school. After returning to Utah, I called home five times a day, if not more frequently. I should have invested in AT&T.

My workdays were long. On an average day, my alarm went off at six-fifteen. A driver came for me at seven and took me to the set. I returned home around eight.

My weight was high, about 153 pounds. That was obviously heavier than I would have preferred, but I'd given up on the idea of being thin. The notion of weighing 125 had been replaced by frustration. I put in just enough time on my treadmill that I wasn't gaining any more weight. Nancy, the show's costume designer, did her best do dress me so that I didn't look frumpy on screen.

I was on automatic pilot and would have stayed that way for a while were it not for the tragic events of September 11. After spending the weekend in L.A., I returned to Utah Monday morning and worked all day. On Tuesday I woke up early, turned the TV on to *Good Morning America,* then went into the bathroom and took a shower. As I walked back into the bedroom, I heard Diane Sawyer saying that, in a terrible accident, a plane had crashed into one of the World Trade Center towers.

I sat down on the bed. At that point it seemed, as Diane had said, like a terrible accident. Then a second plane, United Airlines flight 175, crashed into the other tower. All of a sudden, both towers were on fire. In that instant, life changed. My jaw went slack; I covered my open mouth with my hand. I don't remember getting dressed. I don't remember moving. Like everyone else, I was stunned, shocked, and overcome by confusion. What was going on?

My driver, Pat, knocked on the door. I thought, Oh, shit, I still have to go to work. I left the television on and TiVo'd the news so I could watch when I got back, gathered my stuff, and went out to the car. Pat already had the radio on the news station. We heard President Bush announce that the U.S. was under a terrorist attack. We were halfway through the mountain pass when American Airlines flight 77 crashed into the Pentagon. Pat looked at me sitting shotgun and I blurted out, "What the hell? Are we being attacked by our own airlines?"

Once we got to the set, I dumped my stuff in my dressing room and went to the makeup trailer, where people had gathered around the TV, staring in stone-cold silence and shock as the World Trade Center North Tower collapsed. We listened as airport closures were announced, then the evacuation of federal offices. We heard about a plane crash in Pennsylvania.

We were scheduled to shoot at a local hospital. But I assumed that we weren't going to work. I didn't think that I could. I didn't know how people could keep their focus on work. I wanted to go back to

Park City and figure out how to get home to Wolfie. I'd gotten through to Ed, who was staying home with Wolfie. Even so, I didn't want Wolfie to go through this without me there.

One of the many people in the makeup trailer watching TV reminded me that airports across the U.S. had been shut down indefinitely.

"Then I'll drive," I said. "It takes twelve hours. I don't care."

To my surprise, we had to work. That was followed quickly by an announcement that we were working the next day too. No matter what, we were told, shooting would continue as scheduled. I looked around at people shaking their heads in total bewilderment. I went outside to find one of the executive producers and ask if this was true, and if so, why. Others felt the same way I did: upset, confused, angry, and scared. We wanted to be with our families.

But I was told that we were sticking to the schedule. We had a budget, and so on.

Later I was told that the decision had gone through Roma, who'd said she wanted to work. That made sense to me. She'd grown up amid strife and violence in Ireland and, unlike the rest of us, had lived through war. She dealt with it by clinging to routine, normalcy. Her response made me take a step back and say, "OK, if Roma can do it, I guess we all have to do it too." On the other hand, she would get to hug her daughter when she got home.

Unfortunately, my scenes that day, set inside a hospital, required me to be funny, and I didn't feel like I had an ounce of funny in me. I was too upset, and my thoughts were on the poor people whom I'd seen lose their lives and their families. And, of course, I was concerned that more attacks might happen elsewhere. To get through it, I kept telling myself that this was what we did, what we were doing, and to just put one foot in front of the other.

Between setups, I watched TV in one of the hospital waiting rooms. Everyone else was glued to the news too. Throughout the day, I called home or to my parents or brothers. I wanted to hear their voices. The conversations were all the same: "Are you all right? Isn't this terrible?"

Finally, thirteen and a half hours after picking me up, Pat deposited me back on my doorstep in Park City. The day seemed like it had lasted forever. As I walked to the front door, I felt my legs weaken as the emotions I'd held back all day overtook me like water rushing over a dam. Once inside, I dropped the stuff I'd carried home from the set, sank to the ground, and cried uncontrollably for a half hour.

After watching terror, confusion, and trauma all day on TV, I was affected more than I realized. As a mother and a wife, I empathized deeply with the parents and spouses I'd seen dazed and crying. I'd had a similar ache in my heart after the 1995 Oklahoma City bombing, when I saw the video footage of the ravaged day care center in the Federal Building and thought of those poor parents and children.

Later, as I watched more news and listened to the pundits talk about how the U.S. might respond, I started to cry again. I just wanted to be with Wolfie.

When I was unable to go home, I called Ed through the night to see if he would drive Wolfie up. He couldn't—something about school, and trying to get the kid back on a normal routine. So then we followed the same advice as everyone else and continued with our lives. I did manage to get home that weekend. All I wanted to do was hold my son.

Two weeks later, Ed brought Wolfie to see me in Utah. I was thrilled to see my son, but immediately sensed that Ed wasn't himself. He was trying too hard to appear normal and made an effort to go to bed at the same time I did, which was always his way of showing me that he wasn't doing drugs.

The next day, as Ed and I caught up on things, I noticed that his mouth was doing something funny; that little thing it did when he was doing coke. I'd seen it enough times to know, and it pissed me off. How could he have brought coke with him on the plane when security was at red alert level? How could he have brought it while traveling with Wolfie?

As angry as I was, I didn't say anything to him.

Later that afternoon, though, while Wolfie was playing video games, and Ed was taking a nap, I went up to the loftlike top floor of our cabin, where he'd put his bags. Then I did something that I hadn't done in a long time: I looked through his things.

At that point, I knew we'd reached a new low. Whatever trust I still had in Ed was gone.

Sure enough, I found the coke. It was folded up in a small packet of paper and stuck in his wallet. At first I felt a profound sense of disappointment and sadness. Then the anger hit. I was beyond the fact that he was doing coke and its effect on his health. That was his business now. But fuck him for doing this, for being so unbelievably stupid to fly with drugs on him, and with Wolfie.

After I found the coke, I didn't know what to do next. I just sat there for a few minutes. I didn't want a confrontation—not yet, anyway. We'd gone that route numerous times in the past, and where had they gotten us? Something told me that this was more my problem than Ed's.

I slid the tiny envelope of coke back into his wallet and decided that, even though I was furious with him, I wasn't going to say anything to him.

He wasn't the only guilty party.

Twenty-three

BLACK AND BLUE

For almost two years, I'd been carrying on a friendship with Mark, a businessman who lived in Atlanta but regularly traveled through the West. I'd originally met him through my brother David. After seeing each other at several parties and always having good conversations, we traded emails in which we talked about football, his business, and decorating his apartment in Atlanta. It was mostly him. It was casual and developed into a comfortable online friendship. I enjoyed having someone to talk to. You know what, bottom line, it was nice to have a man pay attention to me.

Yet gradually some of the emails began to carry the hint of flirtation. Those sort of things were buried in talk about music and food, things we liked. It seemed innocent enough. Maybe that doesn't ring true, but I convinced myself it was innocent. I knew the guy was hot. In the back of my mind, I said, "I'd like to—but not gonna."

It seemed safe. We were separated by thousands of miles. It gave me the kind of attention I wasn't getting at home. Was it right or fair to Ed? No, absolutely not. I was letting my emotions stray in a way that would have pissed me off had I discovered Ed doing the same thing.

But I ignored right and wrong in favor of what felt good to me. In March 2001, I hosted an Oscar-watching party at home for friends. In an effort to make Ed jealous, I invited Mark to the party. I was hoping that if Ed saw what my friend Mark looked like—he'd heard about Mark—he'd pay more attention to me.

Mark flew in from Atlanta. He was going to be in L.A. anyway. He had no idea that I was using him. At the party, I introduced him to my one single girlfriend, but otherwise he sat on the sofa and watched the awards, and every so often I came over and chatted with him, always having a good time, laughing and making sure Ed saw.

I'd always prided myself on being a straight shooter when it came to dealing with problems and offering advice to friends. Yet there I was, scheming to make my husband pay attention to me by putting him in the same room with a guy with whom I was carrying on a friendship online. How screwed up was that? I cringe just thinking of the way I behaved then.

At one point during the party, Ed pulled me aside and drilled me with questions. Who was Mark? How did I know him? Why was I talking to him so much? What were we talking about?

He accepted my explanations without questioning me further, but a few weeks later, over spring break, we took the best vacation of our twenty-year marriage. Ed rented a Winnebago, and we took Wolfie to visit my parents in Las Vegas. We visited the Hoover Dam, the Grand Canyon, the crater in Arizona, and then we visited my brother Patrick and his wife in Scottsdale. I didn't think about Mark once.

There wasn't time—or a reason to—because we focused on

spending time with each other as a family. It was real, and memorable, family time, the kind of life that I'd always wanted. It was even fun when Ed fell asleep on the sofa in the back and I had to get behind the wheel of the motor home, but we had loads of fun getting to the KOA campgrounds, hooking up, stopping for burgers, and singing at the top of our lungs to AC/DC's "Big Balls."

Unfortunately that trip was a distant memory by the time I discovered the coke in Ed's wallet. As soon as he returned to L.A., my mind landed in what I thought was a dark place, though in hindsight it may really have been more determined than dark. All I knew was that I wanted out of the marriage. I'd come through the cycle, from avoiding the thought to thinking about it to actually vowing to do it.

Enough was enough, I told myself.

But looking back, finding the coke was only part of the reason I finally decided to leave Ed, and it wasn't the number one reason. The real catalyst was September 11. I know that may sound melodramatic to some people, but it had a profoundly personal effect on me in that as I listened to one news report after another of how the tragedy had brought people closer together, I thought, Yeah, everyone except for me.

Over the next days and weeks, that feeling compounded. Through its complexity also came clarity, as it raised the obvious question: why did I feel distant from Ed? Furthermore, why did that distance seem to increase the more I thought about it? In fact, I began to wonder when the last time had been that I felt close to him.

That raised another, even more important question. Did I want to spend the rest of my life like this—miserable? And making Ed miserable too?

No, not at all. Both of us deserved better. And more importantly, so did Wolfie.

I truly believed that. I still do. Ed and I had compromised for far too long. We all deserved better.

But even knowing all that, as resolved and clear as I was, I still couldn't get to a place where I could have a civil and rational discussion. No, my approach was more convoluted and wrapped up in a lifetime of approaching problems through guilt and insecurity rather than in the direct manner that I imagined as my style. I don't know exactly how to explain it, other than to say that I needed to feel as if splitting up was as much my fault as his, and I also wanted to let him know how much he'd hurt me. In fact, once I found the coke, it was like fuck you, now I get to hurt you.

Enter Mark, who had emailed, saying he was going to be in Utah and wondered if I was going to be there at the same time. I emailed back, yes, I was.

I let him know that I wanted to see him and hang out together. What I didn't tell him was that in my mind I was letting myself cross that line I'd always drawn when thinking about my attraction to him. From the moment I got pregnant, I told myself that I was going to set an example for my child. I wasn't going to be that person who had once cheated on Ed because I was angry. I didn't want to live with that kind of punishing guilt. I remembered all too well how I felt after I miscarried and thought an all-knowing God had pointed his finger at me. Whatever happened in my marriage, I didn't want to go through any of that again.

Yet what was I doing? It's so clear now. For whatever reason, I needed to punish myself before I could leave Ed, and that's what happened.

Mark arrived in Park City and stayed with my brother. Nothing was ever said or spoken, but whether David and his wife and Mark and I were having a glass of wine in that first afternoon he arrived or going out to dinner later that evening, you could feel the attraction between us. At dinner, we joked about my brother's futon bed being uncomfortable. I knew from having slept on it the year before, and Mark agreed. Before leaving, I invited him to stay the next night in my guest room.

And that was his intention when he came over the following day. But we ended up watching TV on the sofa in the living room, and one thing led to another, and that's when I said, "Shit, I should've shaved my legs." It had been a long time since I'd had sex, and I tried to enjoy it. But the whole time I felt like I was in another world.

Looking back, the best part was holding hands, in a cautious, uncertain, new way, as we walked to breakfast. That's the kind of intimacy I liked. Not intimacy. Connection. I appreciated feeling close and *connected* to someone. By the end of breakfast, though, I'd gone through a gamut of emotions, from passion and excitement to oh my God, what have I done, and when is this going to be over?

I knew that I wasn't going to see Mark again—and after saying good-bye as he set out to catch his flight, I didn't.

The next weekend I went home prepared to confront Ed, who still didn't know that I'd found the coke or reached the end of my rope. I'd discussed the situation with Al and our business manager and longtime friend Barbara. I'd need their support if I had any chance of salvaging things with Ed by getting him to fess up and go in for treatment.

The two of them met me at the house on Saturday afternoon, after I got back from taking Wolfie to play with his friend Zach. We walked upstairs to find Ed, who was asleep in bed. Looking in from the doorway, I shook my head in amazement that he was able to sleep with all the coke he was doing.

"It must be the Valium," Al said.

Al and Barbara followed me into the bedroom, lagging behind as I woke up Ed. He opened his eyes slowly. Once he saw Al and Barbara behind me, he knew something was up. His eyes narrowed. He was already on the defensive. I didn't want to waste any time, so I got straight to the point.

"When you came up to Park City, I found your coke," I said.

"What do you mean?" he asked. "What coke?"

"The coke in your wallet."

"I didn't have coke."

I got up from the bed and looked down at him. It was a standoff.

"Ed, I'm not debating the issue. I found it. And if you don't get help and stop doing the coke, I'm going to divorce you."

"Fuck you, divorce me."

Those words went into me like knives. But I think I *wanted* to hear them. I also think he wanted to say them. In reality, we'd arrived at that point much earlier. It had just taken this long to finally force the issue.

"So I'm hearing this right, then," I said. "You're ready to stop."

"Fuck you."

"You're going to choose this over trying to build this family back together."

"Fuck you."

By this time Al and Barbara had slipped out to give us privacy, and I didn't take Ed's cursing as anything more than the angry responses of an addict who'd just had the rug pulled out from under his feet. He could say fuck you all he wanted. We were definitely splitting up this time. I called Zach's mother and checked on Wolfie, who, of course, didn't know what had happened at home. Then I holed up by myself in the house and stewed about what had just gone down with Ed.

I watched TV and read the paper. Again, I kept encountering

stories about the way 9/11 was bringing people closer. Individuals who'd carried grudges against one another for years were finding ways to forgive each other. Family members who hadn't spoken for decades were picking up the phone to apologize and catch up. Old lovers were reconnecting. The more I heard, the more I wondered, God, what's wrong with me that I want exactly the opposite?

Nothing was wrong. That's what I kept telling myself. After twenty years, I was done making excuses for Ed and his reliance on the drugs and alcohol. I was done compromising my own life. I'd spent two decades telling myself that one day he'd get better. If it wasn't that, I was saying, "Poor guy, he's got such a big heart, but look at how much pain he's in." I had an endless supply of excuses. But after that confrontation, the well had run dry.

"You know what?" I told my friend Suzanne one day. "I'm done making excuses and being sympathetic. I've wasted too much time. He's got to grow up. I'm tired of all the pain. Deal with the goddamn pain already."

Going back to work with so much unresolved was hard. I pulled Wolfie out of school for a week and took him with me. I needed him nearby. I cleared it with the school principal and brought his homework. Ed protested but I think deep down he knew he wasn't in any condition to take care of Wolf. Whatever our problems, we were able to put Wolfie's best interests first. To insure that his life didn't change, we agreed to keep news of the split from Wolfie until I found my own house, a process that took almost eight months.

If anything, I saw Wolfie more frequently. I commuted between Salt Lake City and Burbank every weekend, but sometimes I flew home two, three, and even four times during the week just to tuck Wolfie in bed. At night I slept in the bedroom, and Ed stayed in the back room, the studio, or on the downstairs sofa. Not much different than the last ten years, really.

I worried about Ed filling Wolfie's head with crap when I wasn't there. I never said an unkind word about Ed in front of Wolfie, but I suspected there was no controlling the commentary that flowed the other way. Angry, in pain, and still using drugs, Ed badmouthed me nonstop. In person and on the phone. It was years before I quit getting a queasy feeling in my stomach whenever I heard my phone ring.

As far as he was concerned, everything was my fault. Though I argued that his habit of blaming others for his problems was in fact his problem, he made points that got under my skin, and I ran with them. Hadn't I partied alongside him in the early days of our marriage? Had my willingness to repeatedly excuse his drinking and drug use enabled him to keep doing it? Was my complacency over the past ten years as we raised a child part of the reason we never dealt with his problems? Maybe I should have left him earlier. Maybe I should have left him before getting pregnant. One of Ed's arguments was, Why now? Why did I wait until Wolfie was ten? Wasn't it me and not he who was breaking up the family?

I had good, valid answers to each of his points. But still.

For the next couple months, I struggled to get through each day. I wish I could say I went through a difficult period of adjustment, but there was little adjustment. It was mostly just a difficult period. It was hard not being with Wolfie, who was the light of my life. And it was also hard fighting with Ed, who I knew I'd love again one day but hated as we went through the emotional reality of separating.

Too much was going on. I was either working, sleeping, talking on the phone, or running through an airport. I had no appetite through

Christmas, something that had never happened to me before, and although my weight dropped into the mid-140s, I didn't care. In January I started eating again. It coincided with the end of football season. I invited friends over and set out high-calorie spreads that included wings, celery, ranch dressing, chips, and nuts. After everyone went home, I kept working on the leftovers.

Thinking back on that stress-filled, fearful time, I don't remember ever being hungry. Yet I can't remember ever not wanting to eat. I put on 10 to 12 pounds almost immediately. Nancy, the costume designer, bless her heart, bought me size 12s without saying a word. I draped myself in layers, thinking I could cover myself up in shirts, vests, long dresses, coats, and whatever else I could hang on my body. Talk about trying to hide in plain sight.

My managers, who knew the personal stuff I was going through, still had a hard time watching me dress in such an unflattering style. Jack swore that the layers only drew more attention to me. He all but told me straight out that the heavier I got, the harder it would be for me to get work. I didn't care.

Martha Williamson didn't care either. Since I didn't have love scenes, my weight wasn't an issue for the show. Jack asked her to say something to me, but she said no, explaining that I was fine the way I was.

But I wasn't fine. As opposed to previous times when I'd eaten myself to a certain weight and then stopped, this time I couldn't stop eating. Nor did I want to stop. My goal was to get through the season and go back to L.A. in one piece, even if it was a large piece.

One day we were on location, and I was crying: a wreck from fielding call after call from Ed and listening to his verbal assault. It was right before a scene—thankfully, a long shot, so my bloodshot eyes and tear-soaked face wouldn't be visible. Suddenly Della took me aside and said, "Look, whatever happened, you need to forgive him and go back and be his wife. It doesn't matter the cost. You go back and make that marriage work for your little boy."

Just as Ed's calls knocked me one way, her lecture spun me in the opposite direction. It was the kind of thinking that I'd embraced for twenty years. I wanted to say, "You have no idea what you're talking about. I needed to leave that marriage so I could make my little boy's life better." But I bit my tongue. She didn't get it. And I wasn't about to explain it.

Roma, who'd gone through her own divorce, proved more sympathetic and sensible. One day she grabbed me by the shoulders, looked me straight in the eye, and said, "I know it's difficult right now. But I promise you it will get better. It may take two years. There's no telling. But it will get better."

All I heard was "two years."

"Oh God, I can't take two years of this," I said.

With sincerity and love she repeated, "It will get better." I regret now that I was going through so much that I didn't get to know Roma better, because I liked her. She is a good, kind soul. Every so often she sent me a note saying that she was just down the hill, in Salt Lake City, if I wanted to hang out or have a cup of tea.

I never took her up on the offer. If I had free time, I flew back to L.A. But I knew from the few times we talked about her growing up in Ireland and her own tough times that she was a survivor. She knew whereof she spoke. And so I often found myself thinking back to her promise. *It will get better.*

My question was when?

Twenty-four

GOING SOLO

In spring 2002 *Touched* went on hiatus in time for me to catch Wolfie's school talent show. He played drums on Kenny Loggins's song "I'm Alright" while Ed played guitar, and Robby Benson's wife, Karla De-Vito, handled vocals. I was so emotional that I forgot to turn on the video camera.

"You *what?*" Ed asked afterward. "You forgot to tape it?"

I threw up my hands, befuddled.

"I feel bad," I said. "But I was crying."

There was a lot to cry about. I'm not a person who likes change. I didn't feel like I was on my own for the first time in twenty years as much as I felt alone. On weekends, I curled up with a cup of coffee and my two favorite parts of the newspaper: the crossword puzzle and the real estate section. The crossword was my therapy, and the real estate section was a necessity. In April, after seven months of house hunting, I found a five-bedroom ranch-style home. The floor plan was odd, additions had been done without permits, and the house needed work. But it had charm and a spectacular view, which I'd always wanted. After a difficult negotiation, I ended up with the house. Since Wolfie would be living there, Ed checked it out and gave his approval before I signed the papers. As angry as we were at each other, we rose above it for the sake of our child.

The hardest part of ending our marriage was telling Wolfie. We held off as long as possible. Finally, three weeks before I closed escrow, Ed and I decided it was time to break the news to him. We went into his room together. Wolfie was playing a video game. We asked him to take a break and laid out the situation.

"Mommy and Daddy love you very much, but we're having problems," I said.

"We're fighting a lot," Ed added.

"Yeah, I know," said Wolfie.

"We're going to separate for a while," I continued. "You can hang with dad as much as you want, but you're going to live with me in a new house."

We tried to keep things short and to the point, as advised by the experts in the books I'd read. We got the main points across.

"Hopefully after the separation Mommy and Daddy will learn to be better toward each other," I said.

Wolfie was devastated. About an hour after hearing about the separation, he took his yellow belt from karate and tied himself to the balcony outside his bedroom and said he wasn't going to leave. But after moving, he found comfort in playing video games on the big-screen TV in the new house's den, which was the first thing I had the movers unload.

Dressed in sweatpants and a T-shirt, I unpacked boxes until well after midnight. By then Wolfie and his friend Zach had gone to sleep.

When I collapsed onto the bed in my room, I was so exhausted that I didn't mind the lumps in the mattress, which I'd taken from the guest house.

Ed's adjustment was easier. I was out of the house for maybe a couple weeks before he moved a girlfriend in with him. That hurt. But who was I to say anything? I'd left him.

Ed's and my effort to keep our split quiet was blown at the end of June 2002 when *People* magazine broke the news. It was painful to see our personal business in the press. I felt invaded. My mom was quoted. At least Ed said that we were friends, and he loved me. For the rest of the summer, my public profile got no higher than trips to Bed, Bath & Beyond and the grocery store. I hung out with Wolfie and made sure he was OK. Friends gave me encouragement about starting over. But I wasn't ready for that yet.

At the end of August, I had to return to Utah for my second full season of *Touched*. With everything that was going on, I had no interest in doing the show again. Actually, I had no interest in leaving Wolfie, who declined my offer to go to school in Park City. He didn't want to leave his friends, and I didn't blame him. That meant I had to content myself with thrice-daily phone calls and flying back and forth as often as my schedule allowed. Unfortunately, that lifestyle made me really unhappy, and I started to pack on the pounds.

At forty-two, my days of weighing 105 to 110 were long gone. In a perfect world, I saw myself tipping the scale at 125, the same size I was when I had tried to seduce Ed and he told me that I looked good but my ass still needed work. I fantasized about that weight the way some women pictured themselves with Brad Pitt. Never mind great sex. I wanted to be a size 6. I wanted to win the lottery too.

When I went back to *Touched*, I wore a size 12, and, much to my distress, it was snug. I arrived weighing in the low 150s, having spent the past few years battling to stay in the 140s. Finding myself alone and unhappy, I immediately began to eat. I stocked up on fruits and veggies, but the frozen food section was where my willpower—and waistline—met its Waterloo.

What did me in? Jalapeño-and-cheddar-cheese poppers. I piled boxes of them into my cart. It looked like I was stocking up for the entire football season, but they'd last only a couple days. I'd tried the poppers as an alternative to the frozen chicken wings I'd bought the previous football season. I was hooked right away. They were bad, bad, bad—and so delicious.

After a long day on the set, I got home, poured myself a nice glass of vodka and cranberry juice, and put a dozen poppers in the toaster oven. That was dinner. Almost every night. For variety, I branched out to the jalapeño-and-cream-cheese poppers and created combinations. I heated up six jalapeño-and-cheddar and six jalapeño-and-cream-cheese poppers, but I mixed them up, so that I'd get a surprise when I bit into them. I ate, drank, and watched TV till I fell asleep.

Those poppers provided comfort and escape—and about 20 extra pounds. I knew as I shoveled them into my mouth that they weren't good for me. I can still hear myself saying, "These six aren't going to change your life." But if you do six, then eight, and a dozen every day for six months, it *will* change your life. It did mine.

By March 2003 I was up to 170 pounds. My dress size was up to a 14—and it was tight. I prohibited my wardrober Nancy and her assistant Kacie from bringing me anything larger. I vowed I wasn't going up to a 16. No offense to size 16s, but I knew that my life would be over if I got that big. My knees already ached from the weight I carried. I also knew that, if I did get up to 16, I'd never get down to a size 6. It was hard enough to buy a 14. If I hit 16, it was a commitment to being fat forever.

Although I hated being away from home, I would have liked for *Touched* to have run for one more season. I had my deal worked out for the same money but fewer weeks. My head was into getting a regular paycheck and taking care of Wolfie, because I wasn't going to ask Ed for alimony or child support. But when the network didn't pick up the show at the end of its ninth season, I started counting the days till I could go back to L.A. Finally, in March 2003, following the wrap party, I hurried home and started to plan my life as a single mom taking care of Wolfie.

It was pilot season, and I wanted to go out for shows that were based in L.A. Only Jack and Marc Schwartz knew how difficult it was for me to put myself up for scrutiny at that stage of my career. I had not gone through the skin-toughening exercises of going out on three auditions a day and getting rejected since I was a child. With a string of movies that routinely ranked high in the ratings, I'd walk into a casting office, and have other actresses say, "I can't believe you have to read."

It was also difficult to go on auditions given all that was going on in my life. In 2001 I lost out on parts to Courtney Thorne-Smith and Teri Hatcher, both of whom were beautiful and thin. But as I prepared for pilot season again, my managers let me know that casting directors were asking about my weight. As gently as possible, they said it had become a problem in getting me jobs.

Each time they mentioned it, I shut them down. Still, I put myself on the Atkins diet, which let me eat like a linebacker in training camp as long as I stuck to protein. I had bacon and egg whites for breakfast, mozzarella and tomatoes at lunch, and steak with mustard greens and blue cheese for dinner. In two weeks I dropped from 171 to 165 pounds.

I don't know that it helped me get work, though In April I went up for *Crazy Love,* a sitcom about a couple who adopt a baby from China. The script was funny, and Peter MacNicol had been cast in the male lead. Marc arranged for me to submit a film test instead of reading in a room full of network executives.

Then I obsessed. You can see from the note I wrote in my daily organizer that I channeled everything to food:

> Won't hear till Monday. With all the stress, I'm pretty
> impressed about my eating. I'm still doing well. Taking my
> weight down.

But things got worse over the weekend.

> Ordered pizza for the kids. I had cheese and pepperoni
> off a couple of slices. Threw away the bread and the
> crust. But later I had two servings of the Carbolite
> gummies. Felt bloated and sick. Supposed to be at zero
> net carbs. Snack of salami and cheese at 10:15 pm.

On Monday, however, I heard that I got the job. I was elated. I hung up from my talk with Jack and Marc and thought, Oh boy, I'm so lucky I got this part, because I look like a whale. When we shot the pilot, I was down to 160. Knowing that I still didn't look my best, I put pressure on myself to work hard. Peter MacNicol was brilliant and kept me in stitches. The baby we worked with cried every time Peter held her, but she quieted down and smiled whenever she was passed over to me.

Both Peter and I adored Cloris Leachman, who played my mother-in-law. She was like a wild nineteen-year-old party girl trapped in an older woman's body. I heard stories about how she liked to whip off her clothes. I never saw her lady parts, but I didn't doubt that she had a bit of Lady Godiva in her.

All of us were disappointed when *Crazy Love* didn't get picked up. We had a good premise, high hopes, and excellent chemistry. For me, there was a bright side. I'd been able to use that time to start putting my new life together. The work gave me focus and a chance to develop a routine, which I maintained afterward.

Jack remarked that I was a different person since moving away from Ed. Suddenly he could get hold of me, whereas before I rarely answered the phone or returned calls. Sometimes Ed and I had more than sixty messages on the phone machine. At that point, there were so many that we'd erase them. Being more accessible was just one of the baby steps I took toward independence. I also put up a new mailbox that I bought myself at Home Depot. I installed a fountain in the front yard. I took Wolfie to see *X2: X-Men United* and met friends for dinner. At one point, I walked over ten thousand steps four days in a row—a new record for me.

Try to keep that up. You go, girl!

In May Wolfie and I went to see the band Coldplay at the Hollywood Bowl. The funny part was, my dad scored me the hard-to-get tickets. He had made friends with the bass player's father when they had both worked on the Chunnel project in Europe in the early 1990s. My girlfriend Kathy was going with her husband and one of his friends, so we all met at my house before taking a shuttle to the Bowl.

When Ed dropped by to say hi to Wolfie, he cast a jealous eye at the guy who came with Kathy and her husband.

"Who is he?" Ed asked.

"A friend of theirs," I said.

"Are you dating him?"

"I don't even know him," I said.

The idea of dating scared the crap out of me. If one of my girl-friends even hinted at the idea of fixing me up, I cut them off with a sharp "I'm not dating." The full sentence didn't even get out of their mouths. It was pathetic how not ready I was for a social life that included men. One day a sweet guy approached me at the deli section in my local grocery store. As he wheeled his cart up to me, I thought, Oh no, this is like a scene right out of a movie. He looked like a nice fel-low. He was about my age. Very handsome. And brave.

"Are you?" he asked.

"Yes," I said so quickly that I probably interrupted him.

"I'm curious." He looked away for a second, nervous. "I guess it was in *People* magazine awhile ago. I saw that, you know."

"Yeah, it's true."

"So you're single again?"

"Uh-huh." I nodded.

"So what do you do?" he asked. "You know. Because I'm single. I just became single."

"What do you mean, what do I do?"

"For dating?"

"Oh," I said, smiling and shaking my head. "I don't date. I don't do anything like that. I'm a full-time mom. That's it. That's all I do. I don't date."

He nodded.

"Oh, OK," he said. "I thought maybe—"

"No, I don't," I stammered, embarrassed and flattered. "But nice to have met you."

That story got told for weeks. My girlfriends laughed at my amazement that a good-looking guy would be interested in me. I wrote him off as a freak—a good-looking freak. Ordinarily when I was at the grocery store, I only heard whispers about my weight. "Look how big she's gotten." Or: "Is that really her? Oh my, she's gained a ton of weight." Or: "She's still cute. Just bigger."

It was hard to go out in public knowing that people said things like that behind my back. Did they think I couldn't hear? I would think, *Hello,* I have ears—and they work! I kept my head down. My weight stayed in the 150s on a strict diet of sausages and coffee in the morning and sashimi for lunch. Then I'd ruin it with a handful of Jordan almonds every time I passed through the kitchen.

My new life required adjustment. For example, according to my son, I needed to learn how to vary the dinner menu. For almost two months, I made lamb chops nearly every night. I created different marinades and changed up the veggies but it got to the point where I brought a plateful to the table one night, and Wolfie said, "Mom, this is the last night. Don't *ever* make lamb chops again. OK?"

One night Ed came over for dinner and brought Wolfie's drum set. Even though I served lamb chops (instead of asparagus, I made broccolini on the side), Wolfie beamed happily as we watched him play. We weren't a normal family, but neither were we the Osbournes. A year and a half after Eddie had snarled, "Fuck you, divorce me," we were sitting down at the same table again and finding our own way to be a family.

Ed, who now had another new girlfriend, seemed to be getting over his anger toward me. A lot of the tension between us was allevi-ated now that I made a conscious effort not to bug him about his drinking and drug use. Even though I still worried about the effects on Wolfie, I didn't want the responsibility of policing Ed. I'd done that for twenty years, and it hadn't worked for either of us. In this next phase of our lives, Ed and I had to take care of ourselves.

Wolfie commented on the difference. At the time, I was reading Laura Hillenbrand's moving book *Seabiscuit: An American Legend*. I car-ried it with me on errands and put my nose in it every free minute. Wolfie stared at me while I read, monitoring my eyes for tears. He did the same thing when we saw the movie, looking at me every couple minutes and asking, "Mom, are you crying yet?"

I wanted to wring his neck. Finally I had enough.

"I love you, but I'm about to knock your head off," I said. "What is it about me crying that you get off on?"

In the dark theater, he took hold of my hand and laughed.

"At least you aren't crying about dad anymore."

Twenty-five

IT'S ABOUT TIME

On a quiet night at the end of June, I was playing Monopoly with Wolfie, whose smile stretched across his face as he kicked my ass. I hated hearing him say, "Ma, that's my hotel. You owe me." I frowned, but not because he was beating me. I was also on the phone with Ed, discussing Wolfie. The two of us were about to leave for Halifax, Nova Scotia, while I shot the CBS movie *Finding John Christmas* with Peter Falk, and Ed didn't want his son to be gone that long.

"What's he going to do if he stays in California?" I said. "You're working most of the time, anyway. With me, he'll have time to hike and go boating and stuff like that. It's healthier. It'll be like camp."

Ed understood and gave in. It was the kind of conversation that we worked hard to have so that Wolfie wouldn't feel like he bore the brunt of the problems that ended our marriage. Ed and I talked daily, and most of the time worked things out. The Halifax trip was an example of how we could arrive at the right decision. Surrounded by water, full of trees and greenery, Halifax was among the most beautiful places I'd been.

Wolfie and I had a house on a tree-lined street two blocks from the water. When I didn't have to work, we went inner tubing or took long walks. We had seafood dinners on the dock, where we looked out at the boats. The Titanic museum was nearby. It was like a vacation and a relief for me to see Wolfie having fun.

By fall, I was home and back to driving carpools, taking Wolfie to playdates, talking to his friends' mothers, and driving him to baseball practice or chess class. We went surfing on weekends. I cried the first time Wolfie did his first 180. Motherhood was the role I liked best. Occasionally friends invited me to dinner or movies, but I didn't feel social and turned down most of their offers.

Even though home was where I was happiest, my friend Lynn persuaded me to go with her to the Kabbalah Centre, which counted Madonna, Demi Moore, and Ashton Kutcher among its followers. She'd visited the center one evening on her mother's recommendation and listened to a lecture. "It was actually enlightening," she said. "I was surprised."

"Did you see anyone famous?" I asked.

"I didn't even look," she said.

Nor did I upon entering the Beverly Hills temple and situating myself on the floor. Lynn informed me that the lecturer was the same rabbi who'd impressed her and her mother. Pretty soon I understood why. Bearing a vague resemblance to Jake Gyllenhaal, Eitan Yardeni spoke about God and our relationship to the universe with a calm, relatable clarity that made sense to me—so much that I kept going back. His talks and services, though cloaked in Jewish rituals, involved simple, universal truths that echoed the monks I'd heard back at the

Self-Realization Fellowship Center. Actually, the messages went back to the roots of my understanding of the Bible and spirituality:

- Do unto others as you'd want done to you.
- You reap what you sow.
- Sow some damn good seeds.

I liked the red string I wore as part of kabbalah. It reminded me to be kinder. My problem with kabbalah was the language. I didn't understand the rabbis when they spoke Hebrew during services, which made it difficult for me to feel as inspired as I wanted to be. But the friendly scene eased me into a more social frame of mind. I had no thoughts of using the centre as a place to meet men, yet it was while enjoying myself there at a dinner with friends in October that I started talking to a great looking guy.

He caught my eye, and I started to look for him whenever I went there. I enjoyed talking to him about current events, restaurants, music, and kabbalah. A relationship wasn't on my radar, but I surprised myself by thinking about this man who had rugged good looks and I wondered what it would be like to kiss him.

After a couple months of casual chats at the centre, I dropped hints that he should ask me out. He didn't respond. Though I was far from eager to have another man in my life, I was curious why he didn't call, and assumed it had something to do with me. Since meeting him, my weight had increased by 12 pounds to 162 pounds.

He just wasn't that into me, but I wanted to fledge my newly single wings, so I asked him out for dinner and a movie. He was late picking me up—and had a lame excuse that he'd had to get his hair cut.

"If I hadn't asked you out, would you have eventually asked me?" I asked during the evening.

He took a moment to think, and then said, "No. Honestly, I wouldn't have asked you."

OK, fine. That should have been a wake-up right there, but rather than realize that he *really* wasn't into me, I changed the subject and suggested we go out again. Even though neither of us felt an immediate or deep connection, his company and conversation gave me something to look forward to. I felt it was good for me to get back in the dating game. During the first month we dated, I lost 14 pounds just from the butterflies. I swear to God, I lost half that weight the first time we got romantic and I took off my clothes. Three and a half pounds from nerves, and three and a half pounds from sprinting around the room to turn off the lights and pull the shades.

"Does it have to be so dark in here?" he asked.

"Yes," I said. "Even though kabbalah is about letting in the light, no one said anything about the light having to be on in the bedroom."

Dating him was an important step forward for me, but it didn't work out the way I'd hoped. In April he showed up one night as planned. I'd arranged for a sleepover for Wolfie, figuring something fun was going to happen. We watched some TV, I brought out a bottle of wine, and we necked. But just as I thought the passion was building, he got up to go home. He had to get up early the next day, he said.

I walked him outside. He sensed my disappointment. By his car, he apologized for not going further and explained it wasn't that he didn't want to do it, he couldn't. He'd hurt his groin, he said.

"What?" I said, surprised.

He undid his pants and showed me his bandages. I looked down, then at him, and then back down again.

My face revealed a certain confusion.

"I'm sorry," he said.

I couldn't believe that someone might go to the trouble of wrapping his Johnson to get out of sleeping with me.

"Actually, I had an accident with a glass," he said.

"I don't know what to say, but—"

"I just want you to know that it's not like I don't want to sleep with you. I cut myself!"

Weird—that's all I can say. I still don't know what was going on with that. I remember my girlfriend Alyson at the time telling me, without saying the exact words, that he wasn't into me. I probably should've said something along the lines of "Dude, it's okay if you don't want to sleep with me. You don't have to put a bandage around your thing." After that night, everything seemed like challenge. I realized that we had to work too hard to see each other and no longer enjoyed our conversations. Finally, we had a testy argument one night when he accused me of being a typically high-maintenance actress, a type he said he'd dated way too often.

I didn't need that and had certainly never been tagged with that before. I was offended, and lit into him, letting him know that I was the lowest maintenance actress he'd ever meet.

That was the end of my rugged friend—and a turning point in my life with men.

Now I look back at those few months as a gift. He might not have understood me, but I was starting to understand myself. I was a good person and an even better mother, and at forty-three years old, I didn't need him to like me in order for me to like myself. That was an important revelation. I was learning. Had I not met him, I might not have been ready when the real deal came along.

. . .

That summer of 2004, there was no time for me to date, anyway. Ed and Sammy patched things up barely enough to put out a compilation album, *The Best of Both Worlds*, and launch a tour. Ed wanted Wolfie to go on the road and join him onstage at the end of the show to play the last half of his solo on "316." Wolfie knew all the Van Halen songs. The two of them jammed on guitars for hours. I loved seeing Ed's smile when Wolfie caught him playing a part differently and would say, "No, Dad, it goes like this."

Ed had dreamed about one day playing music with his child; hell, he used to play guitar to my stomach when I was pregnant. At nine, Wolfie had picked up the drums, and a few years later Ed taught him how to play the guitar. Wolfie definitely had the Van Halen gene for music. While I had reservations about sending him on tour with grown men who weren't exactly getting along buddy-buddy before the tour had even started, I knew how important it was to Ed, and I gave my consent—on one condition.

"I'll be there too," I said.

Not only was Ed fine with that, he generously offered to foot the bill. Starting in May, I drove Wolfie to rehearsals after school so he could practice his part with Ed. On June 1, they put on a show for friends and family. I got chills watching Wolfie come out and play with his dad. As thrilling as that was, it didn't compare to being on the side of the stage three weeks later at the Worcester Center outside Boston and watching my little thirteen-year-old boy rip through his solo while the crowd cheered.

"How was it?" I asked afterward.

"It was fun," he said.

"Were you nervous?"

"Naw. I was just getting up there with Dad."

"Did you hear the applause?"

"Ma, enough!"

Their end-of-show jam was one of the few times during the show that Ed looked genuinely happy. At odds with Sammy, he drank himself into terrible shape. I was glad I was there to shield Wolfie from the worst of it. The two of us had a terrific time visiting sites like Fenway Park in Boston. When the tour stopped in Chicago, a bunch of us went to Wrigley Field. In spite of those fun excursions, I felt like a third wheel on that tour. I sensed the looks from people asking, What's *she* doing here?

After nearly three weeks, I wondered the same thing. I was gaining weight. It was hard to have a routine on the road other than mealtimes. I'd promised myself that I'd go to the hotel gyms every day, but I didn't go even once. One day I tiptoed onto a scale: 153 pounds. I'd started out a size 10, but I didn't stay that way after a couple weeks of hotel room service, minibar snacks, and the backstage catering. When I got home, the 10s went back on the shelf, and I took out my size 12s.

Two months later, Wolfie rejoined the tour for two weeks, chaperoned by Ed's longtime personal assistant/manager Matt and the band's chief of security and others I had met and felt comfortable with. I heard that Ed was getting in worse and worse shape. God bless people like Matt, who were out there, keeping him alive. Despite my concerns, I kept in mind that Wolfie had two parents. Assured that key people, from Matt to security, would make sure my son was safe, I knew that Wolfie would be OK. As it turned out, he had a wonderful time.

He also had a handful of eye-opening experiences with his father. I don't know all the details concerning the drinking, drugs, and anger. When I asked, Wolfie cut me off with "Mom, I handled it." Later, as I pushed for more details, he would say only that he was able to say,

"Dad, I don't like it when you do this." For the first time, he got an accurate picture of what Ed was really like. After all, I'd protected him his whole life. But this was no-holds-barred. Wolfie saw everything.

In a way, I suppose that I *wanted* him to see everything, warts and all. Why not? He'd seen me in the middle of my problems.

Ed loved having Wolfie on the road. I think it kept him calmer. He probably would have blown up sooner had Wolfie not gone out. In August, I met them in Salt Lake City, where I also helped celebrate my brother Patrick's fortieth birthday. I hadn't seen Wolfie in two weeks. Backstage, where we hugged, he looked like he'd grown two inches and added about ten years of maturity.

After the show, I took Wolfie to Park City for some end-of-summer fun in the mountains. He needed time to readjust to life back on earth following the tour. We spent time hiking mountain trails, riding the Park City Mountain zip line, and playing miniature golf. I liked seeing him outdoors with his feet on the ground, laughing and hanging out with family.

Back in L.A., he started school. I took a step back from my life and saw the personal toll from all the running, worrying, and eating I'd done since the start of summer. On November 1, I weighed 165, up from 154 pounds when I went on tour. I got mad at myself.

Anger is not the best motivation for doing anything, especially going on a diet. Neither is disgust, which I also felt toward myself. How many times in my life had I used those feelings to launch a new diet? How many of those had succeeded? Nevertheless, I vowed to write down everything I put in my mouth and lose 10 pounds by the end of the year. "Today," I wrote on my calendar, "is the first day of the rest of my life."

What I hadn't yet grasped was that the rest of my life had already started. And my weight was not the reason.

Twenty-six

FEEL YOUR WAY TONIGHT

Toward the end of October 2004, my brother Patrick and his wife, Stacy, invited me to a wine-tasting fundraiser in Scottsdale, Arizona, for Phoenix Public Radio. The table they'd purchased seated ten, and they'd put together a group of friends to fill it. I'd made them promise not to fix me up with anyone, something Stacy had hinted at the previous week when on the phone she said, "I have this doctor friend." I'd replied emphatically, "Do not or else I won't come out."

And apparently she kept her word. Even after I began getting dressed at their house, she said, "It's just going to be a group." Before doing my makeup, I went into the kitchen to get a glass of wine that I'd put in the freezer to get super cold, which is the way I prefer it. I ran smack into a good-looking guy in a tuxedo. He was sitting next to the fridge, fiddling with his cell phone.

He looked at me as I came into the room. I stuck out my hand.

"Hi, I'm Valerie," I said. "And your name is?"

"Tom," he said.

I said something else, while also noticing his big brown eyes and thinking, hmm, he's a looker. But to be honest, it was hot out and I wanted my glass of cold wine. Opening the freezer, I continued to talk and ask questions, and then while sipping my wine, I also found out that Tom was a friend of Pat's, lived nearby, and worked in finance.

Then Pat came into the kitchen and noticed the two of us had already met. He said that Tom and Gina, another friend, were going to carpool over to the dinner together. Figuring that Stacy was trying to play matchmaker with Tom and Gina, I made a joke about needing to finish getting ready and excused myself. A short time later, everyone convened in the kitchen. Pat and Stacy elected Tom as the designated driver. We got into his Honda Accord. I slid into the passenger seat on the driver's side, and watched as Tom turned on the air conditioning.

Good move, I said, as he smiled and backed out of the driveway.

The second we hit the sunlight, I made a crack about it still being well over 100 frickin' degrees at the end of October and reached for the AC button on the console.

"It's already on full blast," Tom said.

I kept looking at the controls. To me, the AC didn't seem to be on high. I pushed the button to make sure.

"Hey, don't touch my buttons," Tom said, half-jokingly. "Look, that button there, the one that says Passenger, that's your button. The rest are mine."

I laughed. He was cute, trying to take charge. I could see he had a good sense of humor.

"Okay, mister."

On the drive there, I learned that Tom was a last-minute stand-in for another of Pat's friends, who'd cancelled, and not Gina's date.

The event was in a hotel ballroom. Once there, we found our

table, a large, round top that was typical for large banquets. Tom sat on one side and I ended up on the opposite side. Pat and Stacy hoped I might click with a doctor they'd also invited despite my warning to Stacy, who explained it wasn't a set-up but she was secretly hoping that we'd click. As it turned out, their doctor friend showed up with a date and introduced her around the table as his fiancée.

It was better that way. I wanted to know more about Tom. So I peppered my brother with questions, asking basically what's the deal with this guy? He told me that they rode dirt bikes together. I raised my eyebrows. That wasn't the kind of information I wanted.

"I don't want to hear about your man-love," I said. "I want to know the important stuff. Like who's he dating?"

Pat joked that Tom had turned to the priesthood. After I made a face that said, "come on, tell me the truth," he explained that Tom had gone through a difficult divorce a few years back and wasn't involved with anybody at the moment. I turned and looked at Tom again. He was making Gina laugh.

During dinner, I went to the bathroom and on the way back in I noticed the World Series was on the TV at the bar. I checked to see how the Red Sox were faring. It was early in the game, and I was hooked. Throughout the dinner, I kept getting up to check on the score. Each time I came back, Tom got up and went outside. I didn't mind watching him walk across the room, but I was curious where he was going. At the table, we weren't close enough to each other for me to ask him, but the next time I came back into the room, he was standing up and saying something to Gina before leaving again. I waited a minute, and then instead of going to my seat, I intercepted him.

"Hey, where are you going?" I asked.

"I want to check the score in the Red Sox game," he said. "Where have you been going all those times?"

"Out to the bar to watch the game," I said.

"Want to go with me?" he asked.

"Sure," I said, turning around.

That didn't qualify as a first date, but we got chummy over base-ball at the bar in our formals. After the wine auction, we drove back to Pat and Stacy's and watched TV. The atmosphere was casual, all of us in wind-down mode. Tom and I ended up on the sofa together. At one point, I put my hand on his leg. It was while we talked, and I let it linger there for a friendly moment. A few minutes later, I thought, God, if I just turned around and kissed this guy, what would he do?

Months later, when I told Tom what had been on my mind, he said that wouldn't have been a good idea. It would've been too for-ward for him. The next day we went to the second half of the wine extravaganza with Tom. During the wine tasting, we took pictures. You can see that the body language between Tom and me communi-cated a mutual attraction, which we hadn't yet articulated; I was lean-ing back on him, my head against his shoulder, and he looked happy.

Afterward, the four of us went back to Pat's house and cooked din-ner. It was like a party, with good music, lots of food on the counter, and everyone pitching in—except for Wolfie, who was playing Xbox in the midst of it all. I made miniature bruschetta pizzas, using French bread, buffalo mozzarella, basil, and prosciutto. Tom lent a hand, show-ing off some culinary skills of his own. We worked well together.

Three weeks later Wolfie and I returned to Arizona. I looked at homes around Phoenix for my parents, who lived in Las Vegas but wanted to move closer to family. Then Pat and Stacy and Tom and Gina and I drove to Tucson to watch Wolfie play with Ed in the final show of Van Halen's tour. We hired a driver, who took us in a comfortable van. Tom and I spent the three-hour drive reconnecting, and that was nice.

But the good mood was wiped out by drama at the show. Ed was in terrible shape, and those closest to him on the tour let me know that they were scared for his life. I saw what they meant as soon as I spotted him backstage. Months on the road, the shit storm he created around himself, and the crap he took had ravaged his skinny frame. I saw the damage in his eyes, which were as wild as his long, messy hair.

By this point, Ed also hated Sammy. There always had to be a bad guy in his life, someone responsible for all of his problems, and as far as he was concerned, that was Sammy now. I could feel the tension between them all the way out at the soundboard, where I watched the show with Tom, who put a protective arm around me whenever some unruly guys began getting too close to me.

During one of Ed's solos, the crowd chanted *"Ed-dee! Ed-dee! Ed-dee!"* I leaned over and shouted in Tom's ear, "If they only knew the truth."

That was apparent soon enough. During Sammy's guitar solo on "Eagles Fly," one of his own songs, Ed started in on Pat, who was watching the show from my old perch on Ed's side of the stage. The two of them had always gotten along. But Ed was in a state. He yelled at Pat and then tried to choke my much larger brother. Taken by surprise, Pat defended himself by grabbing Ed's hand and saying, "Don't do this. You don't want to do this."

With his free hand, Ed tried to take a swing at Pat. Pat blocked his punch, took hold of both of Ed's arms, and yelled, "You don't want to do this!" Fortunately, one of the burly backstage security guards agreed. He grabbed Ed and dragged him away. I saw the whole thing unfold from where I was watching with Tom by the soundboard. I couldn't believe it, and then again I knew what Ed was like when he was drinking heavily. I also knew from what we'd been told that he was beyond that point and in some other place. Still.

"What the fuck is going on?" I said to Tom.

He had no idea. I felt bad that he was seeing this . . . this drama that had been and was still part of my life.

"I have to get up there," I said, heading into the crowd.

By the time I got to the side of stage, Pat was walking away and Ed was going back on stage.

"What the hell happened?" Pat said upon seeing me.

"I don't know," I said. "You tell me."

"I can't believe that asshole," Pat muttered. "He's out of his mind. Something's wrong with him."

"Welcome to my life—again," I said.

I stayed on the side of the stage and kept a watchful eye on Wolfie through his solo and then followed him backstage after the show. Ed had destroyed his guitar and screamed at the audience through the microphone. It was a mess. I wanted to get Wolfie out of there as soon as possible. He also wanted to get out of there. Through years of dealing with his dad, he'd learned that you don't try to help or reason with Ed when he's like that. You try to get away.

As Ed ripped up his dressing room, various people expressed their concern to me about him. Ed wasn't my problem anymore. My thoughts were on Wolfie. In the van on the way back to Scottsdale, I tried to talk to Wolfie about what had happened with Ed, but he shut me down with a curt, "No mom, not now." Soon he fell asleep for the remainder of the long drive, and the rest of us talked and dozed until we got back to Pat and Stacy's.

The next day was centered on fun and family as we walked Pat and Stacy's dogs while I focused on decompressing Wolfie. I marveled at his resiliency, but at the same time I worried about how much he could absorb without speaking about it. I made it clear, in terms he could understand, that I didn't want him to inherit the Bertinelli pattern of holding in his feelings and dealing with things on his own. He got it.

"When I'm ready, mom, you're the first one I'm going to talk to," he said.

"Promise?"

"No," he said, smiling.

I laughed. Thank God for a sense of humor.

At dinner, we celebrated Wolfie's performance in front of so many people and the end of the tour. Tom and Gina came over and helped prepare the meal. We grilled salmon, and everyone complimented Tom on the marinade. I made a corny joke about the value of a man who knew how to spice things up. For dessert, Gina and her sister, the original ace of cakes, made a spectacular cake that looked exactly like one of Ed's Frankenstein guitars, which was sweet—and sweeter still was the way Tom made a point of joining Pat the next morning when he took us to the airport.

There was an awkward moment at the curb as we said our good-byes and I got to Tom, who didn't know whether to give me a kiss, hug, or shake my hand as if we'd concluded a successful business meeting. I leaned in and gave him a peck on the lips that seemed natural to me and I hoped the start of something more.

He looked shocked. But it gave him something to think about—and me too.

Not that we had made any plans to get together again. Tom's four children (two boys and two girls) in Scottsdale from his first marriage kept him busy, and he spent Thanksgiving with family in Ohio. But over the long holiday weekend, we swapped text messages during the day ("V, I miss you, T") and talked on the phone at night. Our feelings for each other came out, and we made plans to get together in early December.

"May I drive out to L.A. to see you?" he asked. "I can stay with friends."

"You can stay with me," I said, but then, remembering Tom was old-fashioned in that way, I quickly added, "I have a guest room."

"That's nice," he said.

I found myself wondering if he was a good kisser. If he wasn't, I was going to be so bummed. I was eager to find out.

"Why drive?" I asked. "Why not fly?"

Stacy and Gina called to tease me about his visit. Once in L.A., Tom made it clear that the things they teased me about weren't going to happen that first night. He wanted to show me that he had values. As he put it, he wanted to be cool. That was fine with me as long as I got to find out whether he was a good kisser.

I found that out on the sofa after Wolfie went to sleep. He was an excellent kisser. But he was also a man of his word. At the point when I was getting into it, he got up and excused himself from the room. I wondered if I was adding another chapter to my version of *He's Just Not That into You.* Was I too heavy for him? (I was in the 160s.) Was it something else? Did he think I was an ex-rock-and-roll wife into crazy, wild sex? (A little of that wouldn't have hurt.) Then Tom returned with a present. I opened the tiny gift-wrapped box and found a beautiful antique pin.

"I looked in the magazines at what all the gals were wearing," he said.

"I love it."

"I hope you don't feel . . . you know . . . rejected about this . . ."

"Me? No, no, not at all."

"I don't want to rush," he explained. "I really like you. I want things to be right and comfortable. I'm trying to be sensible."

"I appreciate that," I said, and then added in a joking tone, "but I still feel rejected."

The next day we dropped Wolfie off at a friend's bar mitzvah in Santa Monica and stopped on the way home at the Self-Realization Fellowship Centre, where we sat by the lake and talked for several hours. It was the first time the two of us had been alone, and we made an amazing connection on every level, from family and food, to Gandhi and Jesus. As we got back in the car, I asked myself what was going on. Something big was happening; that's for sure. Was I ready to handle it? I didn't give myself an option. If I wasn't ready to handle it, I'd better get my ass in gear. Because I knew this guy might be the one.

At home, the day continued along those same lines. In addition to our intellectual and spiritual compatibility, we discovered that we were also in sync physically. Everything was nice, gentle, and unhurried. Thankfully, he was amused and patient when I shut the blinds and turned off the lights in order to make the room as dark as possible before I took off my clothes.

"I'm not good with nude scenes," I joked.

"Well, that's going to change," he laughed.

"Good," I said. "As long as the lights are off."

As my situation improved, Ed's got worse. On December 1 Al called me and said they were doing an intervention on him. Ed actually came over for dinner that night, and I saw for myself that he was in bad shape, even worse than he'd been in Tucson. Dealing with him in that condition was tense, but I knew that seeing Wolfie soothed him. He also seemed to feel safe around the both of us.

Ed and I had been getting along better. Even after Al was unable to pull off his intervention after repeated attempts, Ed and I continued on a friendly and supportive path. He felt comfortable coming over and sharing whatever was on his mind. I'd learned to not argue every little point with Ed. He still pissed me off, just as he'd done when we were living together, but I let more things roll off my back. After so many years of fighting, I asked myself, What do I want more, to be right or to be peaceful? I chose peace. I credit Dr. Phil, who I heard say something like you either contribute to a relationship or contaminate it. It's your choice.

On another night when Ed came for dinner, I remarked on the irony of our relationship; two and a half years after separating, we were starting to communicate, something we had failed to do before we got married.

> Had a good talk with Ed. It felt nice to no longer fight.
> Instead of arguing, I told him it's OK, I understand.
> Sometimes that's all he wants to hear.

I was able to connect that idea to what I'd learned at the Self-Realization Fellowship: when you give someone love, there's no room for hate. I loved Ed—and always would. I just couldn't live with him anymore. We spoke almost every day. Sometimes he came over twice a day either to pick up Wolfie or drop off something or just because he needed a break. Then we might not hear from him for a week or two. He approved of Tom. I think he saw the same thing I did, a quality guy who added sanity and stability to our dysfunctional little threesome.

Tom came for the weekend after Christmas. Before he arrived, I studied myself in the mirror and shook my head. I weighed 160 pounds. I wished that I were thinner, but he didn't seem to mind. Nor did he mind my continued insistence that I wanted the bedroom dark. After two days, though, I quit insisting the room be pitch black; a variant of dark gray was fine.

I behaved like a neurotic kook. Tom didn't see the insecurity and misery I was trying to hide by turning out the lights. He was falling in love with the person I was, not the person I wished I were. Did I even know who that person was? After all, I'd been thin before without being happy or liking myself any better. Fitting into a pair of jeans was nice, but it wasn't the be all and end all. I knew who I didn't want to be: I didn't want to be angry. I didn't want to be fat. I didn't want to be unloved. Or unlovable. But who did I want to be? Who was I?

I had to figure that out.

Twenty-seven

I'm Fat

Life was always interesting, but it got a lot more interesting when, at forty-five years old, I realized I was falling in love. Tom and I talked endlessly. That was new to me, and I enjoyed having a friend. I could literally feel myself dismantling the barriers I'd always protected myself with. It was almost involuntary; I wanted him to know me. Something else was brewing. Wolfie liked Tom pretty much from the get-go once he realized we were dating. The three of us sang and talked on the seven-hour drive we made to Scottsdale for New Year's. Wolfie also got on well with Tom's oldest son, Tony, who was just six months older and equally obsessed with the video game Halo.

I flew back and forth to Arizona through early 2005 to visit Tom and to find a home for my parents, who moved there from Las Vegas in the spring. That summer Tom's children, all four of them, who ranged in age from six to fifteen, stayed with us in L.A. for three weeks. From the moment we picked everyone up at the airport, it was like a sitcom.

Unprepared to deal with five children, I had to improvise when they gathered in the kitchen after putting away their suitcases and fired questions at me as if at a press conference: What's there to do? When are we having lunch? What are we doing after lunch? Is there anything to do at night? Can we go to a movie? Can we rent one?

I looked to Tom for help.

"What *is* for lunch?" he asked.

Not him, too, I thought. Realizing I was on my own, I thought fast and then blurted out the first thing that came to mind.

"Everyone in the pool! We'll have lunch later."

Looking back, I must have been eating all the time. By the end of summer, I weighed 170 pounds, almost 20 more than in January. What can I say? I was a social and an emotional eater. I ate when I was miserable, *and* I ate when I was happy. A lot of our life that summer happened around food. Either Tom or I or all or some of the kids were grilling, going out to eat, or snacking. At one point I was starting the morning with a breakfast of scotch eggs: hard-boiled eggs, wrapped in sausage, and then sizzled in the oven. It was really good, and really fattening.

I wasn't working, so I didn't care. My days were filled with the chores that occupy most stay-at-home moms, but my date book contained a recurring note meant just for me: *"Not great with my diet today."* Those entries were balanced out by others: *"A dozen roses arrived today, 'Love Tom.' "*

In August Ed's mom passed away. They had a small, touching ceremony for her on a boat near where they'd said good-bye to Mr. Van Halen. The occasion was extremely sad. I had a lot of fond memories of her. I was also worried about Ed losing his other parent. But my sadness went beyond the immediate situation. I'd never seen a dead body until I went to Mrs. Van Halen's house to pay my respects. Her boys had her lying in bed. I kissed her on the cheek. After my lips touched her skin, I was struck by how cold her body was.

For the next few days, I found myself thinking back to that and how final death was, reminding us how important it was to live each day to the fullest. Yes, that was one of those clichés that I'd scoffed at in the past, but like most clichés, it was true. Time is our most precious asset, the dumbest thing to waste, and I realized I'd wasted more than my share.

After sharing those thoughts with Tom, I was delighted to find that our attraction extended into deeper, more spiritual areas. Long talks about faith, the meaning of life and God made us even closer. I felt blessed to have someone in my life that was available and interested in such conversations. It felt like a natural progression when he moved in permanently in January, and then brought Tony, then sixteen, who wanted a closer relationship with his dad.

A short time later Tom and I decided to go on Weight Watchers together. We counted points and lost a few pounds. Then we stopped counting and let the points add up—and the pounds too. We weren't good dieters. Too much of our life together involved standing in the kitchen and making pasta dishes, meat loaf, tuna melts, and other favorites. Or we went out for Mexican food, burgers, or pizza. Then I finished off the day with my Jordan almonds.

As much as Tom and I loved each other, we also loved to eat. Sooner or later, we needed to confront that issue.

Only once during this period was my weight an issue for anyone other than me. At the end of 2005, I was in discussions to do an infomercial for Victoria Principal, a lovely, nice, smart woman, and her skin care line. I admired the successful business she'd built, but each time we met, I felt uncomfortable. Something wasn't right. I attributed it to the fact that I kept negotiating with her even though I wasn't in love with the product, and I knew that when push came to shove, I couldn't pretend to love something when I didn't.

Victoria had similar reservations, it seemed. Even though she didn't come right out and say she wanted me to be thinner, she volunteered to help me lose weight by sending over her book and advising me what to eat. Suddenly I felt the same pressures to be thin and in shape that I did before making a movie, plus the insecurity of feeling that she wanted me to look some way other than the way I was. In other words, I wasn't good enough. It was the same old story.

We met as the February shoot date approached, and she asked point blank how much I weighed. Nervously, I told her, 168, and it almost took her breath away. It was the kind of politely horrified reaction that had turned me into a Hollywood hermit. Less than a week later, Jack and Marc received a call saying that they weren't going to move forward. I was shopping for a big-screen TV when they relayed the news. The explanation Victoria's people gave? My services were too expensive.

You know what? I allowed my well-honed defense mechanisms to let me believe it was just business. But what do I think really happened? I was fat, and there was no way I could slim down enough before the shoot. If this was the case, I wish she would have told me straight out. She should have just said it: "I think you're too fat."

The next time anyone brought up my weight was in January 2007. I was around 172 at the time, and, without consciously admitting it, I'd given up on the idea of ever returning to single-digit sizes again. I hadn't thought about my weight over the holidays when I sat around watching football while chowing down on heaping bowls of spicy New Orleans–style gumbo. I regretted the day my brother and sister-in-law taught me how to make it, including the can of cold beer she insisted the cook had to drink while preparing the dish (she maintains that the roux turns a certain color in the time it takes to consume the beer). Then Tom brought home various kinds of hot sauce to put on it. Like I needed encouragement to have seconds and thirds.

During the Super Bowl halftime, I huffed and puffed my way enthusiastically through a touch football game at a friend's house. Then a week or so later, Jack and Marc called with an offer.

"Listen, we got an interesting call," Jack said. "You usually aren't open to this, but for some reason we think this time you might be.

"The people from Jenny Craig called."

"Oh God."

"And . . ."

Jack paused, waiting to see if I was going to cut him off.

"I'm still here," I said. "Still listening."

"And they said"—

"They said I'm fat. Of course they said I'm fat. Why else would Jenny Craig be calling me?"

"We thought you were listening," Marc said, laughing.

"Sorry, I am. Go ahead."

Jenny Craig had called before, and their inquiry had mortified me. At that time, I wasn't ready to admit that I was fat, and I wasn't ready to acknowledge that other people might have noticed. I was still horrified as Jack and Marc related their conversation with Jenny Craig's Director of Branding and Advertising, Steven Bellach. I had to fight the urge to grab some Jordan almonds as they gently described what was a backhanded compliment.

"You're their ideal candidate for a new spokeswoman," Jack said.

"You mean they think I'm perfectly fat? Or fat in a perfect way?"

"At least you're joking about it."

"I'm trying to."

The truth was that I liked Kirstie Alley's commercials. Her success on Jenny Craig intrigued me. She'd lost over 70 pounds. And kept it off! We had kids at the same school, and I watched her transformation enviously. The natural thing would have been to go up to her, say how much I admired her courage, and ask about her diet. But I couldn't do that. I didn't want her, of all people, to see me fat. She later admitted having avoided me for the same reason. Who were we fooling?

Finally, Jack and Marc came to me with a deal for enough money to get my ass on TV and say I was fat. But it wasn't only the money that persuaded me to take on such a public challenge. From the moment they brought up Jenny Craig, the vision I had had banging around my brain months earlier of what I wanted to look like came back to me. I saw that picture in my head again: me, much thinner.

Much to my surprise, the undertaking excited me. I wasn't keen on outing myself to the world as a fatty. On the other hand, I knew that the only way I could obtain the results I wanted was to hold myself accountable to people other than Tom, Wolfie, and my family. I needed the threat of total public humiliation. Really. Left to myself, forget it. I'd fail every time. But I'm a helluva team player. I knew that once I signed on, I'd do everything I could to succeed.

On February 9 I met Jenny Craig CEO Patti Larchet, marketing VP Scott Parker, and Steve Bellach. Over breakfast at the Sportsman's Lodge, I listened to them explain the Jenny Craig program and the campaign. The Jenny plan consisted of three Jenny meals and two Jenny snacks a day, and fruit and veggies, totaling 1,200 calories; a daily walking regimen of at least ten thousand steps (for me, that equaled slightly more than four miles); and a weekly weigh-in.

How much weight was I going to lose? We agreed to 30 pounds by September. That seemed daunting. It would take me down to 142 pounds. Privately, though, I knew that I wanted to lose even more. My goal was to end up at 125, about the size I was when Wolfie was in kindergarten—and the weight on my driver's license. But I kept that between God and myself.

There was one question left: was the food any good? They broke out some Jenny snacks—a bag of cheese curls and a bag of bruschetta chips.

"If I like the taste, I'll do it," I said. "If I don't, well, I don't know."

"Try them," Patti said. "I'm typical of the average Jenny Craig customer. I've struggled with my weight. Trust me, they're good."

I had a few of each. Then a few more. And then I grinned.

"I can do this."

The process began when I met with Tania, the Jenny Craig consultant who'd worked with Kirstie. By having me fill out questionnaires, she analyzed my eating habits (they were rotten) and the type of eater I was (emotional and unconscious). She gave me a funny look but understood when I declined her offer to get on the scale, explaining that I wasn't ready for my weigh-in, even a preliminary one. That sort of honesty is what they were buying, I reckoned. The only part of the plan I balked at were required meetings with a consultant. That brought back my bad experience years earlier at Overeaters Anonymous. Tania didn't allow for a choice. She said I had to follow the program.

"OK," I sighed. "If I'm going to do it, I might as well go all the way. It hasn't worked for me so far in forty-six years. I may as well try it your way."

Although clinical in approach, Tania's heart was open, warm, and accepting toward me. At one point, as she told me how even during the maintenance phase someone was always available to talk to if necessary, I started to cry.

"I'm sorry," I said. "But I think for the first time this might actually happen for me."

"It will," she said. "It's the perfect program for you."

"I mean it might happen for longer than just taking the weight off. I might actually keep it off this time."

Before finalizing the deal, I went to the centre closest to me and picked up a week's worth of food. After I lost 3 pounds in the first two days, they told me to stop dieting. I was disappointed. The food was delicious, and I felt good for having dropped that weight so quickly. But they weren't going to shoot any "before" pictures or the first commercial for a few weeks. They didn't want me to get thin yet.

"Have you seen me?" I asked.

Then I met Kirstie, who invited me into her life with open arms. A larger-than-life personality, she had me to her house to work out and talk about Jenny Craig. Dressed in sweats and an oversize sweatshirt, I walked in and said, "I have to see your kitchen." Oprah's designer, Nate Berkus, had given her a complete kitchen makeover, and I was beyond jealous as I touched the green tile that went up to a domed roof and ran a finger over her appliances as if I were looking at jewelry at Tiffany & Co. Her kitchen was frickin' gorgeous.

We worked out in her gym, another eye-popping room that showed off Kirstie's talent as a former interior decorator. Cranking the music, she led me through a tough forty-five-minute workout, talking the whole time. She said that after trying the Jenny food, she signed right up.

Kirstie got me psyched up. Yes, much of what she had to say focused on food and her favorites, like the turkey chili, but she emphasized that if I was anything like her—and both of us had admitted to being raging foodoholics—I should expect and indeed think of this as more of a journey than a diet.

"Yeah, I get it," I said. "I've dieted before."

"No, you haven't. Not in a way that works," she said. "You're going to lose the weight, but it's not the weight that makes you happy. It's who you are and how you let yourself be as you get rid of the layers. What is all that fat?"

"It's the way I've dealt with hurt, pain, stress, and anxiety. I've eaten my way through it."

"Right. Me too. I'm not saying you won't ever be hurt or feel pain or get stressed out. But you'll deal with it differently. As a result, you're going to stop hiding. You're going to find the person you always imagined."

"Why now as opposed to previous times I've gone on diets?" I asked.

"Because you wouldn't be dieting in front of the whole effing world if you weren't ready to come out of your shell, so to speak."

"True," I said.

"You and I know there's no amount of money that can get you to admit that you're fat and risk failure the way I have and you're about to do if you aren't ready to make a change that's much bigger and deeper than a stupid check."

"Absolutely."

"That's why I call this is a journey, not a diet. It's about regaining your life."

When I mentioned proudly that I'd already lost 3 or 4 pounds, Kirstie told me to stop immediately. A look of concern crossed her face. I didn't understand, since we'd just worked up a sweat on her machines. Kirstie said exercise was fine, but she warned me not to diet until after I shot the first commercial.

"Live your life for the next couple of days," she said. "Enjoy yourself. Go out for dinner." Then she reached into her pantry and handed me a stack of boxes. "Oh, here's some of the turkey chili meals I told you about earlier. Take 'em home—and trust me. They're freakin' delicious."

Twenty-eight

LOSING IT

On March 7, I took Tom, Tony, and Wolfie to Morton's steakhouse for dinner. With my diet set to officially start the next day, I wanted to enjoy a both-sides-of-the-menu, guilt-free pig-out, as Kirstie had advised, and that's exactly what I did. I ordered steak *and* lobster and washed it down with not one but two martinis. My calorie count approached my zip code. I didn't care; in fact, that was my intention.

Following a round of toasts, I held up my martini—my first one— and said, "After tonight, you won't see another one of these in my hand until I've lost twenty-five pounds."

"You go, mom!" Wolfie said. "We know you can do it."

It was later, sometime between dessert (chocolate soufflé) and one last mouthful of Jordan almonds before bedtime, that I thought, Oh shit, 25 pounds is a long time. I calmed myself with several deep breaths and reassured myself that that's why I didn't publicly commit to more than 30 pounds. That much weight seemed too daunting to lose at the moment. First I had to get to 25.

But what if I failed?

I wasn't going to fail.

In fact, the next day, as I drove to the Jenny Craig Center in Studio City for my first official weigh-in, I was in a completely different mindset. I was excited, emboldened, pumped up like one of my beloved New Orleans Saints prior to kickoff. I told myself that I was done thinking negatively about myself. That kind of mentality had gotten me to this weight. I had a charmed life. What the hell did I have to be negative about?

I met my consultant, Kathy. She was a mom, like me, from the San Diego area. She watched me peel off my clothes and step on the scale.

"One hundred and. . . . fifty, sixty . . ."

"Seventy-two," Kathy said.

"One hundred and seventy-two pounds?" I said.

Not Kathy, but the other Jenny Craig execs were surprised that I weighed a little more than I had told them the week before. But hey, between the extra gumbo Tom and I had polished off earlier in the week and then my surf 'n turf orgy the night before, I'd added a few pounds. After I'd left, Jack and Marc got a call from the Jenny gang of execs.

"She's gained a few since we told her to stop the diet?" they said.

"You told her to eat," Jack said.

"So she ate," Marc chimed in.

"Yeah, I guess we did tell her," they said.

In the meantime, Kathy and I had a conversation about the numerous diets we'd tried over the years. Between the two of us, we'd literally gone on every diet short of starvation in a Soviet-era prison. Grapefruit, shakes, fruit, all-protein, even nothing but white rice and pineapple. Kathy had finally had success on Jenny and attributed that to the food, the program, and the fact that on Jenny you didn't diet alone. She would always be there for me. That put me in a great frame of mind.

"You've beat yourself up enough," she said. "Let's change that. Our job is to make you feel your best."

A few days later, I had my first photo shoot. I wore a pink button-down shirt and my favorite jeans. They were size 14s. But they were so tight on me that they bulged at the seams on my thighs. I should have worn a size 16, but I was determined to squeeze into those 14s even if they had to paint WD40 up and down my legs and cut those damn jeans off me after we finished.

Ironically, during the shoot, the art director and the photographer told me that they didn't think I looked fat enough. I was like, are you fucking kidding me? I look like Jabba the Hutt. I could've had USDA stamped on my ass. My stomach may as well have been tattooed "Nabisco." I tugged on my shirt.

"See I can't even button the bottom button," I said. "I'm embarrassed to be in front of the camera like this."

They shrugged, gave me a Polaroid to look at, and reiterated that they wished I was fatter.

"Are we looking at the same picture?" I asked. "Because that's the Goodyear blimp I'm seeing."

I have to admit, the diet wasn't a snap, not when I started out. In those early days, I had a hard time getting used to smaller portion sizes, telling myself, No you aren't hungry, not listening to the Jordan almonds in the drawer at night when they whispered, "Psst, Val, come here, I've got something to tell you," and then finally throwing the almonds into the garbage. I also threw out another food I absolutely loved and haven't mentioned because it's like talking about an old boyfriend I'd rather not remember: peanut butter-filled pretzels. Get this, they sold them in the frickin' health food aisle. (See, this is why I haven't mentioned them; I'm craving them right now.) Sometimes I double-fisted them: in one hand, I clutched a bunch of pretzels and in the other hand I held a big Hershey bar. Like the old Reese's commercial ("You got chocolate on my peanut butter; you got peanut butter on my chocolate"), both ended up in my mouth at the same time. So those went in the garbage, too.

I also found it a challenge to exercise every day. It was hard going from zero to 10,000 steps a day. But each night that I looked at my pedometer, achy though I was, I could feel a difference. No pain, no gain—and that was the idea, wasn't it?

On the other hand, I wasn't exactly starving. On the fourth night of my new diet, I ate a chocolate walnut-filled Jenny brownie and made the sort of noises that caused Tom to say, "I'll have what she's having." While he ate two, I held firm and fast to my diet and at the end of the first week, I got on the scale and saw I'd lost 5.8 pounds. That was almost six pounds. I was on my way.

But I stayed calm. As I told Tom and then Kathy and anyone else interested enough to ask, I'd lost 5, 10, and 15 pounds many times in the past and regained them. Plus, Kathy reminded me that the majority of that initial weight loss was water, and a more typical weekly weight loss was 1 to 2 pounds. OK, that made sense to me. I remained focused and determined, and I kept my emotions in check. I wasn't going to be impressed until I passed the 20-pound mark. This was work, and there was a lot still ahead of me. Life didn't happen in a month, and neither did a diet that lasted a lifetime. This was a marathon.

. . .

Indeed, two days after Wolfie turned sixteen, I got my pedometer. By ten o'clock that night, I had walked only eight thousand steps. I wouldn't go to bed before I reached ten thousand. Tom and Wolfie thought I was crazy. Wrong. I was obsessed. A few days later, at my second official weigh-in, I recorded a loss of 1.6 pounds, bringing my total to slightly more than 7 Kathy soothed my disappointment that it wasn't more. I had to stay realistic. A poster outside the ladies' room, which I used before my weigh-in, provided a perfect reminder. It said "Progress—Not Perfection."

I wasn't the only family member trying to clean up, or change, their act. Around this time, Ed put himself into rehab. Finally. Although he'd shown up the previous Christmas sober, he'd relapsed as Van Halen prepared for a summer tour with Dave returning as the singer. The bad-mouthing and politicking behind the scenes by Sammy and Michael Anthony, whom Ed had replaced with Wolfie, drove him back to drinking.

Al made it clear that he didn't want to tour unless Ed was sober. Then the capper was when Wolfie came home extremely upset one day after a photo shoot. He'd also run out of patience and said something like, "That's it. I'm telling Dad that I'm not doing the tour." He didn't want to tell me what happened or whether he'd spoken to his father about it. Soon after, though, Ed checked himself in for treatment.

"Isn't this great," he said during a phone call. "I'm getting sober, and you're getting thin. The two of us are finally getting our shit together."

Strange but true. My first big test came when Tom's kids spent spring break with us, and I filled the pantry with kid-friendly foods. For me that was like planting the kitchen with land mines and walking through blindfolded. The key, as Kathy advised me, was to stay aware and vigilant not just about what I ate but how I ate. I had to remember that I tended to be an unconscious eater, meaning that I ate without thinking about it—eating just because it felt good.

To counter that urge, I prepared a lot of "free foods"—low-calorie dishes and vegetables, like a veggie-stocked Tuscan soup—that kept me feeling full. I ate so much soup that I felt like I was overeating. But I made it through spring break. And when I stepped on the scale at my three-week weigh-in, I cheered the loss of another 2.6 pounds, putting my total loss just beyond 10.

Although that was progress, I was unimpressed. As I told Kathy, I'd lost 10 pounds umpteen times before. My problem was maintaining it. I'd lacked the self-awareness, tools, and support to keep me from putting the weight back on. But this time I felt different from my old life; my outlook and my life were better, brighter. It didn't feel like an accident, either.

"You know something now that makes you a different person," my consultant said.

"What's that?" I asked.

"You've learned that you have a choice in matters. You know that you don't have to settle. And you've chosen to do what's best for you."

On April 5, my diet went from secret to cause célèbre when I appeared on the cover of *People* magazine. Titled "Ready to Get Slim," the magazine let the whole world know I was on a diet. I didn't know whether to laugh, cringe, or hide in the bathroom when I saw myself quoted saying, "I know what you're thinking—I'm fat!" Friends called nonstop to congratulate me. I said, "For what? Being fat?"

Jokes aside, I felt the desired effect. My ass was on the line, and I wasn't going to let anyone down—myself included. Then Kirstie's and my first commercial aired, and the reaction was incredible. She'd come up with the idea of describing me as "sort of fat." It was based on an actual conversation. When a Jenny Craig exec told her that I was going to be the next Jenny Craig spokesperson, she asked, "Is Valerie even fat?" Without measuring his words, he replied, "Well, she's not, you know, fat like you were. She's *sort of* fat."

Kirstie kept me laughing the whole time we worked together. Besides being a riot, she's frighteningly smart and quick. In the past, that would have intimidated me. I would have automatically felt not good enough. This time I found it inspirational. That was a positive, important change in me—and I liked it.

Reaction to both *People* and the commercial was overwhelmingly positive. In truth, it was bizarre. All I'd done was tell people that I was fat and wanted to lose weight. I went on TV's *The View* and *Rachael Ray*—nothing new for me, except that I was talking about being fat. But that was, in a way, liberating. "No one's looking at my thighs (old news by now)," I noted. "People are actually listening to me. So much of this journey is about attitude." On the street and in the malls, people stopped me just to say "Good for you" or "You go, girl" or "You're an inspiration."

Then there were those who said, "You don't look like you need to lose weight." They made me chuckle. Where were they two months earlier when I was hiding in my dressing room at Macy's and overheard a woman say, "Was that Valerie Bertinelli? God, she really let herself go." I understood when people took offense that I referred to a size 14 as fat. They had a point. You could be a size 14 and not be fat. But that just wasn't true for *me*. At 172 pounds, my knees ached, my clothes were tight, and I was out of shape. Add 10 more pounds, and

I would have been the same weight as on the day when I was trying to push Wolfie out of me. I was fat.

By mid-April Tom, my girlfriends Lynn and Suzanne, and even my mom had also signed up with Jenny Craig and started losing. Tom and I turned it into a semicompetition, which I then ignored as soon as I saw that he got bigger results. I reminded him that we weren't on the TV show *The Biggest Loser.* Neither of us faced elimination. One night I got a little miffed when he told me that I was doing my diet wrong. It was a typical guy thing. I said, "Love ya, babe—but get the heck out of my diet."

But it was Tom who ushered me through the biggest hurdle I had to face when on April 13 I came home from the CNN studios in Hollywood after being interviewed by Larry King and found my six-year-old Abyssinian cat, Dexter, meowing in a weird way and crouched in his litter box. He was sick. Even though I was fully made up, wearing eyelashes and heels, we rushed him to the vet, where I paced and worried until the vet told me that Dex needed to have surgery.

At home, I was scared of losing Dex. I was also scared by how much I wanted to eat. That's how I'd always comforted myself in times of stress and strain. But I wouldn't allow myself to use food as a crutch. It was a difficult emotional tug-of-war. Tom helped me through it by making me deal with my emotions, not eat them. At his urging, I opened my new journal and wrote for nearly two hours, something I really hadn't done since my mom had read my diary back when I was seventeen years old.

I guess it's finally time to trust again. It only took 30 years. I'm not stubborn, am I?

On April 18 I brought Dexter back from the vet. At my weekly weigh-in, I posted a drop of almost 4 pounds, obviously a result of all the worrying I'd done about Dexter. I don't recommend such nerve-wracking experiences for losing weight, but they can certainly wreck your appetite. Next was a brief trip to Washington, DC, for the White House Correspondents' Dinner. I wore a black Prada dress and couldn't wait to meet Bush—Reggie Bush, the New Orleans Saints' star running back, who also attended.

Then came my birthday, April 23. In addition to getting a pedicure, I spent the day cleaning my closet. I had 10s, 12s, and 14s hanging in descending order. Seven weeks into my diet, I fit comfortably into my 12 jeans, so as a present to myself, I took out all the 14s and gave them to Goodwill. I had two birthday dinners: one with Tom, Wolfie, and Tony; and another with my girlfriends, who took me to my favorite Italian restaurant. the owner got in on the laughs by bringing out appetizers of Jenny cheese curls and bruschetta chips.

Suzanne gave me a present with a card that said "Do not open until the 25th . . . pound." I had a pretty good idea that the box contained everything needed to make the perfect martini, from olives to glasses. That killed me. At that point, I'd lost 18 pounds.

"It's going to take me another month or more!" I groaned.

"But it's going to be so worth it," she said.

Before reaching that milestone, I faced an unanticipated setback the first week of May when I stepped on the scale at my weekly weigh-in. Instead of losing, as I'd done every weigh-in for seven weeks, I saw the scale move in the opposite direction. I'd gained! Mind you, it was a minuscule 0.4 pounds, but it may as well have been 20. I lost it right there in the center. What had gone wrong? Although I'd pretty much stuck to my diet I'd walked less than the required number of steps on three days. Still . . .

Kathy talked me through my disappointment. She explained that everyone had setbacks at some point. There were a million possible reasons why. Did it matter? No. More importantly, she pointed out how I immediately tended to slip back into my old negative mind-set, the same one that always doomed me to regain the weight. She was right.

"Reframe your thinking," she said. "Don't go sliding into the past. Stay in the present. Look at the positives."

She pointed out that I'd lost more than 18 pounds. Even more, I'd lost four and a half inches the first month and another eight inches the second, even though I'd lost less weight during that second month. Everything was still working. It was the kind of reality check I needed; a true epiphany. Focus on the progress, even if it's slow and steady. Don't let the scale think for you.

That kind of mental framework gave me the courage to hit the mall and look for a new bathing suit for the summer. Like most women, I despised and dreaded shopping for a new bathing suit. But this shopping expedition was more pleasant than in the past. Tom was with me for proof. To my delight, the 12s were too big. I poked my head out of the dressing room and said, "Oh, Tom, can you get me some 10s?" When some of them were also too large, I wanted to knock on all the other dressing room doors and say, "Sorry to bother you, but these 10s were too big on me. I'm now going to try on a few 8s."

Can I just say one thing to the designers out there? Can you please get together and decide what a 10 is, what an 8 is? It's very frustrating, as one of the buying public, not to know what's going to fit you, just because you guys can't agree on the same thing! I'm so tired of hearing sales people say, "Well, this designer runs small," or, "This one runs big." God bless it, can't an 8 just be an 8! OK, rant over.

That was reason to celebrate. According to Tom, I had more definition on my sides, the small of my back was actually small, and two dimples were appearing near the top of my bum. Having lost 22 pounds by the end of May, I was seeing the difference too. But one night, after we fooled around, Tom said he felt like he was cheating on me. I gave him a long, stern look. I wasn't amused. Well, okay, maybe a little.

"Let's hear you talk your way out of this one," I said.

Wearing three different shades of embarrassment, Tom explained that all the weight I'd lost made me feel like a different woman, a whole new person. That was a good thing, he said. I understood. But what about the version of me who was 20 pounds heavier? Didn't he also say he loved me that way?

"What's up with that?" I asked, smiling to let him know I was giving him a hard time.

The truth was that I felt the same way about Tom, who'd lost almost 20 pounds and was about to switch into maintenance. He had a new body as well. Picturing it made me smile. Who said dieting couldn't be fun—and sexy?

Twenty-nine

REGAINING MY LIFE

"Cheers!" I said, holding up a martini glass at Tom. It was the middle of June, and we were in the kitchen at home. As promised, when I reached the 25-pound mark, which happened on the 14th, I fixed myself a martini, using the glass and ingredients Suzanne had given me for my birthday. Then Tom and I got dressed up and went out for another one. It tasted wonderful.

"I still have a ways to go before I get where I want to be," I said.

"Just let yourself enjoy the celebration tonight," Tom said.

Starting with the sexy black Michael Kors cocktail dress I had on, there was much to celebrate in my life that summer. Wolfie was preparing to tour full-time with Van Halen on their rescheduled world tour beginning in the fall. He was already into a heavy rehearsal schedule with his dad, who was doing well since getting out of rehab in the spring. As a measure of how far the two of us had matured, he'd recently come to me for girlfriend advice. We'd had a great talk, and afterward I marveled to Tom, "Something nice happened when I was with Ed."

"What's that?"

"I realized that I kinda like the guy."

That revelation, coming twenty-seven years after we met, was a victory for our entire family, and especially for me. From the time Wolfie was born, I'd wanted to be a better person for my son. Getting to a place where Ed and I not only talked but got along and actually enjoyed each other's company made me feel as if I'd worked through a lot of anger and come to a place where I was doing the right thing for Wolfie. Watching my son mature into a nice young man was all the proof I needed that the effort was paying off.

Only seventeen weeks into the program, I understood what Kirstie meant when she'd described the experience as a journey rather than a diet. Not only was I starting to look different, but I also noticed the subtle and not-so-subtle differences in my way of approaching situations and making choices. I made decisions rationally rather than emotionally or without thinking. As a result, I wasted less time feeling bad about myself or worrying I'd done something wrong or wasn't good enough. This diet was, as Kirstie had promised, like unlocking the person I'd kept trapped inside all my fat. The less of me there was, the more of me I discovered.

When Tom's children came for the summer, I stocked the kitchen with the foods that kids like to eat. We had everything from apples to Doritos to chocolate chip cookies. Even with my Jenny food on the shelves, the kitchen was still *Temptation Island* for me. I had my slips, but I managed to control my impulses better than ever and was down a total of 27 pounds by the end of June. The next month we took everyone to Hawaii except for Wolfie, who stayed in L.A. for rehearsals.

That's when I knew the Van Halen reunion with Dave was really going to fly.

I cried the first four days we were in Hawaii. Without Wolfie, it didn't seem like a vacation. The turning point came when I surfed with Tom and the kids. Their laughter inspired me to get out and enjoy myself. A mai tai at night got me into the vacation spirit. Except for those drinks, I stuck closely to my diet. Once I got past Wolfie's absence, the only downside to the trip were the paparazzi, whose long lenses scoped me out on the beach several days before I spotted them. A not-so-lovely picture of me in a bathing suit ended up in the tabloids as a "Diet Disaster," and another one landed on the TMZ.com website under the headline "Chunk Change."

"I'm only halfway through my diet!" I screamed at my computer screen. "How can you do this to me?"

Well, duh, those pictures ran because I was a diet spokesperson in a bathing suit, and I didn't look attractive. Here's what I didn't understand and still don't! Why does bad and embarrassing stuff like that entertain people? What's so fun about other people's mistakes and misfortune?

I calmed down after seeing that TMZ.com also ran a poll beneath my photo asking readers if they thought my diet was working. Almost 80 percent said it was. That you-go-girl support got me through that hurtful moment. Talking to Tom also helped bring me back to my senses. I didn't need to care what those people thought. As my sweet friend Julie once told me—it's none of your business what other people think of you.

At forty-seven, I was never going to have the body I had at twenty. At the rate I was going, it could end up being *better.* Maybe not as thin, but in better shape. Does that mean you'll see me wearing a bikini on *Oprah*? No way.

My positive attitude carried me through the quarter-pound gain I had following Hawaii. Unlike the last time I'd added weight, I turned this into a lesson. I didn't beat myself up or fall into the frame of mind where I said, Oh, well, since I messed up, I'm going to let myself eat for the rest of the week and then start a new diet on Monday. The new Valerie could slip up and start dieting again the next minute without feeling like a loser. The new Val forgave herself for being human.

On August 1 I reached my original goal of losing 30 pounds. A final loss of 2.6 pounds put me over the top. By then I'd announced a new goal of 40 pounds, although privately, I hoped eventually to lose an even 50. If I managed to get there, I'd be at 122 pounds. But I'd feel pleased if I got anywhere close to that—and stayed there. That's the part that worried me. Staying there. As time drew near for Wolfie to hit the road with his dad's band, I felt my anxiety level ratchet up a thousandfold.

And I knew what that meant. Round-the-clock hunger pains. By September, everything I'd learned since going on Jenny Craig was put to the test. Even with Wolfie's departure still a few weeks off, I felt the dial shift in our relationship. At sixteen and a half, he didn't need me in the same way as when he was younger. I worried about all the different ways he might change on the road. I knew what went on out there, and I didn't like the images that filled my head.

Though I planned to go out for as many dates as possible, I still tried talking to him responsibly about sex and drugs. When I brought up one subject or the other, he snapped, "Ma! I know!" Trying to talk bluntly about his dad, who seemed to be in good shape so far, also went nowhere. "Ma, I can handle things," he said. He impressed others that he could. At one of the few rehearsals I attended, Dave's sisters came up to me and told me what a fine young man they thought

Wolfie was. They said he had an aura of calm. Later, Dave's assistant said that she could see he had a mom.

"A real mom," she said.

Hearing that, I felt like I'd won an Emmy and an Oscar at the same time. I told myself I was doing my job as I bought him new underwear, socks, and T-shirts. After packing his suitcase, I made Wolfie look at it. I wanted him to appreciate the craftwork that went into fitting everything perfectly in that space. All my years of going on location were on display. And Wolfie's reaction?

"Cool, Ma! It'll never look like that again."

Seeing Wolfie onstage with Ed and Dave was like a flashback and flashforward at the same time. Different parts of my life came together all at once. I enjoyed getting reacquainted with Dave, who, now that I was older and wiser, I realized I liked and appreciated. He was a master showman, great at what he did. Back in the eighties, I was too angry with him to see it. Watching him onstage with Ed, it was clear the two were magic together.

I also loved the way Dave treated my son, whose presence onstage clearly had a grounding, stabilizing, and creative effect on Ed. I couldn't remember seeing Ed smile as much when he performed. And those were the rehearsals. On September 22 Wolfie flew to Charlotte, North Carolina, for a week of rehearsals before the tour opened there. As Wolfie walked to the car waiting for him in the driveway, all of us were in tears. Tony worried that Wolfie was going to change or get too good on the video game Guitar Hero, and I worried about everything else, even though he was going to have a chaperone and teacher with him.

"I just fed my baby to the rock-and-roll lions," I said.

"He's going to be fine," Tom said, wrapping his arm around me.

"If he was eighteen, I'd be scared shitless. But he's sixteen, and there are so many people out there watching out for him and making sure he doesn't get into trouble."

"He's a good kid," I said.

"Yeah, he's a good kid."

"He is. He really is." I dried my eyes. "What's in the fridge? I'm starving."

"Honey!"

"I'm kidding," I said.

A week later we were in Charlotte for the start of the tour. As Tom and I entered the arena for the final rehearsal, we stopped halfway across the floor. The place vibrated from the sound of the band playing at full volume. Ed skipped around on his side of the stage, rifling through "Runnin' with the Devil." Dave was taking the day off to rest his voice. Suddenly Wolfie stepped up to the microphone and sang lead. He ripped through "Runnin' " and then went into "Romeo Delight"—my favorite—and "Beautiful Girls."

I turned to Tom. He had been staring at me, studying my awe-struck expression.

"My God, he can sing," I said. "I always told him that he had a beautiful voice. But he can really sing."

Tom pointed to Ed.

"I know," I said. "Look at him. He's cracking up. Who knew Wolfie had that in him?"

"I guess Ed did," said Tom.

Before the first show, Wolfie was too nervous to eat. "Ma, where are you?" he asked in a text message that showed he still needed me. I hurried to his bus. At my suggestion, he managed to keep down a Jenny Craig Sunshine Sandwich, an egg on two English muffins. After a brief workout on Guitar Hero, he joined Ed, Dave, and Al onstage, where they turned in a two-hour-plus performance that won raves in the newspaper and online. "One of the most awesome experiences of my life," declared one fan. "What a blast," said another. I only cared what they said about Wolfie. "The younger Van Halen turned out to be a showy player and a spot-on backing vocalist," noted the critic for the *Charlotte Observer.*

The mood backstage following the show was downright celebratory. The old guys could still bring full-throttle rock to the arena, without being fully throttled themselves. Wolfie, who brought the age of the band down a decade, radiated pure joy as he dried himself with a towel. I stood there, marveling at two things: first at how impossibly unfair it was that these guys—I'm talking about Ed, Dave, and Al— had ravaged their bodies for three decades and they were not just thin, they were cut like young models, while I was on a diet and reminding myself to not go near the food table filled with chips and M&Ms (still no brown ones, thanks to Wolfie, who thought it was funny to carry on the family tradition); and secondly, I marveled at how my own place in this world had run the gamut from the guitarist's girlfriend, to his wife, to his ex-wife, to the bass player's mother. Over twenty-seven years, there'd been times when I'd stood backstage after a Van Halen show and felt thrilled, excited, needed, unwelcome, and uncomfortable. However, I'd never been more proud than when I looked at Wolfie, who was a really strong, fine, solid kid.

They'd turned in a good show.

And I'd done a good job with my boy.

I took a moment to appreciate the connectedness I was feeling to Ed, Al, Dave, and the whole scene. I put my arm around Tom and gave him a kiss. I remember making an observation about blended and extended families, something that seemed warm, insightful, and appropriate. He had four kids. I had Wolfie. This whole backstage rock-

and-roll carnival was also part of my extended family, and I enjoyed it. No, I appreciated it. I hoped it stayed good, too. They had a long haul ahead of them and it was impossible to predict what might happen farther on down the road.

I turned to Tom and said something along the lines of, while things were good now, what if Ed and Dave started to fight? What if Ed began to drink?

"That's your real concern, isn't it?" he said.

I nodded. "Only in so far as it will affect Wolfie."

He wrapped his big arm around me and turned me slightly so that I was staring at Wolfie, who was across the room shaking hands with someone I didn't know.

"Look at him," Tom said. "He's a good kid. He has solid values. He loves you. If anything happens, he will call."

"Yeah . . . and?"

"That's it."

"But I don't have to let him go on a rock tour."

Suddenly Tom sounded like Jack Black in *School of Rock*.

"Rock and roll isn't a choice, babe. It's a calling—and Wolfie's been called." He smiled. "So how's it feel?"

"How's what feel?"

"How's it feel to be so beautiful?"

"Shut up."

"You're right. Let's go back to the hotel."

At the hotel, Tom and I sat with Wolfie, who had his own room but ended up in ours. He was too revved up to go to bed. I remembered those days, when shows had ended, and Ed and I had got back to the hotel at 11:30 pm, but it felt like noon. When I suggested playing cards, he gave me a look that said, "Ma, you've got to be kidding."

We went downstairs. In the elevator, I whispered to Tom, "See, I'm losing him." Tom shook his head. "So how's it feel?"

"Shut up."

We ended up taking Wolfie to the hotel bar, the same place Ed and I had spent many a night following a show. Déjà vu. Only Wolfie ordered a Roy Rogers. A fan in the bar picked up the bill and toasted Wolfie for a great show. Then, as Tom and I got in the elevator to go back to the room, a woman stopped Wolfie and asked for his autograph.

She didn't see me in the elevator, peering out the door on groupie red alert. I breathed a sigh of relief when I saw a teenaged boy and girl with her.

"I wanted to bring my kids because of you," she said. "I think it's great that you love music and get to play with your father."

"Thanks," Wolfie said. "Me too."

If I shut my eyes, I could see Ed doing the same thing twenty-five years earlier. Now our son was signing autographs. After finishing, Wolfie stepped in the elevator.

"Oh!" the woman called after him. "By the way, tell your mother she is gorgeous! She looks so good. Congratulate her on the weight loss."

Even though the doors were closing, I knew my cue when I heard it. I popped my head out and said, "Thank you."

The thanks didn't stop there. The next day Ed, Wolfie, and Tom went golfing at a nearby course. I drove the cart, enjoying the day with my guys. There'd been times in the past when I didn't think I lived such a charmed life. Not anymore. Out on the golf course, I pinched myself. My life contained less struggle and self-doubt than ever. I'd made progress, real progress in all areas of my life, the kind that I'd once thought impossible. How'd I get to this point? I laughed as I realized that it had been nothing less than a journey, exactly as Kirstie had promised.

That journey may not have started with a diet, but it wouldn't have happened without Jenny Craig. Without question, I changed my life from the moment I signed up. Going public with my weight was my way, at age forty-seven, of saying that I was done hiding from the truth, from life, and from myself. I was done hiding, period. Once in the open, I had to face the worst of myself, my self-doubt, insecurity, bad habits, past mistakes, and all the other things that held me back from feeling good about myself.

But I knew those things already. Those were all the things that had held me back and made enjoying life an unending battle. Letting them go was a challenge. The process was couched in a diet. I measured my progress by the amount of weight I lost. The public saw the surface changes, but I saw the personal changes no one else could see. I regained my life one pound at a time. Through my Jenny consultant, I faced the fact that I was an unconscious eater, and I couldn't be that way anymore. I had to be conscious. I had to wake up.

It fascinated me to think that I'd lived my life unconsciously. I joked that I went through life with blinders on. But why? Why not see the things going on around you? It was all about avoiding unpleasantness. Where'd that get me? I was so busy trying to deflect any kind of pain that I hadn't allowed myself much joy, either. I've lost 40 pounds as of the end of November. But the change I've experienced has nothing to do with weight loss.

Nowadays I feel the pain that comes my way and acknowledge my fears. By doing that I have the chance to feel a lot more joy as well. When you're busy blocking out difficult emotions and feelings, you're not going to feel the good stuff, either. And I want all the good stuff I can get. For me, that whole experience can be found hanging in my closet. The size 14s are history. So are the 12s. The jeans hanging in the middle? Those are 8s—and even they're getting kind of loose.

But until recently, I still had a problem with the 12s. For some reason, I couldn't get rid of them. Every day I wondered why they were still there. Why couldn't I throw them out? Did it mean that I didn't believe I'd keep the weight off? Did it mean that I didn't believe in the transformation I'd gone through? Was the journey just a long trek in a circle?

One morning I stood in front of those damn pants, debating the issue. What if I needed them again? Why would I need them? Why was I going back to that place? Questions, questions, questions. Sometimes I made myself crazy by asking so many questions. I walked into the kitchen to get a glass of water. My eyes went straight to a little sign taped to the fridge:

"Leap—and the Net Will Follow."

You know what I did next. After all I've been through and learned, it's the only way I want to live the rest of my life.

ACKNOWLEDGMENTS

All of you know that I'm a freak for Elton John. It was true at fifteen and it's still true today. To paraphrase Elton and his genius collaborator, Bernie Taupin, I thank the Lord for the people I have found throughout my life.

Todd—I thank the Lord there are people out there like you and your beautiful wife and children. This book so obviously could not have been written without you. Thanks for *getting* me. What took you no time would have taken me a procrastinator's lifetime to put down on paper and it still wouldn't be as eloquent, articulate, or funny. You are a master. Not to mention the alacrity with which you approached this project . . . it was contagious (Ha!). Here's to many, many years of friendship and collaboration. Now, step away from the pantry.

Mom and Dad—you made me who I am, and that's such an overwhelming thing to go back and examine, as I did in this book, and I'm delighted to have come out the other end of the process feeling appreciative and grateful. You always gave me so much and asked for nothing in return. With a full heart and much gratitude, I say thank you. I love you both so much. Oh, and Daddy, if I can just get you to re-register as a Democrat . . .

ACKNOWLEDGMENTS

Patrick and Stacy, David, Drew and Laura, Calvin and Bailey my sweet nephew and niece, and my beloved Vispi and Fairweather familia—I love you all so very much. I don't see you as often as I would like, but you are always in my heart.

Jack and Marc—thank you for being there for the long haul . . . both of you truly are the best. And you thought you were retiring . . .

Heidi, Jill, and everyone past and present at PMK/HBH—what a ride, huh? Heidi, thank you for always standing by me and, more important, for being my friend.

Dan—you turned drinks into a book, and in less than a year . . . how'd you do that? You really *are* a good agent! Now, if you could just catch a cab in the rain . . .

To everyone at Free Press and Simon & Schuster—I'm new to publishing, but thanks to Martha, Dominick, Carisa, Suzanne, Nicole, Eric, and my editor, Leslie, for working hard, showing patience, and making this first time a great experience. I also want to thank Donna and Elizabeth for their tireless assistance inputting material. I hope we can do this again. I have so much more to say.

To Patti, Scott, Steve, Amy, Cynthia, Kathy, and all of my Jenny Craig peeps—you have all added important chapters to my life, and the proof is in these pages. I don't believe you can lose weight successfully by going it alone, and I could not have done this without any of you. Thank you.

Kirstie—girl, you kill me. Your brilliance and quick wit are awe inspiring. Here's to maintenance, baby!

Jenny and Sid—truly the best inspiration ever! As your book says, 'one woman changed millions of lives,' so you've changed mine. And I have gained so much more than I've lost.

To Norman, Bonnie, Pat, Mack, and everyone in my ODAAT family—I am so proud to have worked, learned, lived, and loved with all of you and I hope I make you proud.

ACKNOWLEDGMENTS

Martha, Roma, Della, John, and the amazing crew who became my friends and comrades on TBAA—you helped me through a *really* rough patch . . . thank you.

To Jonathan, Nevin, and everyone at Innovative Artists—thank you for believing in me.

Jamie—you da man

Lois, Gabby, Amanda, Craig, Charlotte, and crew at Gelfand, Rennert & Feldman—thank you so much for all your hard work

Terri, Kathy, Abra, Janet, Rachael, and my CBS/Paramount pals— our train has taken off . . . thanks for steering!

Nancy, Kacie, Jetty, Matthew, Roque, Bruce, Linda, Amal, Jonathan, Elaine, Chandra, and all on Team Bertinelli—and what a team you are! Thank you for all you do.

Tom, Nancy, Shane, and Hannah—it wasn't just Halloween that made your family so special to us, thank you for everything.

Kathy and Ron—beautiful music, beautiful people.

Robert and Kerry—from the kiddies to the kitties, we all thank you!

Dave and Lisa—not just my Mac pals but so, so much more! Thank you for always being there for me and Wolf and Dexter and DeeDee . . .

The Kubrs—surf's up!

Larry (Go Saints!), Debbie (Ms. Walkvest!) Carl (plyometrics, baby!), Patrick, Denny, Billy, and all the rest who have helped this bod thru the years . . .

Letty, Debby, Rudy, and Elia, and the Aguilera, Virgen, and Vazquez families—Wolfie and I thank you from the bottom of our hearts.

Larry, Mic, Merrill, Cindy, Tracey, Benjamin—thank you for all your expertise, help, and encouragement when we really needed it.

Peter and Ivo—our birthday dinners at II Tiramisu wouldn't be the same without you. Here's to many more!

My Arizona and Cranium, LCR, and BooRay buds—Gina (my go-to gal!), Liz (don't mess with her when she's playin' cards!), Paul, Colton (pizza!), Carl and Dianne, Dr. Jeffro, Kellee, Stacy, Elizabeth (cake artiste extraordinaire), the Steele Larsen Anderson gang, Phil and everyone at Mountain Valley Church . . . Again, wish I could see you more often, but it's just too damn hot in the summer!

To the awesome Matt's (and I really mean awesome B, G, J & S), Angie, Marc, Liam, Duncan, Craig, Michael, Chris, Christine, Lauren, and every one of you on the VH Road Gang who have taken care of my boy when I can't be there, there are no words of gratitude strong enough.

Barb—you are loved and appreciated.

Jimmy and Phil—what would I have done without you guys? Too many moments go by where I don't say thank you for being in my life. So, thank you.

Faith and Jane—thank you for being there when I really needed a soft shoulder. I miss you both.

To the wonderful women and families I have met because of my son, from pre-school to Oakwood to book group, I feel so blessed to have every one of you in my life and I hope you all know how very grateful I am for our friendships. My heart is deeper and stronger for having known all of you and I truly don't know what I'd do without any of you.

Ed—you are a good man, believe it. When you do, you'll be free. I love you.

T—I love and adore you. And I thank you for bringing your precious children and glorious Italian family into my life. With you, I'm home.

And to my sweet boy, Wolfie—I thank God every day for blessing me with you. You are a strong, beautiful, and courageous young man and I am so very proud of you. My favorite title in life is as "Wolfie's Mom." I love you, to the moon and back . . . and more.

ABOUT THE AUTHOR

VALERIE BERTINELLI has been acting since the age of twelve, appearing in more than two dozen made-for-TV movies. Most recognizably, she appeared on the long-running sitcom *One Day at a Time* and, more recently *Touched by an Angel*. Now a spokesperson for Jenny Craig, Bertinelli was raised in Claymont, Delaware, and the San Fernando Valley, California, and was married for over twenty years to Eddie Van Halen (they split up in 2001). Currently she lives with her son, Wolfgang, in Los Angeles.